Writers on Leadership

John van Maurik

PENGUIN BOOKS

PENGUIN BOOKS

Published by the Penguin Group
Penguin Books Ltd, 27 Wrights Lane, London W8 5TZ, England
Penguin Putnam Inc., 375 Hudson Street, New York, New York 10014, USA
Penguin Books Australia Ltd, Ringwood, Victoria, Australia
Penguin Books Canada Ltd, 10 Alcorn Avenue, Toronto, Ontario, Canada M4V 3B2
Penguin Books India (P) Ltd, 11 Community Centre, Panchsheel Park, New Delhi – 110 017, India
Penguin Books (NZ) Ltd, Private Bag 102902, NSMC, Auckland, New Zealand
Penguin Books (South Africa) (Pty) Ltd, 5 Watkins Street, Denver Ext 4, Johannesburg 2094, South Africa

Penguin Books Ltd, Registered Offices: Harmondsworth, Middlesex, England

First published 2001
1

Set in Linotype Minion and ITC Officina Sans
Typeset by Rowland Phototypesetting Ltd, Bury St Edmunds, Suffolk
Printed in Great Britain by Antony Rowe Ltd, Chippenham, Wiltshire

Contents

Acknowledgements   vii
Introduction   1

Behavioural Theories   7

R. Tannenbaum and W.H. Schmidt; R.R. Blake and
  J.S. Mouton   9
D.M. McGregor   14

Contingency Theories   19

Kenneth Blanchard   21
John Adair   28
John W. Hunt   36
John Kotter   42
Manfred Kets de Vries   51
Judy Rosner, Sandra Bem and Jan Grant   59
CCL Study on Derailment   66

Transformational Theories   75

Team Leadership
Meredith Belbin   77
Rupert Eales-White   84
Jessica Lipnack and Jeffrey Stamps   91

The Leader as a Catalyst of Change
Warren Bennis   99
James Kouzes and Barry Posner   108
Howard Gardner   116

Stephen R. Covey   124
Rupert Eales-White   132
Douglas Ready   140
Robert E. Kelley   147
G. Suarez and J. Hirshberg   154
Ned Herrmann   162
John Harvey-Jones   172
Roger Harrison   180

The Leader as Strategic Visionary
J.M. Stewart; J.A. Collins and J.I. Porras   187
Peter Senge   194
John Whitmore   202
W.H. Drath and C.J. Palus   210
Vision Articles   215

Conclusion: Pointers for Future Leaders and their
    Development   223
Indexes   233

Acknowledgements

I would like to dedicate this book to my wife, Sheila, for her encouragement and patience. I would also like to thank Jane Farmer and Simon Dane for their valuable help and support.

Grateful acknowledgement is given to Rupert Eales-White for permission to reproduce figure 4, and to the Herrmann Institute for permission to reproduce figures 6 and 7.

Acknowledgements

Introduction

Leadership: its study has been the subject of literally thousands of books, papers and other publications over the last century and new works continue to emerge at an astounding rate. In fact in 1996 a staggering total of 187 books and articles were published with the word 'leadership' in their title; and this does not preclude the many manuscripts that were about the subject, but which did not actually mention the dreaded word.

So there is a wealth of material on which to draw when compiling an overview of writings on leadership. Publications on the subject can be found in a wide variety of professional journals, academic treatises and books ranging from the highly academic to the 'pop'. They cover in turn a number of disciplines, including management, psychology, sociology, management education and politics; however, it has been said that nothing new has really been written on the subject of leadership for over 2,000 years. Lao-Tzu, the Chinese philosopher, famously stated: 'When the deed is done, the mission accomplished, of the best leaders the people will say, "We have done it ourselves." ' By the same token, many edicts in the Gospel according to St Matthew are used as a basis for leadership education; along with Lao-Tzu it provides a firm grounding for the fashionable concept of empowerment!

Yet if nothing new has been said about leadership over the years, why does it remain such a potent focus of interest and debate? The fact remains that as a concept it is vital, and the quality of its use or misuse arguably makes it the most important issue in the world today; this at a time when the quality of leadership can radically affect the quality of life for those at work, and when, considering national and political leadership, mankind has the ability to enhance or irrevocably debase his environment, thereby affecting the quality of life on this planet for many generations to come. No wonder that Field Marshal Lord Slim's definition of the subject remains one of the best known and most pertinent: 'There is a difference between leadership and management. Leadership is of the spirit, compounded of personality and vision; its practice is an art. Management is of the mind, a matter of accurate calculation . . . its practice is a science. Managers are necessary; leaders are essential.'

And this is as good a place as any to start. So much has been said and written on the subject that it would be completely impossible to summarize it all in a compendium of this nature – or indeed in any collection or summary. However, it is quite possible to pick out a number of key landmarks, as well as other works that have added specialist insights, in the development of writing and thinking about leadership. What the reader considers to be important may vary from person to person. As a guide: the collection of writings assembled here is aimed at helping both the student and the practising manager (leader?) to advance his or her knowledge of the subject with a view to acquiring further insights as well as being a basis for more effective performance in the future.

STRUCTURE AND APPROACH

The structure of this book sets out to cover writers who represent milestones in the main periods or generations of the development of leadership thinking. These generations can broadly be defined as:

1 Trait theory
2 Behavioural theories
3 Contingency theories
4 Transformational leadership theories.

With the exception of trait theory, which will not be covered in any depth beyond an overview within this introduction, the prevailing thinking behind each theory will be explained in a separate introduction as we reach that section.

However, at this stage it is important to emphasize that none of the four generations are mutually exclusive or totally time bound. Although it is true that the progression of thinking tends to follow a sequential path, it is quite possible for elements of one generation to crop up much later in the writings of someone who would not normally think of himself or herself as being of that school. Consequently, it is fair to say that each generation has added something to the overall debate on leadership and that the debate continues. The structure of the debate will become increasingly obvious as we reach the more recent writers within what would normally be called the transformational period; their work often contains major elements of other schools of thought – and seldom to the detriment of their own arguments. Thus while the writers have been divided into 'generations' that best represent them from both a sequential and intellectual standpoint, do not be surprised to find elements of more than one generation or perspective cropping up in the work of a particular writer.

The whole area of transformational leadership is divided up into a number of sub-themes, such as team leadership, the leader as strategic visionary, etc. This acknowledges the increasing diversity of the whole subject and enables the reader to focus on specific areas of interest.

Each chapter will follow essentially the same overall structure. It will start with a brief biography of the writer or writers in question, followed by a description of their main thesis, drawn from one or more of their better-known works. In addition, I shall attempt to summarize the main messages and contribution of the writer in question to the overall body of knowledge on the subject and also to comment on their relevance both to the reader and to current issues within organizational life. Where relevant, cross reference will be made to the work of other writers. The aim will be to make it easy for the reader to take on board the main messages, as well as to entertain. Specifically, where the content of a chapter is principally concerned with theory, efforts will be made to illustrate that theory's relation to reality. Indeed, as Professor Peter Herriot (formerly of Birkbeck College) was fond of saying: 'There is nothing so practical as a good theory!'

As a final chapter I have been permitted the indulgence of summarizing my own work (and most recent thoughts) on the subject of leadership and of using this summary to reflect on the current state of thinking about leadership. This provides a wonderful opportunity to speculate on what may well be demanded of leaders in this new millennium. However, let us start by examining the prevailing mode of thinking on the subject in the early decades of the last century.

GENERATION ONE – TRAIT THEORY

Although there have been literally hundreds of studies of leadership over the centuries, with such luminaries as Shakespeare, Tennyson and Gibbon taking it as a subject, it was not until the early twentieth century that any attempt was made to subject the phenomenon to genuine analysis.

By the twenties and thirties interest was being shown in the personal attributes of leadership and early theories attributed success in leadership to the possession of extraordinary qualities of energy, courage, foresight and persuasiveness. The prevailing belief was that leaders were born rather than made and so it was only necessary to define the qualities of a born leader in order to pinpoint those individuals who would take the reins of power in the future. Hundreds of trait-based studies were conducted in those early years, but generally the findings were disappointing. One study looked at the 'top people' in industry and commerce in the USA and attempted to measure them against a number of preconceptions, only to find that the single thing they had in common was that they tended to be taller than the average. This tells us more about the type of people likely to be found in leadership positions in those days, i.e. patricians with the benefit of a better diet since childhood, than about the type of people who ought to be successful as leaders; and any student of history would be able to offer a compelling list of leaders – starting with Napoleon, and moving on to Gandhi – who were well short of average height! Consequently, early studies failed to support the premise of the trait approach, namely that a good leader must exhibit a number of relevant traits considered to be essential.

Despite its shaky start trait theory has continued, based on a more sophisticated platform of measures, and findings have revealed a number of relatively consistent results. Individual traits which have been related to effectiveness in positions of responsibility have been highlighted as a high energy level, tolerance of stress, integrity, self-confidence and emotional maturity. Paradoxically, researchers have found that the degree to which any one of these traits is useful may depend on the situation that individual leaders find themselves in. Furthermore, those studying the traits of individual leaders frequently note the need for a leader to balance one trait against another; for example, the need for power versus the need to show emotional maturity.

Although the trait approach has largely been out of favour for several decades the basic premise continues to fascinate students of the subject, as it does begin to explain why some people seek leadership positions and why they act in the way they do when they achieve them. Indeed, there have been a number of occasions where the approach has resurfaced. Recently, a study on whether leaders are born rather than made, carried out at the University of Western Ontario, has hinted at the existence of leadership genes, indicating that they have found a high level of genetic influence. The research is backed up by comparing the results of personality tests on identical twins with the results from non-identical twins; the conclusion was that over 50 per cent of leadership ability differences were linked to genetics.

The researchers found that identical twins were more likely to achieve similar scores for leadership traits on subjects such as charisma, or the ability to inspire others, than with non-identical twins. Although this line of thought can be backed up by pointing to certain families, such as the Churchills and the Kennedys, where there has been a notable tradition of leadership, it does not take into account the fact that there were traditions of leadership in both families; traditions that in the case of the Kennedys were drummed into more than one generation by the redoubtable matriarch, Rose Kennedy. And in many such distinguished families there have been individuals who have *not* lived up to the example of their forebears.

On a far more pragmatic note Sir Bernard Ingham, at the time of writing president of the British Franchise Association, reflecting on his long association with Margaret Thatcher in an interview in *The Times*, pointed to five qualities that she brought to the post of prime minister. They can be summarized as:

Ideological security A strong sense of conviction enabling her policies to flow smoothly from the basis of her philosophy and ideals.
Moral courage This enabled her to stand alone when she felt that it was right to do so.
Constancy More than once she declared, 'The lady's not for turning!'
An iron will An absolute necessity if you want to get things done.
A low need for love Thatcher did not care about being loved, although she did want to be respected.

In studying this list of qualities it is obvious that they are not all born of genetics. While there is no doubt that Mrs Thatcher exhibited them when she was premier it could well be argued that they were traits demanded by the role rather than inborn, and that she was just better than many at bringing them out. So the argument inexorably swings towards the behaviour of the leader being all-important, rather than the influence of any inborn traits.

And indeed it must do, if the act of defining the traits of a good leader has failed to predict future success in certain roles, and if the impact of having an illustrious ancestor may fall foul of the old nature versus nurture debate. Then it is necessary to look further afield in studying the elusive concept of leadership. It is almost impossible to predict how the traits of a leader can influence a group's motivation or performance unless we examine how these traits are expressed in the behaviour of the leader in question.

Although each generation of thinking has undoubtedly contributed to the wealth of knowledge on the subject by setting up a platform for the work of future generations, we will start our detailed look at writers on leadership with an analysis of those who contributed to the second generation: the behavioural debate.

Behavioural Theories

Jones is not a born leader . . . yet.

– from an army officer's assessment

This line of thinking took over from trait theories in the 1940s and remained popular into the 1960s. Much of the thinking developed at the time still holds true, even if subsequent writers have refined and improved on its arguments.

The essential concept behind behavioural thinking was that leadership could be taught and that good leadership was a matter of adopting the right sort of behaviour when attempting to lead other people. The sudden entry of the USA into the Second World War did much to encourage this concept, as following Pearl Harbor the US needed to train a large number of officers and NCOs in a short period of time. At West Point Military Academy and other centres of education it was soon established that leadership could be taught and that those who learned best were not always from what would conventionally be called 'officer-material backgrounds'.

So in the post-war years, while it had been well established that leadership could be taught, the next question that arose was whether there was an ideal type of leadership behaviour and, if so, what made it ideal. A number of academics studied that question and in doing so looked at the ways in which effective leaders set out to get other people to carry out tasks for them. Of the writers examined in this section, probably Blake and Mouton are the best known. They came up with debatably the most flexible measure (and certainly the most widely used) of leadership orientation and activity. However, even this had within it those elements of prescriptiveness that eventually led to the rise of contingency theories.

R. Tannenbaum and W.H. Schmidt; R.R. Blake and J.S. Mouton

A high point in the era of behaviourist theories can be seen in the work of two sets of academics/consultants, Tannenbaum and Schmidt, and Blake and Mouton. Both in their different but complementary ways did much to move forward thinking about the effect of leadership activities and to pave the way for others in the form of situational leadership.

Since the trait theories did not provide any really tangible clues as to what constituted effective leadership behaviour, those interested in the subject began to examine the behaviour certain leaders actually exhibited and set out to differentiate the effective from the ineffective.

One of the first studies of leadership behaviour was done by Kurt Lewin, who set out to look at some leaders' need to display a level of autocratic authority versus the willingness of other leaders to adopt a more democratic role. This study compared the need for some leaders to centralize authority and make unilateral decisions, as against a role that involved the followers in decision-making, where authority was often delegated.

The fundamentals of this idea were further developed by R. Tannenbaum and W.H. Schmidt, who published in the *Harvard Business Review* a feature entitled 'How to Choose a Leadership Pattern' (1958). In their work, the range of leadership styles open to a manager were expressed as a continuum ranging from behaviour that focused on manager-centred leadership through to subordinate-centred leadership (see Figure 1).

In the continuum the focus ranges from one in which the main emphasis is on the use of authority by the manager to one in which the principal focus is on the freedom of the subordinate to take actions and

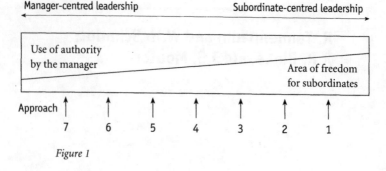

Figure 1

make decisions. It is interesting to note that the range does not go 100 per cent from one corner to the other, because the writers recognized that it is not possible for a manager to have complete authority (except in a non-benevolent tyranny); at the same time it was not advisable for the manager to delegate completely to subordinates as that would in effect become abdication.

The continuum of behaviour, then, from left to right, describes seven different approaches.

1 The manager permits subordinates to function within limits defined by him or her. The manager has confidence in the subordinates and only wishes to conduct an occasional check on activities.
2 The manager defines the limits within which the group is to operate and then allows it to make its own decisions as to how it will undertake the tasks involved.
3 The manager presents a problem to the team, asks members for suggestions about how it should be tackled and then makes a decision as to the way ahead.
4 The manager makes a tentative decision, subject to change. However, the decision has been made before presenting the situation to the group.
5 The manager presents his or her ideas to the group and invites questions about them.
6 The manager 'sells' the decisions that he or she has made about a certain situation but does not give any leeway for discussion or questions.

7 The manager makes a decision and then announces it. Everyone is then expected to start work on it.

Further light on the behaviours open to managers was shed by R.R. Blake and J.S. Mouton, who conducted research at the University of Texas and continued with field work at the Esso Oil Co. They began to cast further doubt on the 'either/or' implications of autocratic as against democratic styles of leadership.

In work published in 1964, Blake and Mouton stated that a leader might put emphasis either on task (getting things done) or relationships (concern for the people involved in the task) when dealing with subordinates, and integrated task and relationships into a grid with five main styles. The key measure of the grid was that leaders could place emphasis on a score from 1 to 9 in their concern both for task and for relationships. From this, a variety of approaches could be identified. The key element of their findings was that leaders in a variety of situations showed a wide range of leadership styles; some were highly production-focused and others were principally people-focused. On the other hand, some leaders exhibited both types of behaviour at the same time, while others seemed to show little interest in either production or relationships.

The range of behaviours was shown by Blake and Mouton not in a continuum but rather as independent dimensions, with the implication that an individual could display any combination of the two basic ingredients of leadership behaviour. The grid, which is shown below, became a measure of manager analysis and personal development. It was based on assessment of scores from completion of questionnaires developed by the writers.

Five main styles or positions were identified from the managerial grid:

Style 1 *Score 9/1. Authority–obedience*
The leader's maximum concern is for task completion and for arranging the conditions of work in such a way that the human elements of it interfere to a minimum. As such, the leader will dictate to the followers what should be done and how it should be done.

Style 2 *Score 1/9. 'Country club' management*
Here there is thoughtful attention to the needs of people, and the focus on satisfying relationships leads to a comfortable and friendly atmosphere with a low-key work tempo. Results can be sacrificed for the achievement of harmonious working relationships.

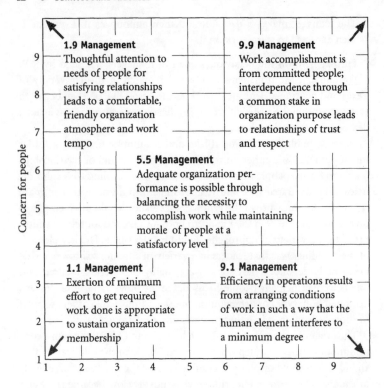

Figure 2

Style 3 *Score 1/1. Impoverished management*
Here the leader exerts the minimum amount of effort needed to sustain organizational membership. There is minimum attention to both task and relationships, and this style is close to abdication.

Style 4 *Score 5/5. 'Organization man' management*
The leader maintains adequate organizational performance by balancing the necessity of maintaining production with that of maintaining morale. This can be regarded as a politically expedient stance, although it is unlikely to change the *status quo*.

Style 5 *Score 9/9. Team leadership*
Work is accomplished by committed people influenced by the leader's strong emphasis on both task and relationships. There is interdependence

through a common stake in the organizational purpose, leading to relationships of trust and respect. The organization is goal-centred and seeks progress through the involvement and participation of all concerned.

Although Style 5 appears to be the ideal, some of the value of the managerial grid has been lost by the tendency of many to assume that a score of 9/9 is the most effective for all occasions without paying attention to differences in the situation in which it might occur. Indeed this style can readily tip over into paternalism, especially when the concern for people operates in isolation from concern for output. Subtle leaders should in fact use a variety of styles interchangeably and with sensitivity.

Blake and Mouton prescribed the 9/9 orientation and linked it to success in a variety of leadership arenas. In a study of over 700 managers they found that 9/9 leaders were more likely to advance their careers and, in a less factual analysis of American presidents, linked this form of behaviour with success – and even greatness.

CONCLUSION

Without doubt Blake and Mouton, as well as Tannenbaum and Schmidt, have done much to advance thinking on the orientation, priorities and concerns of leadership, yet – especially in the case of Blake and Mouton – their work has often been taken as a prescription. It has, however, paved the way for other writers who have placed greater emphasis on behaviour and the choices open to the leader.

D.M. McGregor

For someone who had a comparatively short life as an academic and who did not produce a large volume of published work, Douglas McGregor has had a major impact on thinking about leadership as well as the distinction of adding to the vocabulary of management language in a way that few others have succeeded in emulating.

McGregor's qualifications were in social psychology and led him into two significant posts: those of president of Antioch College and of Professor of Management at MIT. As a key member of the Human Relations School in the 1950s he was a contemporary of such luminaries as Maslow and Hertzberg, and later became a major influence on Warren Bennis. His best-known and most influential work was *The Human Side of Enterprise*. This became a landmark in detailing the influence of thinking and perception, not only in the way people treated each other at work but also in examining the effect that this had on the organization as a whole.

In *The Human Side of Enterprise*, McGregor puts forward two approaches in an examination of managerial thinking and of the leader's mindset in terms of what might motivate people. Broadly they can be defined as the autocratic approach, Theory X, and the soft approach, Theory Y. Each describes a broad philosophy about what motivates people to work and McGregor labelled the exponents of the two approaches as Theory X managers and Theory Y managers.

The Theory X manager believes that:

1 People have a natural dislike of work and will consequently avoid it if possible. Consequently it is necessary for management to adopt a

stick-and-carrot approach to motivation which may be seen in company incentive schemes combined with rules and the measurement of productivity.

2 Because people dislike work, it is naturally necessary to coerce, control, direct and threaten in order to ensure sufficient effort from them to ensure that organizational objectives are met.

3 At the same time, the average worker wishes to avoid responsibility and wants to be directed and controlled, especially if this helps to guarantee a level of security.

This is quite a damning view of human nature and the alternative that McGregor puts forward is quite different.

The Theory Y manager believes that:

1 To the average human being, work is as natural as play.

2 Control by threats or bribes is not the only way to get people to work for organizational objectives. People will direct themselves to be effective and productive in whatever activity they have committed themselves to.

3 Commitment to objectives is a function of the rewards offered for their achievement. Many of the rewards focus on satisfying the individual worker's ego.

4 The average person learns under proper conditions not only to accept but also to seek out responsibility.

5 The capability to exercise imagination, ingenuity and creativity in solving work-based problems is widely, not narrowly, distributed in the population.

6 Under modern conditions of industrial and commercial life, the intellectual potentialities of the average human being are being only partially used.

It is easy to recognize these two extremes. One can be associated with 'tough-minded management' while the other can be seen to categorize 'soft management'. In practice, Theory Y assumptions underlie the behaviour of democratic managers who share leadership responsibilities with subordinates and involve them in the planning and execution of tasks. To allow individuals freedom demands a high degree of personal self-control and a willingness to take risks. However, the fear of losing control through having to trust people is common among many managers and so it is easy to see how some may flirt with Theory Y before reverting to a Theory X approach.

McGregor asserted that Theory X thinking greatly influenced the American work environment of his day with the basic assumption that authority was 'the central indispensable means of managerial control'. This in effect meant that the behaviour often observed in organizations was not a consequence of mankind's inherent nature but rather of the organizations themselves. The organizations had altered the perspectives, nature and behaviour of the people within them.

McGregor was well aware that it was all too easy to think of Theory X and Theory Y as mutually exclusive and at the time of his death he was working on Theory Z, which set out to synthesize the effect of organizational and individual imperatives. In reality, the theories are stereotypes and are at their most useful when one accepts that it is possible to have elements of both approaches in one's own perspective as a leader. It is only natural that there will be some people at work who are lazy and who will shirk responsibility and at the same time there will be others who are the exact opposite. In addition, there are still some jobs where the very nature of the work is so monotonous or menial that no individual would willingly spend his or her time doing them. When McGregor was writing, with a larger industrial sector in the Western world, there were many more process-driven shop-floor jobs of this nature. And here we can see the beginnings of contingency theory: in a development from McGregor's work, John Morse and Jay Lorse stated that 'the appropriate pattern of organization is contingent on the nature of work to be done and the particular needs of the people'.

CONCLUSION

The concepts involved in Theories X and Y while being mainly theoretical must be looked at in the context of other significant work being carried out at roughly the same time. Both Maslow's hierarchy of needs, with its ultimate goal of self-actualization, as well as Hertzberg's concept of hygiene factors, which incorporated autonomy, recognition and the need to do interesting work, fit in well with Theory Y. In a more modern context, Theory Y underpins the concept of empowerment. Empowerment, a word often used but arguably seldom defined and not always put into realistic practice, can best be summed up as giving a subordinate a mixture of three factors when briefing them to complete a task. The factors are:

Direction Sufficient instructions to give confidence, a framework for the work, and purpose.

Challenge An element of stretch that will in turn bring out creativity as well as give satisfaction on completion.

Autonomy/support The confidence to know that there is further help and direction available if required, although not so obvious as to interfere with the individuals' basic need to accomplish the task themselves.

It is easy to see how the component parts of modern empowerment blend a subtle mixture of Theories X and Y; perhaps the time for Theory Y to prevail has finally come. If McGregor were alive today, it is intriguing to speculate what his views on this would be.

Contingency Theories

A leader is like a shepherd; he stays behind the flock letting the most nimble go ahead whereupon the others follow, not realizing that all along they are being directed from behind.

– Nelson Mandela

Those who wish to enjoy enduring success should adjust their behaviour to suit the times. *– Machiavelli*

A common misunderstanding emanating from the behaviourist approach is that the leader should always follow a certain style. This might be democratic, autocratic or some combination of styles dependent on the personality and beliefs of the leader. However, in reality the leadership style that will prove successful in one set of circumstances may well not be as effective in another. For example, in a crisis, a strong assertive leader will probably be called for, but this may not be what is wanted in different circumstances. A prime example here is that of Sir Winston Churchill, who was rejected by the British electorate at the end of the Second World War; or more recently Margaret Thatcher, whose refrain 'The lady's not for turning' actually militated against her when her Cabinet required more flexibility from her over the European single currency.

So in essence a leader can choose to lead from the front, the middle, or the rear and the key concept behind contingency theory thinking is that success in leadership depends on the leader matching his or her style to the demands of the situation. It becomes a matter of making the right choice of attitude and behaviour, and in illustrating judgement and flexibility in so doing.

In this section we will look at a number of writers. These range from Kenneth Blanchard, who is perhaps the best-known and one of the purest exponents of contingency thinking in the form of situational leadership (where the task is completed as the result of a form of transaction between leader and follower), to writers such as Manfred Kets de Vries in whose work the element of choice and transaction is less obvious, but still there.

Kenneth Blanchard

Ken Blanchard is one of those writers who best illustrate the thin line between the academic and popular approaches to writing on leadership. He is a graduate of Cornell University who has managed to put forward an 'easy read' commonsense approach that has had universal appeal. Although many would place him firmly at the 'pop' end of writing on leadership, his work must not be dismissed. As an internationally recognized and respected consultant, author and speaker he is best known for the 'One Minute Manager' series of books which has been broadened to cover leadership, the building of high-performance teams and a number of related areas.

Certainly *The One Minute Manager*, which was published in 1982, has been a massive seller and has influenced a generation of managers in the USA and Europe. Blanchard tends to work in conjunction with other writers and academics and this, while it enables him to preserve the essential themes he holds so dear, allows a wider approach to be established than might otherwise be the case. He has received a multitude of awards in the fields of management and leadership, and in 1979 co-founded Blanchard Training and Development. Through this organization he consults with business leaders across the world and backs up much of his work with his well-known Leader Behavior Analysis questionnaires. It is through his earlier work (especially his collaboration with P. Hersey), and his elaboration and clarification of the theme of situational leadership, that Blanchard has placed himself firmly in the province of contingency theory.

It is from this basic premise, that a leader's style will be most effective when it meets the demands of the situation confronting the leader, that

Blanchard and Hersey developed their thinking and explored the complex interaction of matching the leader's style to both the situation and the environment. They described 'style' as the pattern of behaviour a leader exhibits when attempting to influence the activities of subordinates.

This pattern, they stated, is made up of a combination of task behaviour and relationship behaviour. Task behaviour is the extent to which the leader sets out to organize the roles of individuals and members of his or her group by explaining what activities each must undertake as well as when, where and how tasks are to be accomplished. It further characterizes the extent to which a leader defines patterns of organization and channels of communication. Relationship behaviour, on the other hand, is the extent to which a leader engages in personal relationships with individuals or members of the group, the amount of support that the leader offers, and the extent to which he or she communicates and helps the internal workings of the group.

The leader's natural style preference and range of styles was determined by the questionnaire the writers designed to support their arguments. This identified the individual's dominant style, their supporting style, and the extent to which they used their styles in the most appropriate way. They identified four key styles which were open to any leader. These styles could be summarized as telling, selling, participating, or delegating. Hersey and Blanchard believed that the most important assessment a leader needed to make in deciding his or her approach was on the *maturity* level of the subordinates – this maturity could be defined by the individual's ability and then the individual's willingness to do the job. They stated that it was necessary to look at specific jobs the person was being asked to complete when assessing the most appropriate style to use. For instance, a salesperson might be both willing and competent in front of customers but unwilling and incompetent when asked to complete the post-sale paperwork.

Blanchard went on to elaborate on the arguments and to redesign the approach after his work with Hersey had ended. Most of his arguments were expounded in entertaining fashion in *The One Minute Manager* and subsequent titles, although his main propositions were established in the initial title. The structure of the book is made up of conversations between an appellant manager and the one minute manager, who acts as sage, guru, master of the one-liner and coach in a number of vignettes on the theme of applied situational leadership. The series has given us some classic quotes: 'Catch someone doing something right', and 'There is nothing so unequal as the equal treatment of unequals.' It is highly pragmatic, and very popular.

The basic premise of Blanchard's arguments is that the appropriate choice of leadership style depends on three factors:

1 *The characteristics of the leader*
How does the leader usually lead, and how does he or she perceive the followers? Do they appear competent and does the leader innately trust other human beings (adopting a Theory Y manager approach) to take the initiative and work hard, or does the leader favour a Theory X manager approach and believe that they must be driven as they will try to avoid work? All these factors will influence how the leader chooses to lead. However, as such factors are basically ego-centred rather than other-centred they cannot alone guarantee the best choice of approach.

2 *The characteristics of the follower*
Here the leader must consider the style of leadership the followers are used to. A drastic change of approach by a new leader may well confuse them. In addition, what is the followers' estimation of their own competence? How confident are they? How much ambiguity can they tolerate? Then, of course, there is the situation itself.

3 *The situation*
This is a major determinant. How urgent is it? Is the work new or routine? Do mistakes matter? Is this a minor task, or is it life- or business-threatening?

From here Blanchard and his co-authors went on to define more closely the situational leadership styles he had originally named with Hersey. The styles remained the same, but the basis for measuring them now became the extent to which the leader exhibited either directive or supportive behaviour in dealing with the follower. The leader could exhibit either high support or high direction, or a combination of those approaches. From here, four styles were proposed.

Style 1 *A directive approach*
This is characterized by a great deal of direction to subordinates but little support. They are expected to act fast and not to question orders. This

style was recommended for dealing with work on short time-scales or where staff were new to the job. Alternatively, the work itself might be of a simple or menial nature.

Style 2 *A coaching approach*
Here the approach is both directive and supportive. The approach will be on the following lines: 'Here is a task and here is the way I want you to do it. If you need any help or run into difficulties, come and see me. I will help, support and coach you.'

Style 3 *A supporting style*
This style involves high support but low direction and is often most appropriate where managers of some seniority are working together. Here the approach of the leader is to exhibit trust in the subordinates as they know how to do the work. However, the offer of help and support is always there – the implication is that leader and subordinates can work out any problems together.

Style 4 *A delegating approach*
This style involves low direction and low support. It presupposes that the subordinate has reached a high level of competence and that the leader has considerable trust in that person. Here the words used by the leader might well be, 'You are a senior and experienced person; you do not need to come to me for help or support. You are paid to take both responsibility and decisions.'

The model complements earlier models from Tannenbaum and Schmidt and others, and it also illustrates the choices open to the leader together with the basic components of effectiveness based on making the right choices of behaviour. Blanchard makes the apt point that it is necessary to follow a sequence running from S1 through to S4 when dealing with subordinates. As a subordinate develops, the leader can work his or her way along the sequence. It can be disastrous to apply the wrong style of leadership to any given situation. An S1 style applied too often where the followers are skilled and knowledgeable will frustrate and demotivate, while an S4 style used on unskilled followers will most likely baffle and confuse them, and result in them making serious errors.

Blanchard put his model of situational leadership into a questionnaire, the Leadership Behaviour Analysis II (LBA II), which is widely used in management development training. It illustrates the leader's preferred styles as well as that leader's flexibility of approach and overall effectiveness. Not only does it provide a useful basis for the coaching of the leader, but it also links in with one of Blanchard's favourite topics, that of the leader as coach. Blanchard has linked the LBA II to a diagnosis of someone's leadership style when acting in the role of coach. However, more recently he has branched out to develop his thinking about the coach/leader in greater detail, using his previous ideas as well as ideas he has developed in collaboration with others.

In his collaboration with Don Shula, the celebrated US sports coach, Blanchard takes the concept of the leader as coach several stages further without losing his links to situational leadership. The key concept behind *Everyone's a Coach* is to link the effective coaching practices of Shula with Blanchard's teaching messages, to produce five core messages for the leader coach. The key practices are:

conviction driven Effective leaders stand for something. This means doing the right thing for the right reasons. Sharing one's beliefs, convictions and reasons for wanting something will provide the boundaries as well as the directions people need in order to release exceptional performance.

overlearning Effective leaders help their teams to achieve practice perfection. The essence of good coaching lies in attention to detail and then in the monitoring of results. This scrutiny will help leaders realize their vision as it links in with a philosophy of continuous improvement.

audible – ready Effective leaders, and the people and teams they coach, are ready to change their game plan when the situation demands it. This is really about being adaptable and the key to being adaptable is to be well prepared for the situation in the first place. A series of fixed plans can be catastrophic to both sports teams and organizations.

consistency Effective leaders are predictable in their response to performance. It is necessary for the leader to behave in the same way given similar circumstances. It is not the temporary mood of the leader but the performance of the people at the time that must dictate the response.

honesty-based Effective leaders have high integrity and are clear and straightforward in their interactions with others. In uncertain times, people want their leaders to be straight with them – if they cannot have job security, at least they are entitled to honesty.

The book itself is perhaps too American and too crammed with US cultural examples (especially when making business/sporting comparisons) to have universal appeal. However, Shula makes some interesting points about coaching which are elaborated and re-contexted by Blanchard. Both agree that whereas the old rule in business used to be 'When it's over, it's over', the new rule must be that something is not over until those involved have learnt something from it. People in organizations should be fascinated by what does not work – and then, with coaching, do something about it. Shula has a five-step plan for coaching.

1 Tell people what you want them to do.
2 Show them what good performance looks like.
3 Let them do it.
4 Observe their performance.
5 Praise progress, or redirect.

Blanchard comments that one element often neglected by leaders is step 4. If the leader does not observe, then he or she has no data with which to conduct step 5 successfully. This is in fact the most important step because it is the basis for sound coaching. Indeed, these steps bring out a fundamental dilemma of leadership: it is useful to manage by wandering around, but by being present too often or too continuously (even if this gives the leader the opportunity to catch someone doing something right) does the leader, in effect, disempower the follower?

Blanchard considers that many of the answers to the dilemma lie in the consistency exhibited by the leader. Consistency gives the follower the gift of predictability and he quotes from *Putting the One Minute Manager to Work* to demonstrate that four kinds of consequence can follow a person's performance.

1 *A positive consequence* Positive consequences such as praise or reward are pleasurable and as people tend to move towards pleasure these consequences motivate the nature of future behaviour.
2 *Redirection* Old methods of working are stopped and if a person is positively refocused to do something differently, the effects can be powerful and long-lasting.

3 *A negative consequence* Something bad occurs from the person's perspective. This could be a reprimand, or removal from an activity. People tend to avoid pain and so will take steps to avoid an action or activity if it produces negative consequences of this nature.

4 *No response* If there is no response to an activity then it is likely that this lack of recognition will result in the non-correction of poor methods and the possible discarding of positive activities.

Both Blanchard and Shula conclude that people and performance are influenced most by consequences – that is, the response to their efforts by a leader or coach who is on the scene. The business leader must in turn look to leaders in other areas such as sport to observe and adopt the leadership practices observable there. These will usually involve hands-on, results-focused coaching, a philosophy that produces consistently excellent results.

CONCLUSION

Of late, Blanchard has started to branch out into areas beyond the strict confines of leadership theory. His title *We Are the Beloved* describes his own spiritual journey through life. It is likely, however, that he will be best remembered for his sound, commonsense approach to leadership and for the value he has drawn from working with, and then applying his ideas to those of other talented people. While there are many more academic and more thorough books on leadership, there are few works that so successfully combine accessibility and readability with good common sense as the suite of books authored and co-authored by Kenneth Blanchard.

John Adair

John Adair has been named as one of the forty people worldwide who have contributed most to the development of management thinking. In the UK, however, his reputation has largely been carved out through his works on leadership. *Effective Leadership* is regarded as one of the key modern British works on the subject.

Adair has had a long and varied career in a variety of fields spanning academia, education and consultancy. His experiences include a spell on an Arctic trawler, working as a hospital orderly, and time in the Arab Legion. He has been Professor of Leadership Studies at the University of Surrey; Senior Lecturer in Military History and Leadership Training Adviser at the Royal Military Academy, Sandhurst; Assistant Director of the Industrial Society, and visiting Professor in Leadership at the University of Exeter.

Effective Leadership was first published in 1983 and has been regarded as a landmark British book on the subject. The author's colourful background and interests are evidenced in the form of the wide variety of examples of leadership, many drawn from historical and military arenas, which populate its pages. Adair has gone on to publish a variety of other titles in the 'Effective' series, including areas such as *Time Management* and *Decision-Making*. None, however, has had the impact of his book on leadership. Adair's *Great Leaders*, which set out to trace the history of leadership as a concept and to illustrate it with examples of great leaders, was published in 1989. In many respects the pithy elements of example and practical advice which have characterized the work of Adair came together in *Effective Leadership Masterclass* (1997) in which he took particular examples from *Great Leaders* and used them 'to serve as teachers in a kind of leadership masterclass'.

Although developed in later works, the key tenets of Adair's thinking are found in *Effective Leadership*. While adding valuable insights, it is very much a workbook. Readers are set exercises and challenged to compare their views and reactions to set leadership situations or moral dilemmas. At the same time, Adair does not dismiss trait theory; he believes that personality and character are essential elements of leadership and gives a variety of examples, as well as summarizing the work of previous theorists, to support his views. It is, however, for his concept of the essential tasks for a leader – illustrated in his well-known three circle diagram – that he is best known.

When a leader sets out to get something done there are three principal considerations, and they take the form of needs, needs that the leader must consider simultaneously. First of all, there are the needs of the task. A group comes together when the task is too big for an individual to undertake alone. The nature of the task itself will impose demands and a response from both leader and group that will in fact reveal their nature and ability. The leader must consequently be well aware of the nature and demands of the task.

Then there are the needs of the group. Perhaps not as easy to perceive as the demands of the task, these are needs that may lie below the surface. The group will have a need to promote and maintain a level of group cohesiveness: the maintenance need. Over and above the maintenance need, any group will have to have such things as information, or the right tools for the job.

Finally, there are individual needs. People bring their own needs to any group or task situation. These may well be psychological needs for recognition, for status, or to have a sense of doing something worthwhile. Here Adair uses Maslow's hierarchy of needs to prove his point and states that these needs are usually more profound than most leaders recognize. They spring from the individual's experiences of development into adulthood, as well as their current social and domestic situation. Most important, they will always affect their interaction with the work group to which they belong.

Having laid out his basic premise, this three-circle concept is one to which Adair continually returns, whether he is drawing examples of leadership from modern politicians, or even military leaders from the ancient world. The model is even applicable to the areas of values – which themselves are often the starting-point of action. Consequently it is necessary for both leader and team to search out the answers to questions in three potent areas.

1 *Task* Why is the task worthwhile? What is its value to society? How is the value measured?
2 *Team* What is the commonly accepted framework for values – including ethics – that hold this group together?
3 *Individual* Do I share the same values as this group? Is the task worthwhile in my eyes?

Adair states that different leaders may place different emphases on the components of task, team and individual. For one, the task circle may be a lot larger than the team circle and for another the team circle may be predominant. The writer himself places considerable emphasis on the importance of teams, believing that leadership itself is something of a team effort and the best team is one that is composed of emergent leaders within the organization. An individual leader's style will emerge naturally once he or she has addressed the simple functions of leadership. And the good leader should encourage thought about the task in terms of its values as well as its demands. By doing so, the leader will ensure that the common purpose will overlap with the values of the groups and individuals in the organization to ensure more effective implementation.

Adair has a keen interest in what he refers to as 'leadership characteristics', which are qualities that may be perceived as helping or hindering the achievement of the task. The most important leadership qualities are those, such as enthusiasm, which can be applied to all three circles, as they tend to produce overall commitment to the task. All characteristics, however, will apply in helping to move one of the key circles forward, although their over-use or misuse is likely to be counterproductive. For example, while honesty is admirable, undiplomatic candour may upset people unnecessarily and consequently be counterproductive.

The essential list of leadership qualities is made up of initiative, perseverance, integrity, humour, tact, compassion, efficiency, industry, audacity, honesty, self-confidence, justice, moral courage, and consistency.

The three-circle concept forms the basis of *action-centred leadership*, which has been widely taught and used as the basis for much British leadership development. When compared with the clarity of John Kotter's distinction between leadership and management, some of the areas of leadership prescribed by Adair may seem out of place; but Adair's total

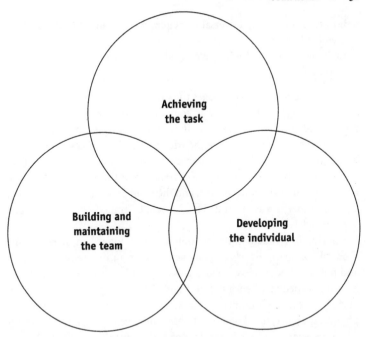

Figure 3

commitment to helping the reader develop as a leader more than makes up for it. He sees it as a process of action and self-development. 'Your leadership development programme should reflect your commitments and burning desire to make the most of your talents. It should focus as much as possible on practical steps. For if you do the right things you will become a leader . . . Do not wait for the right attitudes to appear . . . Actions form attitudes.' By drawing these conclusions Adair sets the scene for his *Effective Leadership Masterclass*, which makes fuller use of the actions, attitudes and capabilities of well-known leaders to complete his thesis.

The concept of the masterclass is an intriguing one; it is by its very nature unscientific, as it draws on the most elusive subtleties of approach revealed by a study of the very best in the field and by the example of their actions. Adair states that the book will give readers a grasp of

• the essential leadership philosophy common to great leaders as revealed in their actions;

● how these enduring universal principles might transfer to the reader's own field of action;
● their own roles as leaders, along with their strengths and areas for improvement.

Although the *Masterclass* abridges the original, it still covers a huge field in its 250 pages. Of necessity it goes over some familiar ground and revisits the three-circle concept. It is at its strongest, however, when dealing with those areas where the wide range of examples (from Hitler to Nelson Mandela) is best exploited. These areas are where the writer wrestles with the elusive concept of charisma, puts the old yet modern idea of the servant leader into context, and then embarks on an exploration of styles of leadership as illustrated by, it could be argued, the good, the bad and the ugly!

Charisma, a much exploited notion when looked at solely in the modern context in which it is characterized as a mixture of good looks and public attractiveness, is like a gloss of fresh paint which soon reveals a lasting inadequacy beneath. But Adair looks at the personal magnetism of such people as Alexander the Great and Napoleon. They had a certain physical presence, they knew how to use symbolism and symbolic gestures when necessary, and (as in the case of Napoleon) they knew the 'power of words over men'. Adair concludes that charisma is a personal magic or aura which attracts a special kind of personal loyalty and enthusiasm from followers. While all leadership is in the gift of the followers, the charismatic phenomenon is a special kind of gift whereby the followers endow the leader with some superhuman characteristics. And some leaders will deliberately try to invoke that reaction by creating a distance between themselves as leaders and their followers while at the same time starting rumours about their own special characteristics – or divinity.

Adair then steps back from these somewhat nebulous remarks by concluding that, while through their personal magnetism some leaders may be able to invoke considerable loyalty, the acid test lies in whether the task is completed successfully, whether at the end of it the team is still held together, and whether individuals feel satisfied with it.

From here the writer comes full circle. Rulers are faced with the dilemma of having to maintain a distance from their followers by virtue of the numbers involved. At the same time they are in danger of having any special aura diminished by the intimacy of modern media – a fate that he feels has befallen the British royal family. But in the end, if the test of leadership comes down to success with the task in hand, is charisma the same thing as leadership? Adair believes that it is not.

When dealing with the concept of the servant leader, Adair is more specific. A common fault with many leaders is a growth of arrogance and a desire to be dominant. However, the teachings of Lao-Tzu and the example of Jesus Christ have indicated a different approach. Both the concepts of Tao and of Christianity have behind them the idea of 'the Way', something that can be broadly defined as 'the order, course or pattern of all things created'. It is the Taoist quality of doing things spontaneously and without worry about their effects on other people's perceptions of oneself that links Lao-Tzu with Jesus. Both loved all living things but did not lord it over them. The emphasis on humility in leadership is unmistakable. A leader therefore is one who listens and meets the needs of the followers. Looked at in this way, it is easier for the leader's conduct to arouse genuine admiration than a loud aggressive approach would evoke. Leaders who divest themselves of the artificial symbols of office are much more powerful than those who cling on to them, for leadership at its most sublime touches people's spirits.

The problem for most leaders is that they have risen to their current position of power because of considerable ability and a dominant spirit. The concept of being humble, of serving rather than ordering, can prove difficult for them. And here is a paradox: to be secure, it is often necessary for the leader to be silent, to listen and not to be in the foreground – to allow others to think that they 'did it themselves'. However, while hierarchies in organizations can work against this, leadership is paradoxical in so far as it works well in formal structures. So good leaders must place themselves on an equal footing with others without losing the respect that stems from their inner leadership qualities. Followers will come to sense the real person within the leadership role and start to respect that person's genuine desire to reflect the equality of all team members in their function of working for the common enterprise.

Adair probes further into the paradoxes of leadership when he sets out to investigate leadership styles more closely. What he is in fact doing here is attempting to distil the elusive concept of greatness. The case studies he uses are those of Abraham Lincoln, Charles de Gaulle, Mahatma Gandhi, and that great misleader, Adolf Hitler.

Greatness can be attributed to rank, knowledge or character. But for a leader to be thought of as great in the historical sense, there needs to have been a really significant achievement. The achievement should have contributed to the total sum of human wellbeing and the accomplishment must have stood the test of time. On the national stage, nations attribute greatness to those leaders who have helped them win or preserve their national freedom. Lincoln is remembered for his achievements, but also for his firmness and generosity of spirit; he genuinely wanted to leave the world a better place than he had found it. De Gaulle, on the other hand, had little of Lincoln's humility; he saw himself as embodying the enduring qualities of the French people and his leadership as stirring the spirit of France. In his work he cultivated aloofness and deliberately did not allow himself to become too close to other people. He would listen to them, but then retire to make the decisions alone. In the end his enormous selflessness outweighed his ego, and his dedication and grand aspirations worked both for him and for France.

Hitler is seen as the great manipulator, setting out to embody all the German virtues. He cultivated an awe-inspiring presence, used the power of the spoken word, and from there manufactured his own charisma. However, vast flaws were to be seen in his leadership abilities: a reliance on fear, an intolerance of error or opposition, a rigidity of approach born of an inability to listen, eventually brought about his downfall. While he undoubtedly had charisma to a mesmeric degree, this was outweighed by his weaknesses as a leader. Adair concludes that there is no true greatness in a leader without moral integrity. Gandhi and Mandela go a long way towards illustrating a quite different approach. This is embodied in utter integrity, courage and a lack of bitterness, even in the face of hardship and persecution. They clearly illustrate that true leadership means staying close to the people, identifying a clear moral purpose and somehow embodying it. By doing this, they were able to alter the perspectives of nations.

Adair points out that some nations have been fortunate enough to find the great leaders they deserve at the right time, but then he writes that all nations need to invest time in exploring the ways in which they can grow leaders for the future. In looking towards the future he suggests that the 'humble', partnership-seeking leaders of the future will need to sense inherent leadership and potential greatness in others – and, as a key task, develop it.

CONCLUSION

Adair ends on a challenging note. His work too is challenging in concept, although those who enjoy left-brained, figure-based analyses may find him indistinct. On the other hand, leadership has always been an elusive idea, and Adair, by using case studies supported by historical examples and analogies from the arts, could be argued to have produced a 'whole-brained' definition.

John W. Hunt

John Hunt is Plowden Professor of Organisational Behaviour at the London Business School, a position he has held for a number of years. Originally from Australia, he has held positions in industry and in business schools in Europe and the USA, all of which has given him a wealth of experience and research to draw on.

Hunt has also consulted at board level in a number of organizations, including 3i, Investors in Industry, where he has concentrated on helping individuals and organizations to improve their performance. *Managing People at Work* (1979) has been Hunt's main contribution to the behavioural literature and is currently in its third edition; it is regarded as one of the best and longest-running texts on behaviour in organizations. An examination of the different editions indicates that Hunt's thinking has moved with the times, including both his views on the place of leadership and the importance of sensitive change management to the well-being of organizations.

In dealing with leadership, Hunt inevitably covers a lot of familiar ground as his intention is to summarize theories and concepts for the reader. There are, however, areas where he explains his own pet theories and where his own research has led him to certain conclusions. These areas include the influence of birth order on the will/ability to lead, the part that politics and power play in making a leader effective, and the processes that a leader should use to ensure the effective implementation of initiatives for change.

Leadership, says Hunt, is 'the capacity to mobilize in competition or conflict a potential need in a follower'. In this sense, leadership is 'a relationship or process of mutual stimulation and elevation that converts arousal into engagement and results'. He points out that many people make it to the top in organizations but not all match these requirements. Those who reach the top in large organizations do have some shared characteristics (but not necessarily personality traits) and what these characteristics tell us is that moving into senior positions is not an equitable process. Much of the conditioning essential to expending energy in the pursuit of career is pre-programmed by an individual's parents and school.

The people who achieve senior leadership positions tend to be:

the first child, or first son First-born children, and notably first-born sons, have a much higher propensity to seek task-orientated roles in organizations, and third- and fourth-born children have a higher likelihood of adopting human relations roles. The family background is a major determinant of style and of balance of styles. Birth order, age differences between children and the effect of adult role models are seen as more influential in role preferences than the sex of the child. There are obvious deviations from the norm, but nevertheless Hunt declares that the above are noticeable trends. An individual's approach to leadership, and debatably his or her success as a leader, is largely a personal behaviour pattern and is developed by family and childhood, as well as organizational, experiences. The individual must then assess the appropriateness of their preferred style to the nature and demands of the organizational situation.

a high achiever These people are motivated by achievement and success.

the possessor of high energy levels This is the energy needed to persist and to push on despite setbacks and disappointment.

able to operate in a longer time span People at the top think longer-term than those lower down the organization.

goal-directed These people are driven by goals and will even create goals where none are necessary.

politically active This is especially the case with first children, who may learn political skills in their families with the arrival of the second child.

loners They do not need the company of others.

field-independent They are able to differentiate what is important from what is unimportant.

Hunt relates the above to the effect of the family on the individual. Children will tend to model their behaviour on their parents' levels of achievement and stretch slightly beyond it. Consequently the child from a background that is already managerial/professional has less far to stretch to get to the top. A look at some of the great leaders of history leads Hunt to ask whether they share the same characteristics that get people to the top in modern organizations. Most of them were first-born children, ranging from Alexander the Great to Churchill and Franklin D. Roosevelt, and he concludes that there is something special about being the first (even Stalin and Hitler, although fourth-born, took first-born status as their elder siblings died at birth). On Hunt's other measures, such as goal direction and energy levels, the historic leaders may have rated high but were not exceptional.

The concept of 'difference', which was the most consistent finding, is often expressed as separateness, and Hunt states that researches have concluded that this stems from childhood experiences which have somehow separated the individual from the rest. Estrangement from their environment makes the potential leader 'turn inward to a private world in order to re-emerge with a new sense of identity'. In contrast, a person with managerial inclinations will see life and work as a search for security and stability rather than as challenge and diversity. Hunt writes that too many managers and too few leaders run large corporations. Managers are typically involved in the day-to-day activities that sustain the central task of the organization, and while leaders will also get involved in the everyday, unlike managers they have the ability to rise to a higher level – thus they will have moments of inspiration and even of glory. This factor is a key difference between management and leadership; managers do not need to be inspirational or glorious in any respect!

Hunt concludes his thoughts on leadership with a word of warning, and here he goes against the grain of much contemporary thinking. Effective leaders do not see themselves as just one of the team; they see themselves as different. A problem with the current obsession with teams is that it reduces the leader's role to that of facilitator – and this robs organizations of the vital difference between leaders and managers. Leaders do not stand out in the way they used to. Too much preoccupation with consensus can encourage a climate of 'anonymous grey figures each unable to be different or separate from the rest. Leadership is about being different and building teams but it is the leader who builds and enthuses the team, not the team that creates the leader.'

Leaders, according to Hunt, have a further vital attribute: they are astute players in the game of organizational politics. They differ from other people in so far as their involvement in political processes is continual. They have to think in political terms all the time. They understand implicitly that organizations are political systems and that consequently leadership is a political process. With this in mind, Hunt (unlike many writers) concentrates on politics as opposed to the exercise of authority. Politics must be mastered. Politics is power in action and is one of the energy sources that actively get things done. Contextual factors in an organization which will affect the level of political activity will include the size of the organization, clarity (or otherwise) of goals, scarcity of resources and different perceptions of the options available. People have to make choices and some goals will be achieved at the expense of others, so people will play politics to influence others as well as to affect the eventual outcomes.

An important role of both leadership and politics is to introduce change. Power and politics make things happen; power and politics enable those who are adept at them to get to the top of the organization. Success in the political arena depends on:

diagnostic skills These are used to develop the database necessary for developing political tactics and include listening, 'wandering around' and networking.

tactical skills These include predicting the outcomes of different tactics and choosing those most likely to bring about the desired results. They include the skills of both listening and prediction.

interpersonal skills These include the ability to influence other people. As power is most effective when used unobtrusively, effective politicians will aim to make their aims more rational and legitimate by sharing their views and expectations with other people and by generating cooperative win/win environments. As studies of effective managers indicate that they are flexible in adjusting their influencing styles to any given situation, Hunt lists a number of political tactics:

- Persuasion and the use of logical arguments.
- Manipulative persuasion, where both the ends and the methods of persuasion become less overt.
- Legitimate requests, made on the basis of the manager's authority.
- Exchange tactics, which contain implicit promises or trades.
- Ingratiation.

● Creative dependency, where one person becomes the confidant of another while simultaneously creating a dependency that can become addictive.

At the same time leaders often will filter information in order to preserve their power. The larger the organization, the greater will be the struggle for influence and promotion. Indeed, by the time an organization has 500 people, every form of political game-playing will be present in it. People will learn to doctor information either to protect themselves or to increase their chances of success or promotion. Tactics for increasing one's chances of success will include 'putting it in writing'; sending positive data about oneself up the hierarchy; sending negative data about peers and rivals up the same hierarchy; and trying to reduce the distance between oneself and one's boss. It is interesting that these tactics can be used both *by* leaders as well as *on* leaders as subordinates jockey for favour with them. However, while politics may have its negative side in organizations, Hunt states that the conflict it generates can have a truly energizing effect. Constructive conflict is essential. There will normally be limits to the use and abuse of power, so, as organizations are political systems, eliminate the politics and you are in danger of eliminating the organization.

It is interesting to note the increasing prominence of change management as a necessary skill in the successive editions of *Managing People at Work* over the years, and in dealing with it Hunt pragmatically advocates the use of effective leadership and effective political skills. The process of change is defined as a series of political manoeuvrings that range from the dictatorial to the democratic. Although change rarely follows a rational planned process, there are a number of ingredients for success, all of which should be deployed.

First of all there should be a *felt pressure for change*. The pressure will energize all concerned; without it, they will not feel any desire or stimulus to make the changes. Then there must be *direction and power*, which could also be termed *leadership and vision*. The vision will point to a desired future state, while the power will refer to the leadership's ability to implement changes. If there is no discernible effective leadership people will be frustrated, especially if they perceive that something needs to be done. There must be people in place with the *capacity to learn the new behaviours or procedures* necessary to make the change happen or to perform well after it has been effected. If the leadership does not prepare for this, the change initiative is likely to flounder.

A further key element is that there must be *actionable first steps* to make the change happen. If people have the skills but do not understand the first things that must be done and how to do them, there will be considerable frustration. And then, finally, there must be *rewards that are relevant to those involved*. If you wish to change behaviour it is necessary to ensure that the rewards match the goals and desires of those involved.

So, successful strategic change will require a crisis or threat to motivate people, a redistribution and centralization of power along with a clear vision/direction for the future. Very important is the ability of the leader both to accurately analyse the situation and to devise strategies and to put them into place. At the same time the leader must have the ability to remain detached and objective in order to enable difficult decisions – especially those involving people – to be made.

CONCLUSION

As ever, John Hunt remains realistic and pragmatic. His leaders are not necessarily 'nice people' or team players; they have the ability to be tough and to play hard games. They also have much of what it takes to be effective and to win through. In describing what makes a leader Hunt leans towards trait theory, and there could be a temptation to put him in that category. However, his philosophy is very much action-based. His leaders must choose to be political and must choose forms of behaviour that will make change happen. Furthermore, his political animals instinctively possess a contingent flexibility that makes them effective change agents.

John Kotter

John Kotter is one of the most prolific and respected writers on leadership today. As Professor of Organizational Behavior and Human Resource Management at the Harvard Business School and previously Konosuke Mashutita Professor of Leadership, he is the author of a number of trail-blazing books and articles on the subject.

Many of Kotter's prime thoughts on the subject spring from a series of works on leadership in the business world. His first examination came in *The General Managers* (1982), which was a systematic study of a group of general managers. This was followed by *Power and Influence* (1985), which argued that to be successful the capabilities needed by general managers were also required of middle managers, as their jobs increasingly demanded the level of leadership usually required in general management jobs. The third and possibly best-known work in the sequence was *The Leadership Factor* (1988), which argued that too few organizations possessed enough people with the necessary attributes and set out to suggest remedies to the problem. More recently Kotter has published *Leading Change* and has been the content expert for a Harvard-produced CD-ROM on 'Realising Change'. His *What Leaders Really Do* was published in 1998. This contained a number of his best-known and most influential articles in the *Harvard Business Review* over the years.

A number of key strands run through Kotter's work. He is fascinated by the reality of leadership and arguably has done more to define the concept than any other writer. He populates his work with case studies taken from major organizations and with the results of detailed question-naires and surveys. For Kotter, a number of other themes must also be addressed. He sees change management as a theme that must underlie all effective leadership behaviour, and this in turn leads on to the need for a leader to be influential and to be adept in the use of power as well as the techniques of persuasion. More than many, Kotter stresses the power of the executive's network of contacts and – perhaps reflecting his teaching responsibilities for Human Resource Management at Harvard – continually links his ideas to the promotion of effective executive development. This can be achieved through a variety of practices ranging from excellence in recruitment to the recognition and exploitation of talent within the organization.

If there is one thing for which Kotter should be valued and remembered, it should be for the fact that he has gone further than his peers to nail down and answer the nagging question: 'What actually is leadership, and how does it differ from management?'

Kotter wrestled with the difference between leadership and management on a number of occasions, starting with a study of US city mayors in 1972. However, his views were expressed most clearly in *The Leadership Factor*, where he used the examples of Lee Iacocca and others to reinforce his thinking. Before clarifying the differences, however, Kotter set out to explain why leadership as a factor in business was now more important than it had been in previous decades. It is interesting to note that his arguments would probably have even more impact now than when they were first expounded.

Writing in 1988, Kotter noted that in the relatively prosperous and stable 1950s and 1960s the need for leadership was not great, either in manufacturing or commerce. Too much leadership could, if anything, have negative consequences by disturbing set and efficient routines. What was needed was stability and control rather than a plethora of new initiatives. However, he concluded that just as leadership becomes more important in an army in wartime than in peacetime, leadership in business becomes more important in times of economic warfare. The rapidly increasing levels of competition, he concluded, had created this wartime scenario when organizations themselves were becoming more complex, and the leadership challenge at the top of many businesses had become almost overwhelming.

From this premise, Kotter sets the scene for his clear definitions of leadership and management. When looking at highly successful middle and senior managers in both the public and private sectors, he found a number of common factors in their approach.

1 A vision of a future that takes into account the legitimate interests of all involved.
2 A strategy in place for achieving that vision that recognizes all the relevant environmental and organizational factors in play.
3 A cooperative network of resources forming a coalition powerful enough to implement the strategy.
4 A highly motivated group of people in place who are committed to implementing the vision.

Kotter states that at the Chief Executive Officer (CEO) level the vision and strategy may be highly complex – leadership with a capital L. At a project level the vision may be diluted to a 'slightly new concept for a product' involving just a few straightforward steps for its implementation. This may require leadership with a small 'l', but it is still leadership.

Effective business leadership in complex organizations can therefore be summarized as having the following elements in common:

1 *Creating an Agenda for Change*
a which includes a vision of what can and should be;
b a vision that takes account of the legitimate long-term interests of the parties involved;
c which includes a strategy for achieving that vision;
d a strategy that takes into account all the organizational and environmental forces.

2 *Building a Strong Implementation Network*
a which includes supportive relationships with the key sources of power needed to implement the strategy;
b relationships strong enough to elicit cooperation, compliance and (where necessary) teamwork;
c which includes a highly motivated core group of people;
d a core group committed to making the vision a reality.

Here Kotter echoes his other iterations on the subject which state that leadership and vision spring from dissatisfaction with the *status quo*. This then requires from the leader the ability to energize, inspire and motivate. How the various actions implied in the above statements can emerge as effective leadership is very much a matter of adjusting the style in which the actions are carried out to the key contingencies of the situation in which the leader must operate.

Kotter goes on to define management (as opposed to leadership) as it has evolved during the twentieth century as the application of four or five key processes:

1 *Planning* The science of logically deducing the means to achieve given ends.
2 *Budgeting* This of course can be regarded as just another part of the planning process.
3 *Organizing* Creating a structure in the organization to help accomplish the plans. This may involve staffing, providing the staff with rewards and incentives, and delegating authority to people where appropriate.
4 *Controlling* This involves looking for deviations from the plan and then using one's authority, as well as methodologies such as review meetings, to solve these problems.

Kotter points out a number of important conclusions to be drawn following these definitions. First of all, management and leadership are not mutually exclusive. They can be complementary and can overlap. (In fact in most people's jobs there will be considerable overlap. That is why the clarity injected by Kotter can be so useful in helping people to define their responsibilities as well as the way in which they plan their time.) However, management and leadership can be very different. Plans do not need to include a vision, and the processes of controlling and motivating can be quite dissimilar. Management is a set of tools based on rational testing and reasoning and they are designed to be used in similar ways across a wide range of business situations. The problem with management is that it does not appear to work well without a great deal of leadership to accompany it in today's volatile and unpredictable environment. Both management and leadership are needed to some degree in all situations, but the leader needs to balance the possible consequences of the 'over tight' with the 'over volatile' to achieve genuine effectiveness.

Kotter suggests that the style of leadership which is effective in most modern organizations is one that is flexible enough to take other people's agendas into account and which recognizes not only how to compete but also how to cooperate. It must be broad in its vision and elicit popular support. The key question then arises, what personal attributes may be needed to provide leadership of this nature?

The list, Kotter says, is a long and complicated one and requires many things to be working on your behalf to ensure success. The main features can be summarized as follows:

- The need for industry and organizational knowledge, which would involve knowledge of products, competitors and technologies.
- Good relationships both in the firm and within the industry.
- Reputation and track record, which should be in a broad range of activities.
- A number of abilities and skills which involve a keen mind, good judgement and the ability to think multidimensionally – this coupled with strong interpersonal skills, including empathy and the ability to sell/persuade.
- Personal values which reflect integrity.
- Motivation, which is exhibited in a high energy level and the desire to achieve, backed by self-confidence.

Many of these qualities are required at middle- and project-manager levels, not just at the very top, and an appreciation of these attributes helps us further to distinguish between leadership and management. Effective management requires considerable knowledge of the disciplines that make up modern management, but does not require an extensive knowledge of the situation being managed. The whole concept of the professional manager who can manage anything is based on this point and from this flows the concept of management competencies.

The Leadership Factor is full of case studies and descriptions designed to illustrate these ideas. It is interesting to note that while some of the case studies have already dated, the original thinking has not. Kotter concludes the book by stating that the concept of leadership with a small 'l' is vital but recognition of this fact would mean that the assessment of leadership potential would be part of all future hiring decisions and the assessment of practices that shape the careers of people in organizations. In turn, individuals need to think about their own careers from a wider perspective, one that helps them bring out their own talents as potential leaders and to match those to the opportunities that may arise.

It is interesting to note how Kotter's thoughts have developed in the series of essays that constitute *What Leaders Really Do*. Here the writer's main themes continue with a further extrapolation of the difference between leadership and management, and the use of power and authority to further the aims of the leader. Because leaders operate through a complex web of dependent relationships, 'managerial work is increasingly becoming a game of dependence upon others instead of just power over others'. He also covers the key techniques of change management.

Although the book consists of separate articles, it is possible to identify a core theme. Kotter states that there is now less confusion about the difference between leadership and management than when he first wrote about it, but that there is still a muddle. For example, people might talk about leadership when they actually mean some combination of leadership and management – and without clarity of meaning, people fail to develop the right skills. Talented people can fail to take the appropriate actions and so manage change without providing leadership. More change demands more leadership and this is difficult to supply if the concept is not fully understood.

Kotter goes back to his original definitions and elaborates on each component of leadership and management, setting each against the other so that the differences are clarified. It is, however, when putting leadership into its essential context of being an agent of change that he is most challenging in his advice to executives. His opening observation is that when managers produce change in an organization the process is both complex and time-consuming. As such, in most successful change initiatives people move through eight stages. They (1) create a sense of urgency; (2) put together a strong enough team to direct the process; (3) create an appropriate vision; (4) communicate the new vision broadly; (5) empower employees to act on that vision; (6) produce sufficient short-term results to give their efforts credibility; (7) build momentum and use that momentum to tackle the tougher change problems; and (8) anchor the new behaviour in organizational culture. But, as Kotter states elsewhere, people can make predictable mistakes when attempting to bring about significant change. This theme is expanded fully when he deals with the reasons why so many transformation efforts fail.

From having studied many organizations whose efforts to change and regenerate can be looked at on a continuum from complete success to utter failure, Kotter concludes that there are eight key reasons for failure:

1 *Not establishing a great enough sense of urgency* Just starting a transformation programme requires the complete cooperation of a number of people. Unless they are well motivated they will not give their help and the overall effort will go nowhere. A paralysed senior

management cadre comes from having too many managers and not enough leaders; as the managers will probably be averse to risk-taking, it is necessary to install genuine leaders in crucial roles. By working on people's opinions, and perhaps even creating artificial crises, it is possible to raise the 'urgency rate' within the organization – the majority must be led to believe that the concept of 'business as usual' is totally unacceptable.

2 *Not creating a powerful enough guiding coalition* It is necessary for a group of senior and influential people to come together and develop a shared commitment to excellent performance via renewal. The importance of teamwork at the top is often undervalued, and the team itself must be led by a dedicated line executive.

3 *Lacking a vision* The vision will say something that helps to clarify the direction in which an organization needs to move. Without it, a transformation initiative can easily dissolve into a series of unrelated and incompatible projects. In failed transformations, states Kotter, you often find plenty of plans and directives, but no vision. The vision itself must be capable of being expressed quickly and succinctly.

4 *Under-communicating the vision by a factor of ten* The net result of under-communication is that cynicism in the organization rises as belief in the vision falls. Executives must use all existing channels to broadcast the message; management education must change to implement courses that focus on the vision. Leaders must walk the talk or they will undermine the change by their inconsistency.

5 *Not removing obstacles to the vision* Too often people understand the overall vision but see huge blocks on the route to implementation. The blocks can be the organizational structure or the compensation of appraisal systems, which can force people to choose between the new vision and their own self-interest. The blocks must be confronted and removed, whether they are organizational or human.

6 *Not systematically planning for and creating short-term wins* People need early evidence that their efforts are succeeding. It is necessary to look for ways of demonstrating clear improvements and to reward those who have helped achieve them. Although obtaining short-term wins can be difficult, the pressure to achieve them will keep the urgency

level high and bring about detailed and analytical thinking that can clarify the vision itself.

7 *Declaring victory too soon* Until the changes have been firmly embedded in the culture for some years it is too early to say that they are permanent. Leaders must use the credibility afforded by short-term wins to tackle bigger, longer-term problems.

8 *Not anchoring the changes in the corporate culture* Until new behaviours are rooted in the norms and values of the organization, they will degrade as soon as the pressure is removed. It is necessary to ensure that the next generation of management truly personifies the new approach – and this in turn has implications for succession and promotion planning.

Ensuring that an organization does not continually fall into these traps could well be taken as part and parcel of its duty to create a culture of leadership. Here Kotter develops a theme that is close to his heart. Most of the work that people do in organizations seems to undermine the qualities needed for good leadership. Career patterns need to be managed, as it is a fact that individuals who are successful leaders often have a number of career experiences in common. These experiences include a significant challenge early in their career, and a broadening experience at a later stage which could involve being assigned to a special task force. Other features include a chance to develop a good network of relationships. Organizations also need to make efforts to spot people with leadership potential.

Such strategies help to create a corporate culture where people value leadership in staff and try hard to develop it. Kotter believes that both the world and business need more people who will work to develop cultures that will in turn create leadership. 'Institutionalizing a leadership-centred culture is the ultimate act of leadership.' With this sentiment, Kotter summarizes much of the thrust of his work.

CONCLUSION

As someone who has done more than most to define the concept of leadership accurately, Kotter has married it successfully to two of his other key themes: the need to be influential and the need for organizations themselves to develop and promote leadership within them.

In many respects it is hard to place Kotter in any one school as he has defined his subject, talked about its development in young people, and also dealt with the contingencies of leadership activity – albeit within a framework of change management. This in itself places much of his work in the arena of transformational leadership. Like many good writers his work defies simple categorization, although this does not prevent its value from shining through.

Manfred Kets de Vries

As a practising psychoanalyst, Manfred F.R. Kets de Vries brings a different, psychologically-based, approach to the study of leadership.

A consultant, academic, conference speaker and author, he is one of the leading European authorities on the subject. His previous experience includes teaching at both Harvard Business School and McGill University, and he currently holds the Raoul de Vitry d'Avaucourt chair of Human Resource Management at the European Institute of Business Administration (INSEAD). He is the author of numerous books and articles on leadership and organizational diagnosis. His titles include *Unstable at the Top* (1989), *The Neurotic Organisation* (1984), *Prisoners of Leadership* (1989) and *Leaders, Fools and Impostors* (1993), and he has written many articles for publications such as the *Harvard Business Review*, *Psychology Today* and *Organisational Dynamics*. He has been a guest speaker in venues as diverse as Management Centre Europe and the Masters' Forum.

As an author, Kets de Vries has tended to specialize in the darker side of leadership as well as in entrepreneurialism and leadership in family businesses. He draws his illustrations of leadership behaviour from a wide range of case studies in politics, business and history, using such diverse characters as Jack Welch, Hitler, Lee Iaccocca, Saddam Hussein and Richard Branson to illustrate the points he makes concerning the positive and negative aspects of leadership. Much of the main thrust of Kets de Vries's thinking on leadership can be observed in *Prisoners of Leadership* and it is expanded in *Leaders, Fools and Impostors*.

In *Prisoners of Leadership*, Kets de Vries sets out to investigate why some leaders succeed while others in similar circumstances fail. Taking a psychological stance, he probes the 'inner theatre' that causes a leader to make certain decisions as well as the complex interplay between a leader and his or her followers. In studying these areas he also looks at the roots of failure and self-destruction, and examines what he calls the 'F Factor' – the failure factor.

In explaining the F Factor, Kets de Vries notes that it is all too easy for the leader to fall victim to the allure of grandiosity. People appear to need leaders and if you are the one actually leading, then it is tempting to assume airs and graces and to develop a need for admiration. But when things go wrong and followers become critical the leader can become irritated – and even slightly paranoid. There are, however, other pressures at work on the leader.

Isolation from reality The concept of the loneliness of command is a real one. While the leader can take care of the dependency needs of the followers, who is there to take care of the dependency needs of the leader? The result can be anger, anxiety and sometimes a wish for revenge at having been left out, all culminating in an irrational desire to blame others. Sometimes the aggression is turned inwards, resulting in equally dire consequences for the organization.

Fear of success Although this phenomenon may be difficult to understand, it is a reality. Success makes you more noticeable; it brings with it greater responsibilities and a change from comfortable routines, as well as a loss of one's old identity. The stress of being in a position of power may then become too hard to handle. The act of failing may then in fact be a cry for help.

A key danger for the leader is that of narcissism. This strange concept is dealt with at length in *Prisoners of Leadership* and then further elaborated in *Leaders, Fools and Impostors*. While Kets de Vries deals with many character traits or dispositions, he is at his most interesting when dealing with this particular reaction to personal glory and power. He regards this desire for admiration, to be noticed, as one of the most important influences on personality style in people in authority. Quoting from the manual *DSM III*, he defines it as 'a pervasive pattern of grandiosity, lack of empathy and hypersensitivity to the evaluation of others'. This can be seen to be present in a variety of contexts and is indicated in at least five of the following:

reacting to criticism with rage or shame;
being interpersonally exploitative;
expecting to be noticed as special without appropriate achievement;
believing his or her problems to be unique;
being preoccupied with fantasies of unlimited success or power;
having an unreasonable expectation of entitlement;
requiring constant attention or admiration;
showing an inability to recognize how others feel;
being preoccupied with feelings of envy.

In short, people with narcissistic tendencies believe they deserve special consideration in life.

Kets de Vries does not believe that an element of narcissism is necessarily all bad; after all, the radiation of confidence and power can be very contagious. While there are obvious downsides, a secure sense of self-esteem can tame feelings of rage and envy of others and provide the building blocks for conviction, purpose and creativity. He quotes John Harvey-Jones as recognizing the siren call of narcissism and as taking steps to avoid excess. The narcissism, if recognized and dealt with, can then be the motor that drives the organization.

There are other, more subtle traps for both leader and organization, and one of them is what Kets de Vries refers to as *folie à deux* – or, to put it bluntly, situations where leaders drive their followers mad.

Using such examples as Hitler and J. Edgar Hoover, Kets de Vries explores the phenomenon of mental contagion, where leaders actually transfer their neuroses and phobias to their followers with shared madness as the result. *Folie à deux* can thrive in closed communities where it is easy to lose touch with reality, and where the outside environment is made out to be hostile. From here it is easy for all involved to develop a culture where compliance is the norm and there are frequent searches for scapegoats. Put these elements together with a leader who has a strong message and followers who feel insecure or who need strong direction, and the stage is set.

While these situations often exist in the political arena, Kets de Vries believes that they are even more likely to emerge in entrepreneurial organizations based on a single powerful individual. The results are predictable: unproductive behaviour, a lack of original thinking and a tendency for the organization to lose touch with its original aims and objectives. Symptoms include:

orders to toe the party line, or else – distrust becomes the prevailing attitude;

a lack of creativity, except in some disfigured form;

a high level of secrecy, as fear is the continual undercurrent;

eccentricities of strategy and planning.

It is possible to cure a *folie à deux* and the easiest approach is to separate the people concerned. The injection of objective outside influences and measurement systems can reassert reality. Here the introduction of the views of auditors, suppliers, consultants and contractors can bring the organization down to earth. However, this particular element of the F Factor is hardest to break down in entrepreneurial organizations.

The concept of the entrepreneur as leader has a particular fascination for Kets de Vries, and he believes that many start their own businesses because they were difficult employees. Consequently they do not welcome suggestions or orders from others as they want to control their own environment. They find it difficult to work with other people in structured situations unless they were responsible for the structure in the first place and can dictate terms. This can result in low tolerance for subordinates who think for themselves, and a general suspicion of others. Put this together with a strong need for recognition and applause (many entrepreneurs come from humble origins) and the individual will tend to see things in extremes when dealing with people. This accounts for the fact that in many entrepreneurial organizations a strong middle management cadre will be seen to be lacking, although those who flourish in such organizations often need the strong, if quirky, leadership they find there and need the risks as well as the potentially high returns. And, as ever, the need for objective counselling and advice for the leader in the form of a consultant, banker, etc., is always present.

The need for an outside influence on the leader, whether that leader is an entrepreneur or working in a different sort of organization, is more fully explained in *Leaders, Fools and Impostors*. In this book, Kets de Vries writes that many entrepreneurs possess the qualities of an impostor, namely being able to pass themselves off as someone other than their true self, and with the ability to dramatize their own actions and aspirations. They also have the capacity to understand how to profit from the wishes and desires of other people. In looking at the psychodynamics of imposture, Ket de Vries states that many leader-impostors have the empathic skills to weave their followers' desires into their own myth, 'creating an increasingly credible tapestry of illusion'. However, at the same time the leader may recognize elements of the impostor within himself or herself and descend into a vicious cycle of doubt, guilt, hard work and procrastination, resulting in self-defeating actions which can be disastrous for an organization – or a nation. Using such characters as Hitler to illustrate these points, the writer paints a bleak picture and states that it is vital for leaders to develop insight into their motivation and to become aware of their blind spots. Only then can the paralysing effects of the syndrome be broken.

Coupled with this are the ongoing effects of narcissism, a preoccupation with power and difficulty in letting go. For many leaders the process of ageing holds special terrors, partly because they have come to identify their whole existence with their role as leader and the prospect of letting go is abhorrent. For the more narcissistic, the realization of eventual mortality through the ageing of one's body is 'the ultimate narcissistic injury'. This self-consciousness can lead to a sense of defect and the waning of sexual powers. Consequently the wielding of power becomes a form of substitute activity or outlet for energies, which can result in its abuse. In other cases the leader may place great significance and invest disproportionate energy on the building of monuments in some form or other – something by which he or she will be remembered.

It is against this complex backdrop that the role of the 'fool' takes on a special significance. The concept of the court jester, or fool, is one that has been around since time immemorial and which has often been used in drama and literature. The basic concept is that of the individual who does not represent a threat of any kind to the king or leader, and who, because of his special position, can give the leader feedback where others cannot. Often the feedback and advice are couched in humorous terms, but it is nevertheless vital in presenting a picture of reality to the leader who may have become isolated and who may have had the truth distorted by sycophants. Hence the fool, by being foolish, can become the guardian of reality and in taking the role can prevent future folly.

In organizational life, the role of the fool can be built into the infrastructure in the form of checks, rules and regulations. However, the role of the individual is often more potent in giving feedback and providing reality checks. The individual could be a member of the organization who is sufficiently confident about his or her future to risk 'playing the fool', or more often an external adviser such as a consultant. Whatever its source, the advice is essential to both leader and organization. Every despot needs one disloyal subject to keep him sane. Kets de Vries concludes his thoughts on this aspect by pointing out that when studying organizations we usually focus on the leader rather than the follower. There is, though, a vital link between the two; 'leaders need followers, the king needs his fool and vice versa'.

What, then, in his examination of the complex morass of organizational difficulties and psychological traps highlighted in his work, is the writer's advice to the would-be leader? Where does effectiveness lie? And how is it achieved? It is in *Prisoners of Leadership* that some of the most concrete advice, as opposed to analysis of problem areas, can be found.

Kets de Vries states that leadership is not only about the leader but also about the complex interaction between the leader, the followers, and the situation, or historical moment, in which they are operating. Although he is doubtful about the value of lists of qualities because leaders may possess different qualities in various combinations, he does accept that there are a number of things to look out for. Using the example of Charles de Gaulle, whom he also quotes, he points out that great leaders have always managed their effects – to an extent, they are showmen. At the same time they must demonstrate their readiness to launch great undertakings, be prepared to show that they have vision and to see things through to the end. All this adds up to demonstrating a compelling self-confidence that will draw others to the cause. These characteristics contribute to the leader's charisma, and once established this charisma can be maintained through dramatic appeals to action backed up by good stagecraft.

The leader can draw strength from his or her inner images to sustain the action and this is where the vision plays its part. It is up to the leader to create a shared reality that is transmitted to the followers, often by describing the way ahead and the goals as a journey or path to follow. This sometimes magnificent obsession, which is fuelled by images from the leader's inner world, then mobilizes followers to pursue a course of action leading to the desired conclusion. But at the same time it is up to the leader to 'manage the meaning' of the overall situation.

In doing this, leaders must articulate the dream and at the same time make it attractive to others, and it is here that the theatrical elements of leadership come to the fore. Following on from this, effective leaders create in their followers a need to be taken care of; they awaken dependency needs, and even become the repository of their followers' fantasies. In doing so, they display an acute sense of timing and use simple yet hard-hitting language to enable their message to come across clearly. Consequently the group of followers will be prone neither to doubt nor uncertainty. Kets de Vries cites a number of political leaders, such as Churchill, in making these points but also stresses that business leaders can do the same thing, albeit on a less grandiose scale.

In addition, effective leaders are good at building and maintaining networks of communication. They manage their relationships with key subordinates very carefully, even to the point of engineering conflict between them. The resultant fracas, in the case of Roosevelt, enabled him to see the choices that they found difficult to make – and the well-advertised quarrels provided him with sound information. When it comes to information, effective leaders are good at bringing order to the chaos of information overload. They are reducers, and from this reduction – part of the ability to manage cognitive complexity – comes clarity and novel solutions.

Other statements about leadership effectiveness fall into Kets de Vries's original ideas about charisma. Empowerment is defined by the leader's demonstration of confidence in subordinates. Statements of intent on the grand scale are reinforced by individual assertions of confidence and thus by 'harnessing the energies of their followers and translating intention into sustained reality, they encourage them to achieve unexpected results'.

Good leaders know how to manage stress, they know how to wait, and they do not give up easily. With this staying power they can go beyond simply being visionaries and become positive 'doers' – with the doing itself based on a realistic knowledge of the organization and how it works. All the qualities described above help the leader avoid the F-Dimension as the best leaders possess special qualities at both the conscious and unconscious level and can address these two levels in their followers. If the leader can do this and use self-insight as a restraining force against the seductive call of power, then he or she is likely to be successful.

CONCLUSION

The concepts of self-insight, inner theatre, conscious and unconscious desires, and other features of a psychological dimension are in many ways peculiar to Kets de Vries. Many of them are complex and require a fuller explanation than can be afforded here. However, they provide powerful insights and examples for the reader, as well as (in a number of instances) a series of stark warnings. In outlining them he provides a useful service to both the student of leadership and the practitioner.

Judy Rosner, Sandra Bem and Jan Grant

In the last few decades and most noticeably since the resurgence of the feminist movement in the 1960s there has been considerable debate as to whether women are sufficiently well represented in the higher echelons of management and leadership. Certainly as more women entered middle levels of management the focus shifted to the 'glass ceiling' which prevents women reaching the most senior positions. However, the question addressed by those writers who wished to move beyond opinion into analysis has been not so much whether women should reach senior positions as to whether there are elements of female behaviour and thinking that differentiate them from men as leaders. If so, will these characteristics increasingly come to the fore and provide answers to tomorrow's problems? Some argue that women by their very gender bring different qualities to leadership, while others argue that both sexes have a masculine and feminine side which can be reflected in their leadership style. If the latter is the case, then it follows that organizations should create a climate in which both masculine and feminine attributes can be expressed.

In this section, the work of three women who have contributed to the debate is examined. Judy Loden Rosner, as a faculty member of the Graduate School of Management at the University of California and author of *Workforce America* (1990), based her views on a study of men and women leaders she carried out on behalf of the Leadership Foundation of the International Women's Forum. Sandra Bem's interest in the fact that men and women might display the same characteristics led her to write 'The Measurement of Psychological Androgyny' (*Journal of Consulting and Clinical Psychology*, Vol. 42, 1974), a study that was backed by questionnaires to determine thinking styles. Finally, as contrast and endorsement, we will look at the work of Jan Grant, who studied what women could offer organizations.

Judy Rosner states that women who have managed to break the glass ceiling in their organizations have proved that leaders do not come from one mould. Those women who were successful had shown that a non-traditional leadership style is well suited to some environments and can improve an organization's chances of succeeding in an uncertain world. Consequently there is strength in an organization having a diversity of leadership styles. Men are more likely to describe themselves as transactional leaders, while the way in which women describe themselves tends to conform more to concepts of transformational leadership. This means that women are more likely to get subordinates to transform their own self-interest into the interest of the group for a broader goal. At the same time, women leaders attributed their power to personal characteristics like charisma, interpersonal skills and networking rather than to organizational position.

A major differentiator between men and women noticed by Rosner was that women's leadership style was interactive; the women surveyed worked hard to make their interaction with subordinates positive for all involved. They also encouraged power-sharing, participation and information exchange. They tended to allow all employees to contribute in powerful and important ways, thereby generating a win/win situation that was good for both employees and the organization (it is interesting to note the similarity with Stephen Covey's 'fourth habit' of effective people – see page 126). Women leaders were keen to promote participation because they believed that people performed better when they felt good about themselves, but what they did went beyond conventional participation as their actions enhanced other people's sense of self-worth and therefore energized followers.

Inclusion is at the heart of this interactive leadership, an idea that would be close to John Whitmore's heart (see pages 202–3). And women leaders worked to instil a sense of group identity in a variety of ways, by instituting mechanisms that made people participate and by using conversational styles that facilitated greater involvement by all. There is always a danger that participation can be seen to be merely symbolic, yet most of the women in Rosner's survey defused this risk by asking for suggestions, using the feedback to test their own hypotheses and to clarify their views before making decisions. On the other hand, where participation did not work the women leaders had the flexibility to act unilaterally.

Women's attitudes to power were also different from those of men. They were willing to share power and information rather than guard it, and they were willing to share the reasoning behind their decisions. But sharing power and information has its risks; people may reject or challenge what the leader has to say, and those who have been listened to but who see the leader subsequently taking a different course of action may become disillusioned. The women leaders tended to acknowledge these risks but felt that they were worth taking because the positive outcomes were overwhelming.

One of the positive outcomes was that employees felt important. Their leaders added to this by refraining from asserting their own superiority or doing things that set them apart from others. They did not covet formal authority because they had learnt how to lead effectively without it. At the same time they spoke of their enthusiasm for work and how they aimed to spread their enthusiasm to others. Enthusiasm was a clear theme that ran through Rosner's findings and writings. However, to steer clear of leadership styles that could be criticized as mere cheer-leading, they ensured that they preserved their credibility by achieving results that could be easily measured.

Rosner remarked on the ease with which the women leaders she studied adapted their beliefs and styles to their socialization and the career paths they had chosen. Women traditionally have been in the gentler professions, which tend to use cooperative and supportive behaviour; thus their interactive leadership has its roots firmly in their socialization. They now have power and control over resources but they still see the sharing of power and information as an asset rather than a liability. They believe that what people really want (over and above pay and promotion) is to feel that they are contributing to a higher purpose, and that as individuals they have the opportunity to learn and grow.

The 'best' leadership style depends on the organizational context and Rosner concludes that the degree of change in organizations is an important factor in creating opportunities for women. The higher the level of change, the better the opportunities for the women involved. As the economic environment demands rapid change and the workforce demands participation, interactive leadership may well emerge as the style of choice. For this to happen, more organizations need to challenge their own assumption that command and control is the best approach. Because more women than men are likely to be interactive leaders there is a risk that some organizations may perceive this style as 'feminine' in nature and therefore resist it. By valuing a diversity of leadership styles (and particularly the interactive) organizations will find the strength and flexibility to survive in the uncertain and competitive future. In saying this, Rosner puts women firmly in the driving-seat as generators of future prosperity. It is, however, interesting to contrast her views with those of Sandra Bem, who sheds more light on style flexibility with her concept of psychological androgyny.

To put this concept into perspective, it may be helpful to recall the time when men joked that the only truly successful women they knew were more aggressively masculine in attitude and behaviour than the men they worked alongside. This may well have been true for some who would have seen it as the only way to get ahead, but it does not seem to be the way in which most women – and in fact many men – wish to lead.

In her article on psychological androgyny Sandra Bem defined a number of characteristics that could be defined as masculine or feminine. She did not mean that certain characteristics were the sole province of one sex but that a particular characteristic was more likely to be found in one or other of the sexes. Bem listed a number of male and female characteristics and some that were neutral. A sample of the more powerful male and female characteristics is given below:

Male	*Female*
Self-reliant	Yielding
Defends own beliefs	Cheerful
Independent	Shy
Assertive	Flatterable
Strong personality	Loyal
Forceful	Warm
Analytical	Sympathetic
Dominant	Sensitive to others' needs
Willing to take risks	Understanding
Makes decisions easily	Compassionate
Willing to take a stand	Soothes hurt feelings

Bem believed that those people who had the flexibility to use both masculine and feminine qualities would be the most effective because they could choose from a wider range of behaviour according to the demands of the situation. The effective leader will be capable of dominant behaviour when necessary and of a sympathetic approach when appropriate. The ability to move between styles is what Bem calls 'androgyny' and she suggests that those who need to be more effective as leaders must acquire a broader range of androgynous skills, irrespective of their sex. The overall philosophy of flexibility and 'wholeness' is similar to that of both Kenneth Blanchard and Ned Herrmann, although Bem places it in a different dimension.

A somewhat different view of this male/female debate is put forward by Jan Grant in 'Women as Managers: What they can offer organisations' (*Organisational Dynamics*, Winter, 1988). Grant believes that many women have had to suppress their feminine characteristics on their way up through organizations because these characteristics make them appear ill-suited for leadership roles. There are, however, negative consequences for the women and the organizations concerned; the very behaviours that have been repressed or undervalued are those that help an organization become more responsive to human needs 'for a sense of connectedness, community, purpose, affiliation and nurturing'. Grant argues that over and above biological influences, it is women's experiences in the family, community and political structure that have led to the development of a number of valuable psychological qualities that are especially relevant to effectiveness in modern organizations:

Communication and cooperation As women have had a lot of practice from an early age in communicating with and caring for other people they are often very good at it and can find means of reconciliation rather than confrontation. This helps to make behaviour in meetings more cooperative than competitive and can lead to a better exchange of information.

Affiliation and attachment There is evidence that women have developed a different psychic starting-point from men, one in which affiliation is valued equally or more highly than self-enhancement. This strong sense of ties to and concern for others can be a useful resource in organizations whose members are often prey to feelings of alienation and isolation. Women's greater ease in the field of relationships could change organizations and make them places where egocentricity and an all-out push for personal success become less important and where affiliation, friendship and 'personhood' become more highly valued.

Power While men tend to equate power with aggression and assertion, women tend to equate it with giving and caring, or with nurturing and strength. For them, it is much more a transforming force from within the organization than anything hierarchical.

Physicality The physical make-up of women, 'tied as it is to nature's images of birth, blood, pregnancy, lactation and nurturing of growth', can be an asset for women in organization and leadership roles. This is because it 'grounds women in the day-to-day realities of growth and development', giving them a sharp perception of reality and a down-to-earth perspective on life in the organization that can be immensely helpful to the organization itself.

Emotionality, vulnerability and lack of self-confidence Women find it far easier than men to express their fears, their emotions and their lack of self-confidence. These weaknesses may in fact be solid strengths, as by not entering into denial women are in a stronger position to develop strengths out of the so-called weaknesses. This starting-point has also allowed for a far more accurate assessment of one's self and of one's own strengths and weaknesses. Women's ability to express emotion as well as vulnerability may make the organizations to which they belong more human as environments by placing the same stress on interpersonal accomplishments as they do on other achievements.

Intimacy and nurturing Grant argues that girls reach maturity with a greater capacity for empathy with others and a greater sense of connectedness to the wider world than men. This leads them to value closeness and to nurture intimacy with others in a way that can seem very challenging to men, who value rationality and separateness. Organizations need to acknowledge the value of the important skills associated with 'the more reproductive processes of society'.

Grant concludes that the case must continually be made for moving women out of the traditional nurturing and expressive roles and for building their innate qualities into strengths that can be used in the upper echelons of organizations. If organizations are to become more humane, less alienating towards their people and more responsive to those individuals, they will need to learn to value process as much as product. At the same time, women must learn to value their experiences and learn to speak with their own voice if they are to make a significant and liberating impact on the organizations in which they work.

And thus we return to Judy Rosner who could be said to be talking about the enactment of Grant's qualities.

CONCLUSION

The literature on women as leaders is growing and will continue to do so. At the same time, while debate continues over a number of different aspects covering the approach of women to leadership as well as their impact in the role, it is axiomatic that although the glass ceiling has existed,

● many women have made highly successful leaders by behaving differently from men;
● many women have made highly successful leaders by behaving just like men – or more so;
● there are a number of characteristics that more commonly apply to men and others that more commonly apply to women;
● on the other hand, no two women and no two men are alike;
● there are many men working in so-called 'male characteristic environments' who would dearly like to see female characteristics displayed by both the men and women leaders or colleagues they work with.

So the overall situation is still far from clear-cut. This writer can only conclude that a great deal more work needs to be done on the subject – work to ensure that women can reach the top, and on the different characteristics that make for effective leadership by both women and men when the top is finally reached. It is facile to blame all the ills of organizations on 'male characteristics', but at the same time it is dangerous not to think in terms of both individual and organizational androgyny. Diversity, as ever, is the key.

CCL Study on Derailment

(Morgan W. McCall, Jr, and Michael Lombardo; Robert E. Kaplan with Wilfred H. Drath and Joan R. Kofodimos)

A major focus for the study of leadership and a thriving centre for the development of would-be leaders is the Center for Creative Leadership (CCL) at Greensboro, North Carolina, USA. Founded in 1970 through the sponsorship of Smith Richardson, who gave the world Vicks VapoRub and was a major benefactor of several other emergent businesses in the area, CCL has since then built up a powerful name in the world of leadership development. It has also contributed significantly to the overall state of knowledge of the subject via its influential research team. CCL research has over the years covered such diverse subjects as entrepreneurs and inter-cultural values. One of its most powerful studies, however, has been in the subject of 'executive derailment' – the phenomenon in which executives whose careers start with great promise fail to live up to that promise and eventually do not make the grade as top-level business leaders. This has been the subject of technical reports issued by the centre spanning some six years, and of a book that moved the debate from causes to cures published eight years after the first report. All the writers mentioned here are either employed by CCL or have been associated with it in an 'adjunct' status.

Morgan McCall and Michael Lombardo were the key researchers behind Technical Report No. 21, 'Off the Track: Why and How Successful Executives Get Derailed'. In their study they found that those executives whose careers left the fast track on a non-voluntary basis differed only slightly from those who actually reached the top. Some executives found that earlier strengths suddenly became liabilities, while others found that what they had believed to be weaknesses became exactly what was required of them as strengths in a different context. The researchers worked with several Fortune 500 corporations to identify people who had a good overview of the successes and failures of other executives and interviewed those people who made succession decisions. Respondents were asked to describe the features of both success stories and derailments.

The results of the interviews set out to answer four questions. Why were those who eventually derailed successful in the first place? What was it that brought their latent weaknesses to the surface? Why did they derail? In what ways did they differ from those who remained successful?

Initial reasons for success were seen as many and varied, but the researchers eventually honed them down to the fact that a successful executive would possess two or three of the following seven characteristics:

1 Outstanding track record – identified early as having high potential and having a string of successes.
2 Outgoing, well-liked, charming.
3 Technically brilliant.
4 Loyal and helpful to management, willing to make sacrifices.
5 Ambitious, managed career well.
6 Moved up during reorganization or merger.
7 Excellent at motivating or directing subordinates.

Sometimes those who were seen as well-liked and charming were regarded with some suspicion, and it was also felt that those who had done well during mergers had moved up at a time when performance was particularly hard to measure. In fact the researchers concluded that nobody was without faults; both the successful and the derailed had faults, but they wished to study what might cause these faults to surface – and to be significant – well on into a career. In general, the flaws of both the successful and the derailed tended to show up when one or more of the following five things happened:

● they lost a boss who had shielded them or covered for them in some way;
● they entered a new job for which they were not fully prepared, and this was usually coupled with having a new boss whose style was different;
● they left behind them a number of little problems, or of 'bruised people' whom they had handled poorly or failed to handle at all;
● they were promoted in some way during a shake-up of the organization and their behaviour was not examined for some time after the promotion;

● they entered a level of seniority where getting on with other people under highly stressful conditions became extremely important.

The events listed above began to sort out the two groups of successful and derailed, and the researchers concluded that how an executive deals with his faults in times of stress is critically important. They cited a mixture of ten managerial and personal flaws as reasons for derailment and added, somewhat chillingly, that only two need apply to the average derailment.

1 *Specific performance problems with the business*
The stress of a business that was not reaching its targets was likely to put an individual's performance under the microscope.

2 *Insensitivity to others; an abrasive, bullying style*
This was a major cause of derailment, and under stress some of the derailed managers became abrasive and intimidating. This was often characterized by extreme impatience and disregard for the feelings or priorities of others.

3 *Cold, aloof, arrogant*
Some began to intimidate other people by their technical brilliance, making them feel stupid, and not listening to their viewpoints. It was felt that they had no time for those they did not consider as brilliant as themselves.

4 *Betrayal of trust*
This was regarded as a cardinal sin although it was seldom connected with basic honesty. Rather it was about 'one-upping' others or failing to follow through on promises.

5 *Overmanaging – failing to delegate or build a team*
This flaw was seen to be fatal at higher levels, when the meddlers were dealing with more senior people who were likely to have higher levels of expertise in their subject than their bosses. Consequently, they were liable to upset people and to be vulnerable in any subsequent conflicts or arguments.

6 *Over-ambitious – thinking of the next job, playing politics*
This was a complex area as the executives bruised others in their haste to get ahead but also spent too much time trying to please upper management. They were left with few allies.

7 *Failing to staff effectively*
This was the flaw found in so many managers, who were unable to pick good people or who selected staff in their own image; both would rebound.

8 *Unable to think strategically*
The inability to think strategically often emerged in over-attention to detail; these managers could not make the move from being doers to being planners.

9 *Unable to adapt to a boss with a different style*
The key difference between the successful and unsuccessful was that the successful were more adaptive; they did not go to war with their new bosses and did not let issues become personal.

10 *Over-dependent on an advocate or mentor*
Some stayed with an advocate too long and became over-associated with that person. This made other people start to question that executive's ability to stand alone, and, of course, sometimes the mentors left or fell out of favour themselves.

The researchers noticed a pattern by which some combinations of strengths became weaknesses that eventually caused failure. Paradoxically, the same attributes that had got these people to the top eventually undermined them. The drive that had at first supported them made them moody and volatile under pressure, they became defensive when they made mistakes and often tried to hide those mistakes. At other times they were seen as political, or as direct yet tactless. The survivors, on the other hand, usually had more diversity in their track record and this appeared to give them greater flexibility in handling a variety of organizational and interpersonal issues. Those who derailed usually did so for four basic reasons: over-use of their strengths turned them into weaknesses; their deficiencies eventually came to matter; they allowed success to go to their heads; and, of course, events could conspire against them. The researchers concluded that there was an element of luck in the equation but at the same time there was often a period in which the fatal flaws began to surface, a time when the executive concerned was either unaware of them or did nothing about them.

While the report concluded that there is no one best way to succeed – or to fail, for that matter – it was possible that two key elements truly differentiated the successful from the derailed – total integrity and the ability to understand other people.

The story was taken up again by Robert E. Kaplan, supported by Wilfred H. Drath and Joan R. Kofodimos, in *Beyond Ambition: How Driven Managers can Lead Better and Live Better* (1991). At that time, Kaplan was a senior fellow at CCL, Drath was the publications director and research associate, while Kofodimos was an independent consultant and researcher.

Kaplan, building on the work already done by the Center, set out to explain how the drive to excel could actually derail the careers of talented managers. He set out antidotes to derailment and burnout for leaders by illustrating how executives on the fast track could shift to an 'inner fifth gear' and avoid the pitfalls. Based on an intensive study of forty senior executives whose drive to excel was actually damaging their performance and prospects, he set out to show how personality traits could be changed for people to achieve more effective performance as leaders.

Many of the problems came from what Kaplan described as the *expansive* character of the executives concerned. This was something that was inherent in the people themselves and could be accentuated by the character of the organization. He reiterated many of the flaws already identified in previous CCL reports and added 'focusing on empire-building and other kinds of self-aggrandisement', 'pushing themselves too hard', and 'having an inflated sense of their own importance'. All this added up to a particular type of character: an expansive character. Character might be described as a fundamental pattern that unites what might otherwise appear to be a set of disparate traits. An expansive character is concerned with the drive for mastery. Combined with this drive is a willingness to expend great energy in its pursuit and to push other people hard in order to attain it. As the executive may see himself or herself as lacking in mastery, this then becomes a theory of motivation. It is interesting to contrast these thoughts with Bennis's theories of a slower and more paced progress towards mastery (see pages 99ff) and with Kets de Vries's theories of executive decline.

The individual in pursuit of mastery is likely to be extremely focused and intense as well as aggressive in pursuit of objectives. Kaplan gives the example of Margaret Thatcher as an expansive character, while her contemporary Ronald Reagan is seen as too passive and *laissez-faire* to be considered as such. The expansive personality can be intensified by the executives' environment; they sit in the upper echelons of the organization and receive treatment that can amplify already well-developed expansive tendencies, or bring out latent ones. While power and prestige can fortify people as leaders, they can as easily inflate expansive tendencies out of all proportion to the requirements of the situation. So if a manager has bad habits they may get worse, but conversely if a manager had previously lacked a commanding presence he might emerge with the capability to succeed in the senior role. It is an ambiguous situation and a slippery slope.

To be expansive is to possess the drive that can push an organization forward by overcoming the inertia that can stand in the way of change. And this sheds further light on the difference between the characters of those managers who become leaders, and those managers who remain mere managers; if leadership is about making change happen, then expansive characters are indispensable as prime movers. To make a difference to an organization, executives must be highly motivated, even driven. But this character trait is seldom a total blessing; the driven manager may be responding to an underlying sense of insecurity and feeling of low self-worth. In some cases this anxiety may prevent the executive from seeing beyond it or from caring much about anyone or anything else. The consequences of this expansiveness for an individual's leadership style may emerge in a number of ways:

1 High ambition for mastery – seen in ambition for oneself and also for the organization. In both cases this may result in the setting of next to impossible targets.
2 Extraordinary effort in the pursuit of mastery. This can be seen in pushing oneself and others too hard. This individual would be seen as working to his or her own agenda, and as exploitative.
3 Hunger for the rewards of mastery. A strong need for recognition and the need for heroic standing, high visibility and the trappings of power are common here.
4 Resistance to experiencing oneself as lacking in mastery. This emerges as a resistance to criticism, being self-protective, with poor self-awareness and an inability to recognize one's own mistakes.

When the above traits are exaggerated the organization's performance is damaged and its human capability is degraded. Pushing for short-term results at the expense of longer-term considerations can be dangerous. While those who are insufficiently expansive may sacrifice results in favour of the scrupulous treatment of people, those who are over-expansive will sacrifice people and the organization for results.

So what is to be done? Kaplan argues that driven people may become lopsided in their character traits and that it is necessary to regain balance. This can be done by identifying one's system of values and reordering the hierarchy of those values in such a way that the quest for worth can be satisfied by exhibiting characteristics previously assigned a low value. This requires insight and is not easy, but leaders able to grow in this deeply personal way can become more versatile, flexible and adaptable without losing the capacity to be resolute. In becoming more adaptable, they begin to see things less in black-and-white terms and obtain a better perspective on people and situations.

What, then, are the stages of this personal evolution? Essentially they are four in number, but Kaplan makes the point that they are tough and best made with the help of coaches and mentors.

The first stage is one of stabilization, maintaining the old self. But the function of the second and third phases is that of destabilization, where the individual separates from the old self and stands outside it in order to see more clearly the problem with the existing state of the self. At the same time it is necessary to develop an interest in reorganizing it. This is an unsettling period, but concentration must still be maintained on the search for the new self. Once there is insight into the possibilities of the new self, this must be mobilized into action. However, the journey into the new self is not complete until the individual answers the challenge – phase four – and sets out to stabilize the new self and integrate it into his or her character.

This is a tough journey, a hero's journey, and the individual must have a positive attitude towards change, though as a leader this attitude to change should already exist. To make the point Kaplan quotes Jung: 'Without necessity nothing budges, personality least of all.'

There are additional challenges for development as a leader and they principally concern developing balance. Often the expansive, driven character has a number of anxieties which make that person take extreme and self-orientated measures to demonstrate their worth. Leadership is about redressing the balance, and although perfect balance in the individual is an unlikely outcome it is realistic to expect a better balance.

While there is no one best style, it is possible to hope for better adjusted versions of the different types of leader.

For leaders to achieve a better balance in their work, Kaplan suggests that they must contend with two phenomena: the Big Doubt and the Big Worry.

The Big Doubt is that nobody can really make personal changes for the better. However, changes can be made if the individual is not beyond reach and the intervention itself is fairly powerful. Change in personality in middle age is not only possible but may be necessary for survival, and executives can evolve out of even extreme behaviour patterns when it is really necessary.

The Big Worry is that if change does occur, it will be for the worse – it is part of a natural reluctance to tamper with a winning formula and is understandable when the executive possesses strengths that at the time outweigh weaknesses. The change could cause that manager to lose effectiveness! Perhaps from being too driven the executive may become insufficiently driven. Kaplan suggests that in order to overcome this worry it is necessary to understand what it means to be 'less driven'.

Being less driven simply means eliminating the excessive portions of the drive. The leader remains highly motivated and tries as hard as is necessary – but not too hard! Thus instead of losing the edge it is retained and the individual gains the ability to use it better. What does this mean? For a start it means being able to use one's abundant energy more economically and deftly. This can result in a more astute approach to challenges and in that person becoming a better judge of when to insert himself or herself into a project or discussion. The job of empowering others then becomes more manageable. Organizations should not worry about the consequences of their leaders and executives moderating their drive; instead they should worry more about the opposite – the consequences of expecting too much and feeding huge appetites for accomplishment, thereby pushing their people even beyond the point of diminishing returns.

CONCLUSION

The messages from all the CCL writers remain the same. There are common characteristics that bring about career downfalls, fatal flaws that can emerge, as well as certain antidotes to them. Although the initial studies now go back some time, it would appear that with increasing levels of competition both between and within businesses the consensus of analysis and advice provided by these writers is becoming ever more relevant.

Transformational Theories

The only way to be able to predict the future is to create it.
— Chief Executive Officer, Sony

Change is down to unreasonable people, reasonable people accept
life as it is.   *— George Bernard Shaw*

Here the idea of the leader as an agent of change takes over from the
more transactional bases of earlier schools of thought. The focus of
thinking, while not in disagreement with the ideas behind transactional
leadership, now points towards a series of more sophisticated demands
being made on leaders. These demands centre around the high levels of
uncertainty experienced by leaders, their staff and indeed whole organizations in the final decades of the last century (and still today).

Many of the old truisms have been abandoned and few new certainties
take their place, apart from the fact that constantly increasing levels of
change and uncertainty will continue. The planet shrinks, the environment suffers, the global economy becomes a reality and life at work
becomes more demanding for everybody, not least the leaders.

A number of expectations and demands being made on business and
society's leaders can be listed as follows:

* to change organizations and the systems within them;
* to empower others and create organizational cultures that support this
  alteration in stance;
* to work with, in and through teams in de-layered and increasingly
  technological environments;

- to change people's mindsets and to give them clarity of purpose and direction by 'managing the meaning' of situations;
- to drive forward adventurous, visionary strategies.

This section is divided into those writers who have concentrated on teams, those who have looked at the leader as an agent of change, and those who have examined the leader as a visionary – or even looked at the concept of vision as an abstract term. In fact it becomes increasingly difficult to separate these elements. Teams need vision, organizations need to change and they too need visions of the future to help them reach their new objectives. The demands made on leaders multiply almost on a daily basis. Perhaps those who wish to enjoy enduring success should remember the following three thoughts.

Team. The word can be broken down into:

Together
Everyone
Achieves
More

Change. This can be defined as the process of making or becoming different – and different need not be a threat, it can mean progress.

Vision. Jonathan Swift wrote, 'Vision is the art of seeing things invisible.' Not an easy call for either leader or follower, but without a vision and the sense of meaning and purpose it engenders, nations, business and even people perish.

Meredith Belbin

Dr R. Meredith Belbin is currently Chairman of Belbin Associates Ltd, based in Cambridge, England.

His current position as a celebrated independent consultant is largely the product of his earlier work and success in research into teams. Having gained a doctorate in gerontology and entered industry in engineering production, Belbin went on to accumulate a wide range of experience in both academic and practical fields. He has been a research fellow at Cranfield Institute of Technology and a consultant at the Organization for Economic Co-operation and Development in Paris, where he specialized in employment and re-training. During this period he published two books, but without doubt he is best known for his contribution to current research on teams, the clear definition of team roles, and their implications for leaders.

The material from which Belbin amassed his data on teams was largely accumulated during nine years of research at the Administrative Staff College, Henley, and at the Industrial Research Unit from Cambridge. Although the work was founded on research the findings were addressed not so much to the academic world as to practising managers, and large numbers of real-life managers figured in the research itself. Consequently the work has from time to time been criticized by the academic world but has been much loved by the management community for whom it was intended. Indeed if there are grounds for criticism it is perhaps because the Belbin team-roles measure is over-used in the workplace, possibly resulting in a lack of rigour in the interpretation of results in some cases.

Belbin's research into teams came about through an interest in the functioning of syndicate groups on senior management training pro-grammes at Henley College. The college had long recognized that some syndicates functioned better than others and the directing staff were intrigued by the fact that team performance in addressing various exer-cises did not appear to correlate with the perceived quality of the team's members. Belbin records that a series of closely observed studies were set up to observe the behaviour of syndicate members within the college's executive management exercise and later in a game called Teamopoly. This put players under pressure, and significantly, at the end of each game, there was a team inquest.

Soon after this, Belbin looked more closely at the talents and qualities of the various team members he was able to observe. Some teams, which he called Apollo teams, were filled with members who had the highest mental ability and Belbin was intrigued by the degree to which these teams frequently under-performed. He then moved on to look at the personality types of the people within the teams, initially at the character-istics of extroversion and introversion, and then at anxiety levels. The level of analysis was strengthened as team members were invited to complete a battery of tests, most notably the 16 Personality Factors, the Professional Personality Questionnaire and the Cognitive Task Analysis. From these studies and tests came the eight celebrated team roles.

1 *The Coordinator*

This role was originally entitled 'the Chairman' but Belbin has sub-sequently bowed to the demands of political correctness and given it its current title. Essentially the behaviour of the coordinator is to pull together and focus the team's efforts. People with high coordinator scores tend to be stable, extrovert, good judges of people and adept at organizing the efforts of others. They are also adept at getting things done through other people. They like harmony and order, and are often better at bringing out creativity in others rather than exhibiting originality them-selves. The coordinator is a leadership role and one that is useful when the team needs to focus on purpose, objectives and process.

2 *The Shaper*

People with a high score here will be the drivers within the team. Shapers are anxious, impatient, extremely task-focused and they tend to dominate others. Belbin recognized that these people would put the attainment of the team's objective over and above the maintenance of good relationships or the protection of other people's feelings. They could make life uncomfortable, but they were useful in ensuring action and application. Belbin called these people shapers because they 'shaped' the team's efforts.

3 *The Plant*

Belbin observed that some members of a team were more introverted than others, yet tended to contribute more in the way of ideas and creativity. Often these team members had higher scores in intelligence tests than others, but their ideas were not always adopted as they could be overruled, put down or ignored by more vocal participants. When this happened, Belbin observed that the plants tended to withdraw into themselves and did not contribute any more ideas. He gave plants their title because they planted ideas in the team and also because an effective team would nurture its plants as a rare and valuable resource.

4 *The Monitor Evaluator*

This is another role in which high intelligence was exhibited. The monitor evaluator is a critical intelligence in the team, yet can appear aloof and uninterested. Belbin noted that these people often hung back from the discussion but then came in on a point of order, logic or fact – often being quite undiplomatic in the way they did so. They were vital to the team as a means of quality control, but not always popular. Monitor evaluators often came from legal or accountancy backgrounds.

5 *The Company Worker*

This role, which Belbin noted was often undervalued by organizations and the teams within them, plays a vital role in turning the plans and ideas of the team into reality. The company worker, now more often called the 'implementer', Belbin observed to be talented at scheduling, charting, budgeting and generally making things happen, though tending to be unimaginative, unexciting and not a visionary. They may be competitive in a group but are most interested in the subsequent practical application of the team's deliberations.

6 *The Team Worker*

Certain people in the team are not dominant, yet enjoy being team members. They will support other people's ideas and foster harmony between members, but – unlike shapers – will not challenge for the leadership. While unlikely to make a major impact on the direction of the team, they are nevertheless important in so far as they help to provide the groundswell of opinion and support for the agreed objectives and direction of the team.

7 *The Resource Investigator*

People who fill this role are extrovert and sociable. They enjoy making contacts and derive great pleasure from going outside the group in order to obtain information or to influence people. Belbin stated that they were useful for exploring and reporting on ideas as well as developing external contacts that might prove useful for the team; they would report on progress and conduct any subsequent negotiations. These people tended to be diplomatic, but poor on detail.

8 *The Completer Finisher*

As a team role, the completer finisher ensures that the team is protected from its own mistakes (both of omission and commission) and that it meets its deadlines. Completer finishers are useful in so far as they inject a sense of urgency into proceedings. However, because of the nature of their anxiety coupled with a tendency to nag, they can make themselves unpopular.

The eight roles, which at the time Belbin said were the only roles to emerge from his studies, have become the basis for much subsequent team-building both within organizations and in centres of management education and development. At the end of *Management Teams*, Belbin set out the Self Perception Inventory of team roles that had been designed to give Henley members a simple but effective means of assessment. Unfortunately, he did not copyright the Inventory, which is now extensively used, although subsequently he has brought out computerized versions with an extra role – 'The Specialist' – and at the same time refined the feedback through personalized printouts. Many users, however, see this extra role as more job-related than behaviour-related and so tend to stick to the original set when using them for team-building purposes.

Over and above his insight into team roles *per se*, Belbin used his findings to comment on a number of other areas more closely connected to individual leadership. In looking at the ways in which both coordinators and shapers set out to influence proceedings during the various business games conducted at Henley, Belbin looked at mental ability, communication and control as well as the distinctive approach of both coordinators and shapers in various situations. He noted that coordinators often found themselves in a dilemma of their own making. If they were clever, their teams did not always perform better; if they were also dominant, they became increasingly detached from their teams despite dominating the discussion and decision-making. In these cases few tears were shed when the plans eventually misfired.

Shapers, on the other hand, tended to do well when formal authority was bestowed on them, although this to some extent depended on the exercise (or situation) the team was tackling. Where the situation demanded their drive, persistence and high-pressure negotiating skills they succeeded and were capable of outmanoeuvring other companies in the business games. But when these tactics failed, they had less to fall back on than the more conventional coordinators. Belbin concluded that 'just as there are horses for courses, there are leaders for teams'. Of the two classic team-leader roles of coordinator and shaper, the nature of the challenge and the characteristics of the members of the team clearly have a bearing on which of the two leadership roles best suits the situation. Here, Belbin's work can be compared with that of Hersey and Blanchard who took this approach far further in concept and analysis.

Belbin concluded that with the aid of the psychometric instruments he used, he believed he had detected three types of team leader. One type was suited to the balanced team, which due to the composition of team roles within it is capable of dealing with a variety of complex multidimensional problems. Another fitted the team that had the capability to do well, but which faced obstacles that were either internal or external. The third type was most relevant to the 'think tank' type of team; usually the classic co-ordinator and shaper types were appropriate here. But what about situations where the personal qualities demanded of the leader are altogether different? Here the successful manager must learn to act in the way required to cope with the demands, or develop a convincing style of leadership that suits his or her personality. The leader must at the same time learn what style the team needs and be aware of the range of contributions from team members themselves that will keep that team in balance.

After looking at the dynamics of taking team roles in pairs and examining the effect of missing team roles, Belbin established that the useful people to have in teams were those who possessed strengths which served a need without duplicating the roles already filled. What was needed was not so much well-balanced individuals but individuals who balanced well with one another – in that way, human frailties could be underpinned and strengths used to full advantage. However, a new demand does emerge for the leader, one that requires far more analysis and human understanding based on an assessment of team roles.

From here, Belbin moves into the arena of winning teams and team design – areas that have become more important in the increasingly competitive business world since the studies were conducted. A winning team, he concluded, was characterized by:

1 the person in the chair;
2 the existence of one strong plant in the group;
3 a fair spread of mental abilities;
4 a spread of personal attributes offering wide role coverage;
5 a good match between the attributes of members and their responsibilities in the team;
6 a recognition of imbalance where it occurs.

As an overview, Belbin concluded that the classic mixed role team provides the most consistently good results. He backed this up through examination of teams in Marks and Spencer, the BBC and ICI, among others. These balanced teams had the advantage that their members could be placed in other teams without much loss of efficiency, but putting the right team together required a high degree of skill from the selector (leader?). Belbin also examined the 'super led' team where one leader dominates team members and leads from the front. He concluded that this form of leadership might be appropriate for small firms, but that over-dependence on a single individual is a prescription for everlasting uncertainty over what the future may bring.

Belbin looks at various team formats, given the different purposes of the teams considered; these ranged from project management to innovatory work. He gives as examples two teams, one set up to design a new model and prepare a prototype, the other to streamline the processes needed to produce it. The requirements ranged from the management of innovation in one case to getting things done in a politically sensitive area in the other. One team, rich in talent, merely needed control of its balance with the occasional firm touch, while the other was set up for control from the front, needing a leader with drive who would ensure that schedules were met.

Belbin concludes that establishing the right climate in which well-formed teams can flourish is the foundation stone on which good teams *will* flourish. Only then does it become possible to explore the questions and opportunities involved in trying to create an optimum combination of people; of finding potential contributors who are good examples of their type and then using them to best effect. This has been and always will be a challenge to team leaders.

CONCLUSION

Belbin has undoubtedly produced the definitive work on teams and it is widely used in the UK and the English-speaking world. The team roles are easy to relate to and other conclusions about team-building, team membership and team leadership are also easy to assimilate. At times Belbin has been accused of over-simplification, and Charles Magerison and Dick McCann (who founded Team Management Systems) have produced a more complex study of team roles and processes, linked to a useful interpretation of the Myers Briggs Type Indicator, which describes potential behaviour and linkages between roles more deeply than Belbin. However, any such measures must stand up to the practitioner test. Is it user-friendly? Can it be remembered easily? In this case the Belbin team roles beat all other measures in that they are immediately identifiable to team leaders and followers alike.

The philosophy of team roles and team-building also fits in well with other approaches such as the forming–storming–norming–performing analysis of Tuckman, where the impact of various roles can be seen as helping to move a team through the four stages. It is especially appropriate as an aid to the climate, goals, roles, leadership and relationship processes method of diagnosis by Robin L. Eltedge and Steven L. Philips in their *Team Building for the Future*. Consequently, although Belbin may have his detractors who accuse him of over-simplification or of poor research, most have failed to put anything better in its place. Belbin's work must therefore go down as a milestone in the work on teams and team leadership.

Rupert Eales-White

Discussion of the work of Rupert Eales-White is to be found elsewhere in this book (see pages 132–9), but here we consider him as one of the UK's most enthusiastic exponents of team working. He constantly puts his theories of team creativity and team leadership into practice through the successful management development programmes he runs, and he builds on and reinforces the key beliefs he expounds in his writings on the subject. Eales-White has published two books on teams: *Building Your Team* – part of the *Sunday Times* Leadership Skills series (1995), and *How To Be a Better Teambuilder* (Kogan Page, 1996). Both books deal with Eales-White's preoccupations: his desire to see business effectiveness brought about by good leadership, and a love of creativity used as a basis for making business processes work more effectively.

His main thesis is that a leader can adopt two roles when working with a team. It is desirable to be an effective team leader (ETL) but to be one it is necessary to be an effective team-builder (ETB) – the roles are intermingled, although an individual's success as an ETL will be dependent on his or her skill as an ETB. Many of the themes in Eales-White's *Creating Growth from Change* (1994) and *Ask the Right Question* (1997) emerge in a team context and so the summary here will concentrate on some of the writer's other views; specifically those on the leader's role in team-building and implementing effective processes. In the 'Team' books, Eales-White specifically looks at what constitutes an effective team. He deals with recognizing and developing one's strengths and the skills of team leadership and then at building the team itself. He is also strong on techniques of using the power of process as a vehicle for team leadership.

As a starting point, it is necessary for a leader to have a clear picture of what constitutes an effective team, and the author puts forward some key components to be looked for in individual members of the team itself:

enthusiastic
energetic
humorous
willing to support
resistant
decisive
wishing to plan
questioning
open to learning and feedback
honest
clear about their role

At this stage he does not mention leadership, but the start of both effective team leadership and team-building lies in leaders having a sound knowledge of their own strengths and weaknesses. It is the effective application of the leader's strengths in the context of the strengths and weaknesses of the team members that will generate good performance. Personality clashes can be anticipated and overcome, so the leader can ensure the team moves forward from the conflict, or storming, stage of development.

Eales-White states that both the leader and team members will have:

- a need to be in control of situations;
- a need to be supportive;
- an overall team orientation.

He provides questionnaires to help readers assess themselves against these criteria. The higher an individual's team orientation score is, the more likely they are to be an ETL. However, people with a low need to control coupled with a high need to support may well be poor at decision-making. The problem facing many leaders is that of the 'perception gap'; they may, for example, perceive themselves to have a high team orientation while in fact they have a high need to be in control.

Team strength is then broken down into eight complementary components which are loosely based on the Belbin team roles. These are:

investigating
innovating

evaluating
focusing
implementing
finishing
supporting
coordinating

These strengths, while similar to the Belbin roles, tend to focus on the positive and to lend themselves more readily to the range of behaviours needed in modern project management and innovation-focused groups. Team members will be able to maximize performance if, when operating together as a team, they can deploy the complete range of strengths. If a strength is missing, then the ETL must somehow ensure that it is brought out in one or more team members. At the same time, if the team's overall process is right it will probably elicit at least two strengths from each team member. Recognition of the team's strengths and weaknesses is vital at the recruitment stage when the ETL has the ability to readjust the overall chemistry of the team and to bring in abilities that are lacking.

Duplication of strengths can, on the other hand, lead to conflict. But if the ETL allows those who have a single predominant strength to lead in a particular situation and then breaks the team into sub-groups to allow other special talents to be shared around, then the project should move reasonably smoothly towards its conclusion. All strengths are necessary for team performance but the two that an ETL needs to ensure are present (and is also able to exhibit personally) are focusing and coordinating. Indeed, if a team member is stronger on focusing the group, this will represent a leadership challenge and the team leader may need to exaggerate this behaviour – or change team members.

Coordinating is a vital role. It plays to the need for facilitation at the team-building stage and is much needed at the idea-generation stage. Team leaders who are not strong here may need to delegate the role, and learn not to lose face, if they want their team to become creative faster. The key skills needed of an ETL are those of promoting discovery through effective questioning and listening, managing creativity, and understanding the power and nature of process. In many respects the ETL must help to create a team climate where it is acceptable to question all assumptions, while at the same time describing the original task clearly and monitoring progress and performance. There is, however, a dilemma: it is vital that the innovative project team is empowered to question all assumptions, to stand back from the problems and issues it faces, and to think, question and uncover new possibilities before anything is actually done. 'We need to break the rules before we make the rules – break out to break in.'

The team process of 'breaking free' can be summarized as follows:

THINK   Identify the issue, be objective
QUESTION   What are the assumptions/constraints?
UNCOVER   assumptions/constraints
REMOVE   those that are invalid
DISCOVER   new principles/better solutions.

The implicit skills, which the leader must foster in his or her team, will include group action thinking or brainstorming.

As the team gains skills and a level of maturity, the role of the ETL must change. This may involve a move from that of leading from the front to leading from the middle – acting as the occasional co-ordinator, while others increasingly take on the role of process facilitators. This in turn will help to develop all other team members in basic leadership skills. As the team develops and members learn to take on certain leadership roles within it, the impact of a new team member can be quite uncomfortable and put it back into conflict mode. At this stage it is necessary for the ETL to step into the breach and go back to basics. It may be necessary to regenerate the team's vision, reconsider task and process, and recreate the bonding stage. It is far better to form a new team with a new life and energy of its own.

In building the 'living team', Eales-White says that the power of process cannot be underestimated. At present everything is subject to change and organizations often ignore the good things already in place in the rush to meet new objectives. The issue is not then *what* should be done so much as *how* it should be done. Increasingly, organizations are recognizing the need to apply simple, powerful processes to achieve tasks, thereby working smarter rather than harder. Therefore the ETL needs to develop and apply a process to build the team, and then, under the ETL's guidance, the team needs to apply processes to achieve its tasks. The quality of the process thinking will have a major impact on ultimate success or failure.

The task process will vary according to the complexity and time horizon of the project. However, for an effective process in general, there are many steps that must be taken, including thinking and planning, over a number of phases before the action starts. Eales-White gives a comprehensive description of a full team task process, as follows.

A team task process

Share information
Distil key points
Clarify and confirm the nature of tasks
Agree objectives and interim milestone
Develop time plan
Brainstorm alternatives
Summarize options
Evaluate options and agree actions
Agree work roles and resource requirements
Agree initial phase and first deadline
Set time for feedback and review
Execute first phase
Feedback and review.

The team-building process, on the other hand, will be different and it is essentially the responsibility of the leader to build the team. Before starting, a number of building blocks must be in place.

Belief The ETB must believe in the power of teamwork. This will involve acknowledging the uncertainty that starting this process will entail, but accepting that every member will have a potential contribution to make.

Knowledge ETBs must understand their own strengths and weaknesses as well as those of the team. Empowerment of the team can only occur when this knowledge is shared, as this will generate consistency between what ETBs say they expect from others and how they behave themselves.

Skills Key skills of an ETB as well as of an ETL are to be able to be open, to put probing questions which promote discovery and force others to think for themselves, to listen effectively and to apply the power of process.

Eales-White then describes his own ideas for an effective team-building process.

From the start of the first meeting, it is necessary for the leader to have a firm idea, or vision, of the meeting's objectives. This clarity of vision will enable the leader to operate initially at a higher level than the team members. Subsequently the process of the meeting could well be as follows:

1 *Acknowledge uncertainty* The ETB may need to act as facilitator to steer the team through the initial uncertainty. This will force the ETB to adopt the right behaviours and to demonstrate the consistency mentioned earlier.

2 *Agree the objective* With a new team, a key objective should be to agree what steps now need to be taken to build the team. Team-building, however, should not be isolated from the ultimate task and it is important that a supporting objective should be that of developing a shared understanding of the task, vision and mission.

3 *Share knowledge* The ETB must explain what an effective team should look like and get agreement that this is a valid goal. There must be a task vision and mission, but also a team vision and mission. The group needs to understand the what, where, when and why of the task, as well as that of the team itself. The focus of the first meeting must be on the latter. Later the 'how' of the task must be addressed through applying an agreed process.

4 *Clarify role* The job of the ETB will be to manage expectations – expectations of the leader's and team members' behaviours.

5 *Apply techniques* Techniques of brainstorming and group action thinking must be explained and used immediately.

6 *Agree process* The importance of process must be explained and agreed. If the team gets the process right it will get its performance right.

7 *Apply process* The right process is the one the leader and team are comfortable with. Eales-White suggests one that works is as follows:
   * a social event, get to know one another;
   * collect information on both task and team;
   * share the information, including team strengths and implications of skill mix;
   * develop task vision and mission – this will undoubtedly come to include the team's mission as well as its emergent shared values;

- agree interim milestones;
- brainstorm technical requirements, actions and timings;
- complete the resources audit – what is needed and who does what?
- implement agreed first phase.

8 *Agree actions* Before the meeting ends, there should be a review to summarize what has taken place. This will serve to consolidate how the team will work together in the future.

9 *Agree time and place of next meeting* Basic, but essential.

CONCLUSION

The fact that there is so much overlap between Eales-White's team task process, the process for team creativity and the team-building process serves to underline his key thesis. This is that teams, tasks, creativity and the deployment of effective processes are inextricably intertwined, and essential for effectiveness in project-driven organizations that are striving to succeed in a fast-changing world. Although the processes described are quite basic, it is interesting to note how often they are ignored in the business world. Eales-White would say that they are ignored because members of senior management are often too individualistic, and ignore the benefits of team-building and well-thought-out team working. He may well have a point!

It is also interesting to compare Eales-White's emphasis on process and purpose with the tripartite stress on people, purpose and links made by Lipnack and Stamps in *Virtual Teams* (see pages 92–4). Eales-White was not specifically thinking about virtual teams, but the noticeable similarity of conclusions reinforces the fact that there are key consistent features for effective leadership in a team context that should not be overlooked.

Jessica Lipnack and Jeffrey Stamps

Jessica Lipnack and Jeffrey Stamps are respectively President and co-founder of the Networking Institute. They are authors of a wide range of books dealing with networks within organizations, and the impact of modern technology on the way people and organizations work, both now and in the future. Having met as students at Oxford University, they have been gathering information on networked organizations since 1979 and published their first book on the subject in 1982. They are frequent conference speakers, widely used consultants and acknowledged experts in this specialized field, having collected information on the subject from networkers in every continent, including Antarctica.

In 1993 they published *The TeamNet Factor*, the first book in a trilogy on network organizations. In this book they concentrated on the network as a form of organization and gave illustrations drawn from small groups through to large alliances. In *The Age of the Network* (1994) they showed how companies use networks to their strategic advantage, and in *Virtual Teams* (1997) they completed the trilogy by examining how the team is undergoing a transformation in the twenty-first century. Here they concentrate on how small groups of people working across boundaries, supported by new computer and communications technology, are transforming the way people will work in the future. They also make challenging predictions about the forms of leadership that will be effective in these situations and address the 'people' side of the organization/technology relationship.

Lipnack and Stamps's purpose in writing *Virtual Teams* is to present good examples of virtual teams and to illustrate how they can work in a future where the prime challenge will be to transform from the hierarchy–

bureaucracy format to one of networks. They start by describing the evolution of teams into virtual entities, set against the vast changes in the business and social scenarios.

The authors define a virtual team as a 'group of people who interact through interdependent tasks guided by common purpose'. This may sound like any other team, but they further define the concept by stating that a virtual team also 'works across space, time and organizational boundaries with links strengthened by webs of communication technologies'. In the new order, people no longer need to be working together in the same place: electronic communication and digital technologies give them unprecedented opportunities to work together at a distance. Enablers such as personal computers, voice mail, mobile phones, and of course the Internet and the World Wide Web, are growing faster than anyone predicted. For the first time since nomads first moved into towns, work is diffusing rather than concentrating across both space and time. The World Wide Web in particular has allowed virtual teams to create electronic homes in the form of protected intranets as private islands of communication within the larger Internet.

The reason why so many teams do not work well in today's environment is because people do not make allowances for how difficult it can be when they no longer work face-to-face. Virtuality, the authors state, starts when people are only fifty feet apart. The greater the distance separating people, the more time zones they have to cross to communicate. When teams are spread over the world the window of actual/real communication time can shrink to zero, yet even so-called collated teams, such as call centres, can cross time boundaries and need to 'think virtually'. Indeed, many work practices, such as supply-chain management and product development, require people to work virtually across organizational boundaries.

There are, however, a number of prescriptions and principles for successful virtual team working. The team must:

- involve the right *people* from both internal organizations and from outside companies;
- carefully define its *purpose* and use it as a compass when it gets off track;
- establish excellent communication *links* among team members, using various media as well as face-to-face meetings when possible.

The three words that capture the essence of teams, including successful virtual teams, are: people, purpose, links.

For the virtual team, the task – the work that expresses the shared goals – is the purpose that holds the group together. The links then are the channels, interactions and relationships that weave the living fabric of a team unfolding over time. The nature and variety of the links is the biggest differentiator between a virtual and a normal team.

The people–purpose–links model involves nine virtual team principles with three slants on each of the three key prescriptions. The slants on the 'people' side are:

• Independent members	People as parts
• Shared leadership	Parts drawn together as wholes
• Integrated levels	Team becomes a 'whole' entity

Virtual teams are made up of independent members with a measure of autonomy and self-reliance. The leadership within them tends to be informal and the diverse mixture of technical and managerial work required means that most members of the team will take on a leadership role at some stage in the process; so shared leadership is the norm. Finally, the team will have two levels of organization – the level of the members and the level of the group as a whole. The team will have grown out of its membership but will also be part of the larger organization. To be successful, it must integrate levels both internally in terms of sub-groups and members, and also externally in terms of peers and supergroups.

Purpose is divided into:

• Cooperative goals	Do
• Interdependent tasks	Doing
• Concrete results	Done

The purpose defines why a particular group wants to work together and virtual teams are far more dependent on having a clear purpose than face-to-face teams. Because they normally operate outside bureaucratic rules, members must rely on their common purpose to stay in tune with one another. The interdependent tasks connect the purpose and desires with the final outcome, and when the task is over the team needs evidence of concrete results. These three elements help the team to be focused and productive.

Finally there is the web of links:

- Multimedia
- Boundary-crossing interactions
- Trusting relationships

Channels
Communicating
Patterns

The term 'links' bridges three key areas of communication. People need the actual physical connections which make boundary-crossing possible. The process of frequent communication facilitated by the links constitutes the actual process of the work and the interactions gradually grow into trusting relationships. People's patterns of behaviour define the outlines of their relationships, and patterns of interaction based on trust become a substitute for hierarchical controls. With the break-up of old channels of information which relied on hierarchy, more information is becoming available to a greater number of people; this in turn feeds the move towards virtual teamworking.

The authors conclude that virtual teams are basically the same as ordinary teams, and for them to be viable they must include what is timeless and enduring in other human groups. At the same time they include features that are already evident in the turbulent years at the turn of the millennium.

The authors move on to describe the differing pressures of the task on virtual teams, and conclude that the greatest difference between virtual and normal teams lies in the use of links. For the first time, teams can virtually collate all the information they need in order to work together and put it all into context, thereby achieving things that normal teams could never do in the normal nine-to-five day.

Nothing is more important to the team than a clear sense of purpose. Members need more than rules and regulations to hold them together and the writers chart the development of authority in virtual teams. While both individuals at the top and bureaucracies have the power to reward and punish, in the information era the purpose of the team takes on a new aura as the source of legitimacy. Virtual teams develop an inner authority based on the members' commitment to the shared purpose. As such, then, it is possible that no central figure of authority will bind the team together until CEO level is reached. The central power will stem from the information and expertise held within the team – 'multiple knowledge' will come to equate to power and also legitimize it.

When it comes to leadership itself, team members need to think not only in terms of themselves but also in terms of the team. They need to look inwards and outwards at the same time. The leaders sit on boundaries – they look up and down as well as in and out. From the Janus leader's viewpoint, people are 'holons', they are both wholes (as individuals) and parts (as part of the team). In virtual teams, people are seen to operate as holons in three ways:

1 as members – the parts of the team;
2 as leaders – forming the connective tissue between the parts and the whole;
3 as levels – the successive wholes that make up complex networks.

For virtual teams, however, entirely new roles have sprung up to encourage productivity and provide cohesion. Old roles still exist but must be performed in new ways, and this is especially true of the key role of leadership. It is here that the struggle between the independent 'me' and the interdependent 'we' becomes part of the group persona and must be dealt with. Owing to the structure of organizations that employ virtual teams, the leadership role will only be successful if everybody understands and assumes part of the expanded virtual leadership burden. Research has shown that the only role universally observed in groups is that of the leader; paradoxically, virtual teams that are very self-motivated and self-managed are leader-ful, not leader-less. When the leadership structure is examined, it is found to be made up of an inclusive set of related roles of leaders and followers. Six basic leadership roles required by virtual teams have been identified:

coordinator
designer
disseminator
tech-net manager
socio-tech manager
executive champion

The writers state that the transformation of people into a group by way of a leadership role is a 'miracle of social construction'. Leaders are convenient 'handles' to help insiders and outsiders to identify groups. This habit of simplifying complexity by seizing on a prominent part of the group translates into the assumption of a single focus of leadership. However, this is not normally the case. In virtual teams multiple leaders are the norm rather than the exception. The process of dealing with the complex tasks and issues calls for shared leadership, even if the team is named after a particular person for the sake of convenience.

On the other hand, small groups will have at least two observable types of leader: social and task leaders.

Task leadership is focused on expertise and activities required to produce results. The measure of success is productivity. This form of leadership is central to task-focused small groups. Social leadership arises from activities that generate feelings of group identity and satisfaction. The measure of success here is cohesion.

But how do you convey rank online? Too much rank in a virtual team is stultifying and frequently a team will not coalesce until it has identified the right people to accomplish its tasks. It will often define its expertise roles before it locates the people to hold them. This in itself is a step to virtuality as the writers challenge us to imagine a team that does not yet exist. This team must search for the right people – those with the relevant expertise – and this in turn will probably lead to the recruitment of people from differing locations and organizations: the start-up of a virtual team.

And the start-up of a virtual team can be a leadership challenge in itself. It is vital to invest in beginnings because lack of clarity about goals, tasks and leadership makes it harder for the team to perform. It is necessary to establish criteria for the measurement of results, to punctuate progress with opportunities to measure and assess progress, then finally to celebrate when the task is complete. Clear goals drive the process and aid cooperation and interdependence. There is a further impact here on the forms of leadership that are most likely to be successful. While the traditionally hierarchical forms of boss-like leadership *contract*, virtual teams and networks demand *more* leadership, not less. The leadership roles themselves may be changing; virtual leaders must act more as coaches than bosses and are more likely to be successful through persuasion than coercion. The 'private places' needed by most leaders must come through membership of special competence- or status-based networks that are by invitation only, as opposed to general access by the team.

Enabling a virtual team to work smart subsequently involves the creation of a team identity, such as the adoption of a name and, more importantly, the publication of a clear statement of purpose. This statement of purpose can then be used to focus on the team's understanding of the desired results and anticipated delivery dates. The team's sense of identity can also be enhanced by giving it a sense of location, even if this is only an electronic address and web location. After this, responsibilities can be clarified and the key roles of task and process leadership can be allocated. It is vital to ensure that each task has at least one leader. Virtual teams increase their overall leadership capability as they subdivide their work – it may enter a planning session with one leader and emerge with several. However, task leadership alone is not sufficient for team success. Process leadership is also necessary and will involve the overview of various types of activities, such as generating, planning, choosing and negotiating tasks, and executing them.

The authors conclude with an interesting debate on virtual values and the elements of social capital necessary to make such teams really work. Trust is seen as the glue that binds together the three team elements of people–purpose–links. People must be trusted for their implicit competence, the purpose must be linked to shared rewards to be truly unifying, and finally team members must trust information they receive as well as the channels of dissemination. The information itself will be mistrusted if it is suspected that the organization is not releasing it in the quantity and quality expected. The success of any small group leaves a legacy to the organization of which it is part, and this legacy of relationship success accrues as social capital.

Social capital is made up of trust, norms of reciprocity (i.e. agreements about how people will interact and bargain with each other), and then through dense social networks. It is an enabler of good team working as well as an outcome. Individuals on their own cannot possess social capital; it lies in the web of relationships between people and mingles with other means of generating wealth. The writers conclude that all virtual teams can increase both social and knowledge capital. Social capital accumulates as team members expand the number and diversity of their relationships. Because of their separation, they have an obligation to make knowledge capital explicit and available. By stretching the bounds of generally accepted means of knowledge generation and task fulfilment, virtual teams offer great value in a broad range of situations and point to possibilities not yet seen in the history of work.

In considering virtual teams, it is arguable that Lipnack and Stamps have not invented any new leadership requirements; what changes are needed are certainly more a matter of emphasis. Team leaders need to be more flexible, more aware that the roles required of them may alter, and that both process and purpose need to be stressed over and over again. Then implicitly the team leader needs to be as technologically skilled as each member of the team – and probably more aware of the possibilities of the technology than any other team member.

CONCLUSION

The authors have made a broad-based statement of the future requirements for both better teamworking and leadership. However, when analysed outside the technological context it would appear that the old truisms still count, even though they must be viewed in the light of new applications and changed emphases if they are to survive in dynamic new circumstances.

The Leader as a Catalyst of Change

Warren Bennis

Warren Bennis is without doubt one of the twentieth century's foremost thinkers and writers on the subject of leadership. With some twenty books published to date on the subject (three of which appeared in 1989 alone), together with a tally of over 750 articles, he has successfully bridged the gaps between academia, journalism, pragmatism and common sense.

In a long career as an academic, Bennis has held a number of significant posts. He has been Distinguished Professor of Business Administration at the University of Southern California; he has served on the faculties of MIT's Sloan School of Management, where he succeeded Douglas MacGregor as chairman of the Organizational Studies Department, and on the faculties of Harvard and Boston Universities. In addition he has had a wide international career, having held posts at IMEDE, INSEAD and the Indian Institute of Management at Calcutta, among others. In the commercial world, Bennis has consulted at Rockwell International, Chase Manhattan Bank, the Ford Motor Company and Polaroid. He has served four US presidents in an advisory capacity and then done the same thing in industry, where he has advised John Harvey-Jones and others. Bennis has served on the national boards of the US Chamber of Commerce and the American Management Association. He has received many honorary degrees and has been the recipient of the Distinguished Service Award by the American Board of Professional Psychologists, among a host of other accolades.

In 1985 Bennis cooperated with Burt Nanus, founder and director of the Center for Futures Research at the University of California, on the highly acclaimed publication *Leaders: the Strategies for Taking Charge* (1985). This work set out lessons on how to become successful, based on

Bennis's research with ninety of America's leaders. The key messages from the work were that leadership is open to all, and that it embodies the management of attention, of meaning, of trust and of self. These elements constitute a 'mastery over present confusion', and the good leader knows that leadership is a skill that can be learnt and that it involves the deployment of self which is a matter of full commitment and a willingness to learn from everything. *Leaders*, despite having been accused of being populist, helped move the trend of thinking about leadership towards the concept of transformation.

The focus here will be on the main work that followed the publication of *Leaders* and emanated from Bennis's 'purple patch' at the end of the eighties – a spell of writing that helped move thinking on the subject further into the fields of change management, transformation and personal development.

For *On Becoming a Leader* Bennis interviewed forty executives from an eclectic variety of backgrounds, including Richard Ferry, co-founder of Korn/Ferry; Barbara Corday, then vice-president programming at CBS; and Herb Alpert, musician and business leader. He focused on two main questions: How do people learn the skills of leadership? What do organizations do to promote or discourage the conditions under which people can learn these skills? In posing such questions, Bennis places his work in both the contingency and transformational camps. The leader can make his or her behaviour contingent to the situation, and by doing so emerge as a transformational leader.

Leadership, Bennis writes, is difficult to define. It is like beauty, hard to describe but you know it when you see it. Consequently, becoming a leader is not easy, yet learning to lead is much easier than many people think because leadership, like art, can be demonstrated. Bennis says that much of the book is about adult learning; he disagrees with psychologists that most learning happens when you are very young, and believes that taking charge of your learning is about taking control of your own life. Therefore anyone of any age can transform himself or herself if they want to. Becoming the kind of person who is a leader is the 'ultimate act of free will'.

Bennis declares that it is necessary for a leader to master the context in which he or she must practise. The context, he states, in terms of US business is moribund. It is geared towards the short term and delivery of the next quarter's results – consequently everybody persists in grasping neat, simple answers when in fact they should be questioning everything (it is interesting to see that the overall context has hardly changed since Bennis's book was written). Driven by the pressures that occur when people reach high office they become bosses, not leaders – they are driven but going nowhere. The first step in becoming a leader is to recognize the context as a trap for leaders rather than a launching-pad, and to declare independence from it. As Bennis says, conventionalists and rationalists wear a metaphorical square hard hat; leaders must be different and wear sombreros.

To master the context, as opposed to being its slave, it is necessary to

- become self expressive;
- listen to the inner voice;
- learn from the right mentors;
- give oneself over to a guiding vision.

The above steps are closely linked to the development of a distinct sense of purpose. Leaders not only challenge the context but also change it. They refuse to be deployed by others and choose to deploy themselves.

From here, Bennis goes on to describe the basic ingredients of leadership.

1 *A guiding vision* A leader has a clear idea of what he or she wants to do and the strength to persist.
2 *Passion* The leader who communicates passion gives hope and inspiration to others.
3 *Integrity* Candour about your own strengths and weaknesses is the key to self-knowledge and then to 'inventing yourself'. Integrity is the basis of trust. This, however, cannot be acquired; it must be earned.
4 *Curiosity and daring* The leader must wonder about everything, be willing to take risks and embrace error as a basis for learning.

A clear understanding of the context stems from the full deployment of oneself along the lines described above, and being fully deployed ensures true self-expression – being an original and not a copy of someone else. From here, Bennis expounds his well-known list of differences between leadership and management:

- The manager administers; the leader innovates.
- The manager is a copy; the leader is an original.

- The manager maintains; the leader develops.
- The manager focuses on systems and structure; the leader focuses on people.
- The manager focuses on control; the leader inspires trust.
- The manager has a short-range view; the leader has a long-term perspective.
- The manager asks how and when; the leader asks what and why.
- The manager has his eye always on the bottom line; the leader has his eye upon the horizon.
- The manager imitates; the leader originates.
- The manager accepts the *status quo*; the leader challenges it.
- The manager is the classic good soldier; the leader is his own person.
- The manager does things right; the leader does the right thing.

Bennis concludes that in making the shift from manager to leader, individuals are their own raw material. It is necessary to know yourself and then to become the maker of your own life in order to fulfil that leadership potential. He then moves on to offer lessons from his own years of study and observation.

The leaders Bennis talked to all agreed that self-knowledge and self-invention are lifetime processes and that although no one can teach you how to achieve them, there are some things which others have done that are helpful. Bennis lists them as the four lessons of self-knowledge.

1 *You are your own best teacher* This is expressed as achieving a personal transformation. Here it helps to have a sense of role from which a perception of the gap between what the individual perceives himself or herself to be and what he or she ought to be can be studied. After that it is necessary to assume personal responsibility for the re-education.

2 *Accept responsibility. Blame no one* Major stumbling blocks on the path to self-knowledge and the development of leadership are denial and blame. It is necessary to accept responsibility for oneself.

3 *You can learn anything you want to learn* Bennis defined this as 'seeing the world simultaneously as it is and as it can be, understanding what you see and acting on your understanding'. It is necessary to embrace new and potentially unsettling things and not to be afraid of failure.

4 *Understanding comes from reflecting on your experience* This means

having a dialogue with yourself, asking yourself tough questions at the appropriate time in order to seek out the truth, and acquiring or recovering knowledge. Nothing is truly yours until you understand it. Reflecting leads to understanding, and when you understand you know what to do.

Bennis adds that it is necessary not to be designed by one's own experiences but to become one's own designer; to become cause and effect rather than just effect – true stages in the development of self-expression and genuine leadership.

Further development of leadership potential comes from a realistic knowledge of the world and all it has to offer. This involves seeking to fill in the gaps in your education and experience, by reading or by any other method so long as that method is active and the involvement passionate. Bennis concludes that leaders must learn from their own experiences and that this means looking back on childhood in order to become master of your life and of what has happened to you. It means consciously seeking broadening experiences in the present, taking risks as a matter of habit and seeing the future as an opportunity to do new things rather than as a trial to be endured. In addition, Bennis states that the process of learning from one's experiences must help the leader to operate on instinct when necessary, to use intuition and to follow an impulse even when that may appear risky. Here, and in the examples he gives to back his premise, Bennis's thinking is close to that of Ned Herrmann, who advocates the development of the D-Brain Quadrant (see page 164) in the growth of personal leadership characteristics.

There are two further key elements in Bennis's argument; both are about turning the power of personal transformation into action and results in an ever-moving and chaotic world. First of all it is necessary to move from self-knowledge to self-exhortation, to deploy one's self and to strike hard, with energy and passion.

There are a number of ingredients in the deployment of self and these can be put together in a definitive process – a process which could be described as the self and leadership development process for effective action. The ingredients are:

Resolution and reflection To make the process conscious by reflecting on your self, reflecting on the task and coming to a resolution after having subjected it to both logic and intuition.

Perspective Take the same set of facts, shift the vantage point and see just how different everything now looks. A point of view starts to develop.

Tests and measures If the leader first answers the basic question, 'What do you want?' the subsequent tests and measures should flow smoothly.

Desire This probably exists in everybody; it is about self-expression and cannot be taught. Yet it can be activated and separated from drive (which is about proving oneself). Drive coupled with desire, however, is productive.

Mastery It is necessary to have true mastery of the task in hand, then to have the ability to articulate it, as well as a level of human sensitivity, tact and compassion.

Strategic thinking If the overview and subsequent planning are done properly it is possible to be more pragmatic about the risks involved in realizing the vision as well as more philosophical about mistakes on the route to success.

Synthesis Finally it is necessary for the leader to combine all of the above means of expression in order to act effectively.

Consequently, Bennis summarizes that the means of expression are the steps to leadership. Leadership is first a matter of being, then of doing.

1 Reflection leads to resolution.
2 Resolution leads to perspective.
3 Perspective leads to points of view.
4 Points of view lead to tests and measures.
5 Tests and measures lead to desire.
6 Desire leads to mastery.
7 Mastery leads to strategic thinking.
8 Strategic thinking leads to full self-expression.
9 The synthesis of full self-expression equals leadership.

The developmental process is now set out. It is a matter of personal transformation that once completed will enable the leader to be an effective agent of change, someone who can think beyond the conventional bounds of the immediate situation and spot opportunities for growth and increased effectiveness. In short, a transformational leader.

Bennis also deals with the art of getting people on your side. He says that a 'leader's ability to galvanize his workers resides both in his understanding of himself and his understanding of his co-workers' needs and wants along with his understanding of their mission. Competence, vision and virtue must exist in perfect balance. Competence or knowledge without vision and virtue breeds technocrats. Virtue, without vision and knowledge, breeds ideologies. Vision, without virtue and knowledge breeds demagogues.'

Trust is an essential element in aligning people to your aims, and there are four ingredients that leaders need in order to generate and sustain it. These are: constancy – they stay the course; congruity – they walk their talk; reliability – they are always ready to support their co-workers when it counts; integrity – they honour their promises.

It is in the final chapter, concerned with the skills and attitudes that the leader needs to make change happen, that Bennis really deals with the transformational skills required of a leader. Business and personal life are increasingly made up of dilemmas and ambiguity and he addresses the question of how a leader can learn to thrive in such situations, forging a new future and creating learning organizations. He sets out ten organizational and personal factors for doing so:

1 *Leaders manage the dream* The leaders he spoke to all had the ability to create a compelling vision and to translate it into reality. The vision must be communicated and then people must be recruited, rewarded, retrained and reorganized. In turning the vision into reality the organization itself must be transformed.

2 *Leaders embrace error* Good leaders create an atmosphere in which risk-taking is encouraged. Failure is not the crime. Low aim is.

3 *Leaders encourage reflective backtalk* In other words they listen, and in listening they find out more about themselves.

4 *Leaders encourage dissent* Leaders need devil's advocates – 'variance sensors', people who are able and willing to give candid opinions about the vision and policies, as opposed to clones who will simply mirror the leader's opinions.

5 *Leaders possess optimism, faith and hope* These characteristics provide choices – the opposite of hope is despair, Bennis writes, and 'when we despair it is because we feel there are no choices'.

6 *Leaders understand the Pygmalion effect in management* Leaders expect the best from those around them and know that people can change and grow. They understand just how much to stretch them

without straining them when shooting for goals.

7 *Leaders have a 'certain touch'* This can be an instinctive combi-nation of what the organization's culture must be if it is to grow combined with a degree of political instinct.

8 *Leaders see the long view* This is made up of vision – and, in particular, patience.

9 *Leaders must understand stakeholder symmetry* This means that when making decisions, they must know how to balance the various claims and demands of all the groups, internal and external, who have a stake in the organization.

10 *Leaders create strategic alliances and partnerships* They recognize the need to create alliances with other organizations whose futures run parallel with their own.

Bennis concludes that the ten features involved in forging the future are the basis on which his sample of leaders thrive. Future successful leaders will need all their qualities – and more.

The central themes of *On Becoming a Leader* are picked up again in *Why Leaders Can't Lead*, in which Bennis continues his crusade by stating that the central reasons why leaders often fail to lead effectively start with an obsession with the bottom line. He develops his argument by pointing out that there are often too many chiefs, coming off a production line like fast food; these he calls 'McLeaders'. More seriously, he bemoans what he describes as a high degree of untapped human potential in the USA, and expresses worry at the level of yes-man-ism and the greed that promotes a desire for quick profits over value generation. Most of the personal advice given to the would-be leader fits in closely with the more elaborate counsel given in *On Becoming a Leader*. It is towards the end of the book, however, that Bennis moves from examining the characteristics required of leaders to giving pragmatic advice about how to avoid disaster during periods of change. He comes up with a number of tips based on his own research and experience.

1 Recruit with scrupulous honesty. When reality does not match expec-tations you will be faced with a number of disappointed and disillu-sioned new recruits.

2 Guard against the crazies. When you set out to promote innovation, it is all too easy to attract people who will distort the prevailing ideas; people must be agents of change but not agitators.

3 Build support among like-minded people. Some people act as if the organization came into being the day they arrived. Use everyone, new hands and old hands alike.

4 Plan change from a solid conceptual base. In other words, have a good understanding of how to change as well as what to change. If change is to be permanent it must be planned and gradual.

5 Don't settle for rhetorical change. Significant change cannot simply be decreed. It is a matter of balancing the demands of different intramural factions.

6 Don't allow those who are opposed to change to appropriate basic issues. To ensure that this does not happen it is necessary to make certain that people are not frightened by the changes proposed.

7 Know the territory. Find out everything there is to know about the organization and its environment.

8 Appreciate the importance of environmental factors. Worthwhile changes if they increase discomfort are probably going to fail.

9 Avoid future shock. If the leader, when planning the future, forgets the past or neglects the present, shock will follow. It is therefore necessary to proceed carefully.

10 Change is most successful when those who are affected by it are involved in the planning. They will resist if they think it is being imposed on them.

CONCLUSION

Warren Bennis has produced a huge volume of work on the subject of leadership. He has made a number of definitive statements about it, and in the writer's opinion, none more useful than those in *On Becoming a Leader*. In many respects, *Why Leaders Can't Lead* is an 'overflow' from the earlier volume. Some have criticized the former work as being merely 'a flow of consciousness'. Those who do tend to forget the series of interviews on which it is based, interviews which give his advice a strong foundation of facts and research. In many respects his work here is hard to measure but is often masterful – like Bennis's own definition of leadership and beauty: hard to define but you know the quality when you see it.

James Kouzes and Barry Posner

The work of James Kouzes and Barry Posner has been the inspiration of many an organization. In so far as they have set out to show that leadership is something that can be learnt and mastered, they have laid the foundation for a number of organizations' development programmes, notably in a leadership development programme set up by Texas Instruments for its middle managers across the globe.

Their major joint work has been the acclaimed *The Leadership Challenge* (1987), which was described by Tom Peters as a 'tough read' because it was so challenging. More specifically, it was summarized by Rosabeth Moss Kanter as a 'path-breaking study of successful leaders – male and female, young and old, corporate and entrepreneurial'. The value of these inspiring role models is enhanced by the authors' compelling insights and practical experience empowering people to 'find and nurture their own leadership'. In fact what Kouzes and Posner achieve through research, and reports on interviews which distil the experience of literally hundreds of managers, show that leadership is a process that can be mastered by all. But first, the writers themselves.

James Kouzes is the author of many articles on management education, leadership and organizational development. He is a former director of the Executive Development Center at the Leavey School of Business and Administration, Santa Clara University; he is also an experienced consultant and management educator who has trained many thousands of managers. He has also served on the American Management Association's Human Resource Council.

Barry Posner has been Professor of Management and Director of Graduate Education and Customer Service at the Leavey School of Management, with responsibility for the school's MBA programme. As a recognized scholar and educator he is the author of many articles and of *Effective Project Planning* and (with W. Alan Randolph) *Getting the Job Done: Managing project teams and task forces for success* (1991). He is a member of the American Psychological Association and has been president of the Western Academy of Management. He has served on the boards of a number of organizations, and is a frequent conference speaker.

The authors introduce *The Leadership Challenge* as a book about how people get extraordinary things done within organizations. They define leadership as starting where management ends, where systems of control, reward, incentive and overseeing give way to innovation, and where individual character and courage of convictions can achieve great things. They anticipate Warren Bennis to some extent by stating that leadership does not come from any special powers within the leader but from 'a strong belief in a purpose and a willingness to express that purpose'. Leadership, they say, is not a place or position within an organization, it is a process.

The process the authors themselves followed to research and compile the work began as a project in 1983, when they set out to find what it was that leaders did when they achieved their personal best in leading rather than managing others. They constructed a 'personal best' survey in which leaders were asked to reflect on their experiences and what these had taught them about leadership itself. More than 550 in-depth surveys plus an additional 780 shorter surveys were collected, and 42 in-depth interviews. From their analysis the authors developed a model of leadership which became the foundation of the book and then drew up the *Leadership Practices Inventory* to enable them to measure the behaviours they had observed. They have subsequently marketed this inventory on a commercial basis. Finally they tested out their research by asking over 3,000 colleagues and subordinates to assess the extent to which those leaders they had studied actually used the practices they had discussed.

The book then examines the five practices of excellent leadership revealed by the research and subsequently condenses them into ten commitments for leadership – ten ways in which the reader can apply the practices pragmatically in their organizations. The final chapters deal with learning to be a leader, as the authors believe leadership itself to be a learnable set of practices.

In introducing their initial five practices, the authors use examples of leaders from Apple Computers and North American Tool and Die and show that effective executives followed a three-step strategy of vision–involvement–persistence. From this process they move on to discover five fundamental practices that enable their leaders to get things done. They:

1 *Challenged the process* The leader rises to the challenge, moves away from the *status quo* and recognizes good ideas in other people. As adapters and innovators, leaders were prepared to take the risk of failing, but at the same time they were always open to learn from both their mistakes and successes.

2 *Inspired a shared vision* Leaders have a desire to make something happen and often have a mental picture of what the end result should look like before they start the project. However, at the same time they must be able to share the vision with their followers and to involve them in it. They must 'know their followers and speak their language' – yet they must also exhibit their own belief in and enthusiasm for the outcome in order to infect and motivate others.

3 *Enabled others to act* In 91 per cent of the cases Kouzes and Posner analysed, the leaders revealed how teamwork and collaboration had been essential in achieving success. The authors considered this to be the most significant of their five practices. The effect of enabling others to act is to make them feel empowered and capable; from this flows commitment.

4 *Modelled the way* This is all about leading from example, being clear about one's vision and values, and then acting consistently with them. It is also important that leaders remain vigilant about the little things that make a big difference.

5 *Encouraged the heart* The writers observed that leaders must encourage people to persevere with the job and to do so will involve genuine acts of caring, carried out publicly and with sincerity. 'Love of their products, their people, their customers, their work' – this may just be one of the best-kept secrets of exemplary leadership.

These practices, Kouzes and Posner concluded, were open to anybody who wanted to accept the challenge of being a leader. Their research had shown that leadership is a learnable, observable set of practices and that there are a number of behavioural commitments that can be broken down into action plans in the 'personal best' leadership cases. These are as follows:

Challenging the process
1 Search for opportunities.
2 Experiment and take risks.

Inspiring a shared vision
3 Envision the future.
4 Enlist others.

Enabling others to act
5 Foster collaboration.
6 Strengthen others.

Modelling the way
7 Set the example.
8 Plan small wins.

Encouraging the heart
9 Recognize individual contribution.
10 Celebrate accomplishments.

The authors then give examples and further advice, taking each commitment in sequence. The advice is fleshed out with examples and quotes from the data collected during their many interviews. Much of what the authors conclude, while being perfectly valid, can be found elsewhere in this book. Consequently only a relatively small sample will be dealt with here, beginning with the indisputable fact that leadership is in reality defined by the followers, who determine whether their leader actually possesses good leadership qualities.

Here Kouzes and Posner review a separate survey of some 1,500 managers, sponsored by the American Management Association, and a follow-up study of another 800 senior executives, in which they set out to determine what values/traits/characteristics they admired in their superiors. Although more than 225 characteristics were identified, these were reduced to fifteen categories. Later studies, in which they asked senior executives to complete a survey of superior leader characteristics, identified twenty attributes. The top four, which correlated with their earlier studies, indicated that a leader should be honest, competent, forward-looking and inspiring.

These characteristics also tallied exactly with a study carried out with AT&T employees; the authors therefore concluded that they were very much 'a given'. In essence, these qualities can be summed up as 'credibility'. This is one of the hardest attributes to earn but it is also fragile, easily lost and hard to regain. Credibility is the basis upon which long-term persuasion is built – credible leaders do not get people to do; they get them to *want* to do. This essential leadership credibility is, they state, built on the effective carrying out of the leadership practices they have defined.

The writers subsequently move on to deal with each of the ten characteristics in turn. While a number of the behaviours dealt with are common to most treatises on leadership, and in fact dealt with by other authors, they broke new ground in certain areas at the time the book was written.

In the related areas of innovation and risk-taking they are particularly strong. They assert that the leader must be aware of employees' need for challenge and how this can be stultified by excessive routine and boring tasks. Leaders must make rules but must also seek out opportunities to bend or break them. In this, Kouzes and Posner echo the work of Rosemary Stewart, who in *Choices for the Manager* (1982) made the case that effective executives should examine the demands, constraints and choices that make up their working lives and then seek to meet their demands by challenging the constraints and making choices. But choices involve risk; and risk and innovation often go hand-in-hand.

The authors write that it is a duty of leaders to encourage people to be risk-takers and to risk failure. When something fails they should not seek to apportion blame but ask what opportunities to learn can be gleaned from the event. Every innovation will expose the organization and its people to some degree of risk, but it is the people's ability to grow and learn under stressful and risky situations that will determine how they view change. Consequently it is necessary for everyone to be 'psychologically hardy' and it is a challenge to leaders to create an environment that breeds hardiness and motivation. To do this, they themselves must be masters of uncertainty. The authors then set out a number of ways in which leaders can promote an environment in which uncertainty can be changed into an opportunity for experimentation, innovation and controlled risk-taking:

1 Institutionalize processes for collecting innovative ideas.
2 Put idea-gathering on your own agenda – foster the creative champions within the organization. Be very visible in the role of chief listener.

3 Set up little experiments. This helps the leader find out which teams within the organization are better prepared or able to accept or assist innovation.

4 Renew your teams – switch people around between teams and also train members of existing teams; doing so will refresh perspective.

5 Honour your risk-takers. This means honouring good attempts as well as outright successes.

6 Analyse every failure as well as every success.

7 Model risk-taking. It is necessary for the leaders to encourage others to take risks by being seen to take them themselves. Outward-bound development training, the authors believe, can facilitate this process.

8 Foster hardiness. Leaders must always stress the benefits of change, and foster an atmosphere of commitment, control and challenge by making public statements of their own commitment. They must also seek to illustrate how the present challenge will lead to better things in the future. This, of course, is linked to the power of the shared vision for the future.

At a later stage, Kouzes and Posner examine the role of the leader from the follower's point of view. The message about what really counts in an organization, they say, is emphasized by the leader's 'moments of truth' – a phrase they borrow from Jan Carlzon of SAS and which means seizing opportunities to demonstrate personal commitment. And for leaders, every interaction with an employee, vendor or customer must become a moment of truth as these interactions will clearly demonstrate the leader's core values better than any written statements. Typically such moments of truth will be found in how leaders spend their time, the questions that they ask, their reaction to critical incidents, and finally, what they reward. It is through these actions and processes that the leaders make intangible statements tangible.

Within these four areas are incorporated earlier words of wisdom from Tom Peters with his MBWA philosophy of 'walking the talk'. More specifically, in looking at the questions that leaders ask, Kouzes and Posner point out that the type of questions asked will send clear messages about the focus of the company and the values that should be pursued, as well as the leader's memory and interest. Here they anticipate the later work of people like Rupert Eales-White, who emphatically state that the technique of asking the right question is a key to good leadership and strategic thinking.

And, of course, when there is success it is necessary to celebrate the accomplishments. In initiating the celebration it also helps if the leader personally knows a wide range of people within the organization, and here Kouzes and Posner emphasize the fact that effective leaders must also be good networkers.

The writers expand on the concept of the leader's network of contacts and offer unique advice and insight. To be effective and to be able to know where and how to obtain information, it is necessary for leaders to examine the extent to which they have, or use part of, an extensive network of contacts. They add practical advice on how readers can draw diagrams that represent their networks. They also conclude that without doubt all managers should be members of networks of relationships. Effective use of a network will mean that individuals must seek to use the contacts identified within it to influence bosses and subordinates as well as peers and people in external groups, where they may lack positional authority. The influence brought about by effective networking can be crucial.

Building on John Kotter's study, which concluded that networking was one of a manager's critical challenges, Kouzes and Posner noted that when managers develop an effective web of relationships, especially with peers and with those external to the organization, they are more likely to be successful in their careers. Peers can be a valuable source of information and can also serve as advisers and counsellors. Use everyone in your network to the fullest extent possible, conclude Kouzes and Posner – and learn from as many sources as possible.

The writers end the main body of the work with their thoughts on how to become a leader who cares and makes a difference. Based on their research and in-depth discussions, they concluded that leaders who had used the five key practices frequently were seen to:

● have a higher degree of personal credibility than those who did not;
● be more effective in meeting job-related demands;
● be more successful in representing their units to upper management;
● have higher-performing teams.

Leadership practices, they say, fall most closely into the area of transformational, as opposed to transactional, leadership. But the individual must take a cognitive step in order to become a transformational leader. This step involves learning to lead, which can mean formal training as well as learning by doing – the process of trial and error. 'Then once you act like a leader, the more likely it is that you will have a positive influence on others in the organization. Leaders can indeed make a difference.' Finally, they say, there is self-belief. That is where the whole process of leadership and learning starts.

CONCLUSION

The Leadership Challenge has survived the test of time in so far as it was a key work in the emergent literature on transformational leadership. What has made it stand out is the high degree of practicality of both thinking and advice it contains; this has ensured its place in lists of recommended reading more than a decade after its publication.

Howard Gardner

Howard Gardner is one of the world's most accomplished psychologists. Moreover, in a writing career that has spanned over twenty-five years, he is one of the most abundant thinkers and authors in the field of human psychology.

Gardner's books have a common theme, that of the mind. Starting with *The Quest for Mind* (1973), he has published eighteen books, dealing with such diverse topics as multiple intelligences, creativity, and the development of the mind through the process of maturation from child to adult. He is also the author of several hundred articles and is much in demand as a speaker on topics such as creativity, leadership and the arts. He was awarded a MacArthur Prize fellowship in 1981 and became the first American to receive the Louisville Grawenmayer Award in Education in 1990. At the time of publication of *Leading Minds* in 1997, he was Professor of Education and co-director of Project Zero at the Harvard Graduate School of Education (where he is at present Professor of Cognition), and Adjunct Professor of Neurology at the Boston University School of Medicine. He has been awarded honorary degrees from fourteen universities.

In *Leading Minds*, Gardner adopted a psychological approach to the phenomenon of leadership, examining the minds and histories of the famous and eminent; the work was undertaken in collaboration with Emma Laskin, a researcher at Project Zero which has the mission to enhance creativity, learning and thinking in the arts as well as scientific disciplines at individual and institutional levels.

Gardner's key goal in *Leading Minds* was to describe features of effective leadership, irrespective of whether or not he admired the leader in question. The work is subsequently divided into chapters that describe the various concepts with which he wishes to deal before moving on to give short biographies of eleven famous leaders from politics, science, religion and the military. Those dealt with range from Margaret Thatcher to Margaret Mead, and from J. Robert Oppenheimer to Mahatma Gandhi. Gardner defends his choice of the famous by pointing out that most works deal with 'ordinary leadership' and then extrapolate to the 'heights of achievement'; he believes that it will be easier to understand and bring out lessons for the ordinary by first focusing on the extraordinary. Regrettably there is insufficient space here to deal with the biographies (although they are worth reading both for their interest and their historical perspective); rather the emphasis will be to summarize the key messages about leadership and followership that Gardner extracts from his examinations.

A leader, says Gardner, is an individual 'who significantly affects the thoughts, feelings and/or behaviours of a significant number of individuals'. He goes on to make the distinction between direct leadership, where the leader addresses his public face-to-face, and indirect leadership, where leaders cause an impact through the work that they are doing. Churchill, Stalin and Roosevelt, when they met during the Second World War, were three powerful direct leaders who by their words and actions set out to change the world. Einstein, for instance, was not a leader as such but has influenced the world hugely by his work. Churchill and Einstein consequently both qualify as leaders, albeit from different ends of the direct–indirect spectrum. In general, there is a movement among leaders to move towards the direct form of leadership, and in doing so their technical expertise may suffer or be sacrificed. All leaders, however, influence the thinking of other people by the stories they tell, and the concept of the 'leader's story' is one that differentiates Gardner's study from most other works on the subject.

Leaders achieve their aims and are effective largely through the stories they relate. In order to understand their significance, it is first necessary to explore Gardner's concept of a 'cognitive approach to leadership'. The arena in which leadership occurs is that of the human mind, the minds of the leader and of the followers – the audience. Leaders must set out to alter the minds of their audiences in order to resolve important issues. A cognitive approach focuses on how thoughts, views and images develop and how they are stored, rearranged and sometimes distorted. The

complete cognitivist wishes to explain more complex forms of information, such as stories, scenarios, dreams and visions. Therefore when
confronted with leadership a cognitive scientist is likely to ask, 'What are
the ideas, or stories, of the leader? How have they developed? How do
they affect the thoughts or feelings of other individuals?' These are key
questions to ask about leaders and leadership; they concern influence and
are the mainstays of power. The leader's personality may be an important
factor in his or her success, but there is a missing piece of the puzzle. The
cognitive approach, which deals with the mental structures activated in
leaders and followers, provides the link.

Because of Gardner's cognitive approach, the concept of the leaders'
stories takes on a particular importance. Stories may appeal to different
levels of human sophistication, and the concept of the unschooled or
five-year-old mind is explained. The unschooled mind tends to think of
things in terms of black and white, as opposed to a more discerning
approach which sees shades of grey. When considering stories leaders
tell, Gardner's studies indicate that those aimed at the unsophisticated
mind triumph. Humans like clear statements, clear (if simplistic) explanations and unequivocal pointers to the way ahead.

Stories emerge in three broad categories: there are stories about the
self, the group, and about values and meaning. Although no one story
necessarily addresses all three needs, stories leaders tell are created in
response to the human need for better self-understanding, the need to
understand the position of their group, and the need to latch on to values
and meaning as a basis for action, or even existence. Most humans crave
a clear statement of value; an insight on what is true, good and ultimately
worthwhile. The chances of success are greater if the story becomes the
central mission for a leader. It is also more likely to succeed if it can be
put forward over a long period of time, if it can be allowed to take hold
during a period of non-crisis, and if it encourages individuals to think of
themselves as part of a broader community.

In times of crisis or change, this need in individuals is exaggerated.
And from here the challenge is set for the leader to produce a story that
can be incorporated in a vision that 'builds on the most credible of past
syntheses, revisits them in the light of present concerns, leaves open a
place for future events and allows individual contributions by the persons
of the group'. The example Gardner gives is that of Martin Luther, whose
ideas spread so rapidly because he built on the strengths of Catholicism,

addressed legitimate concerns about inequities that were prevalent at the time, and invited his audience to think personally about their own potential contributions to the new order. However, the greatest challenge facing a leader is to bring about significant changes in a large and heterogeneous group. Here the best chances for success come through a steadfast concentration on the same core message, along with a measure of flexibility regarding the manner and sophistication of its presentation.

But where does the phenomenon of leadership itself come from? There are foundations in the actual primate status of humankind. Primates organize themselves into hierarchies with clear dominance structures and relationships. They also have a tendency to imitate. These characteristics are all plainly visible in pre-school humans – and so the ground is set for leadership as such, and for leaders to emerge. When it comes to signs of future leadership in humans, a number of features appear. Although these early markers are by no means common to all great leaders, as generalizations they pose some interesting questions. Many had child-hoods that were marked by loneliness or some form of isolation; school-days were difficult. Future leaders have also often lost fathers at an early age. Often there was ambivalence in relationships with parents and it is conjectured that the desire to wield power in later life is an attempt to resolve these anxiety-producing situations. Irrespective of source, how-ever, a desire to gain power – either for its own sake or in pursuit of an external aim – is usually present. Leaders have often stood apart from their contemporaries from an early age; they have felt that they were somehow special and capable of feats that were beyond the reach of other people. They know a lot about how to reach and influence other human beings – and this knowledge is not easily locked inside: it must be expressed. Consequently, nearly all direct leaders were eloquent. They had linguistic intelligence which was linked to other forms of intelligence in order to make them sophisticated and effective communicators.

Gardner also deals with the concept of followership. Are followers cut from a different cloth than leaders? Napoleon is quoted as saying that he had become a good leader because he had been an outstanding follower. What does bind leaders and followers together is their common need for a structure, a hierarchy and a mission – needs that stem from their common primate heritage. Admittedly these needs may be less binding for those who are not so anxious about being in a closely-knit group.

Gardner then moves on to deal with what he considers to be the key attributes of a developed leader. Although it could be argued, he says, that no leader ever fully reaches their ultimate potential, there are characteristics that appear crucial to the practice of effective leadership.

1 *A tie with the community (or audience)* A leader needs followers, and the relationship between leader and followers must be active and dynamic. Each is affected by the other and leaders must alter their stories to take the changing features of followers and the overall situation into account. Ultimately, if the tie between leader and followers is to endure, both must work together to construct some kind of institution or organization that embodies their common values.

2 *A certain rhythm of life* The leader must not only maintain contact with his or her community but also find the time to achieve a distance from the mission or action. Gardner refers to this as 'going to the mountain top' – a much-needed time for reflection and introspection. This may happen quite naturally for the indirect leader but it is something the busy direct leader may have to fight for.

3 *An evident relation between stories and embodiments* Leaders exercise their influence in two principal ways: through the stories or messages they communicate and through the traits they display. Churchill is held up as a leader who gave out a fighting message of opposition to Nazi Germany and embodied it in everything he did. However, other leaders may exhibit a tension between words and actions. Stories may grow out of the leader's life experiences and therefore may become embodied in the leader's self – this is when the greatest sincerity is evident to followers and when there is most likelihood of an enthusiastic reception.

4 *A centrality of choice* Some individuals attain positions of leadership in situations where they and their followers exercise some kind of choice, without the need to use naked power or instruments of terror. 'Only in such instances of "leadership through choice" does it make sense to think of stories being told, virtues being embodied, or opinions being changed through example and persuasion.' Although both Stalin and Saddam Hussein may have reached positions that embodied some of the better points of leadership, they lost the perspective that would have enabled them to pull back from their more draconian actions before being corrupted by power.

So what does the exemplary leader look like? Gardner lists the characteristics of an imaginary leader who embodies the best qualities of the leaders he has examined as well as the most potent qualities of leadership he himself has put forward.

First of all there is a willingness to challenge and confront authority. It is almost a feeling of entitlement to challenge and although the challenge may entail risks, the leader is not risk-averse. At the same time the exemplary leader (or EL) stands out early in life because of a concern with moral issues, competitiveness and a wish to attain power. This will not be for power's sake, but as an aid to attaining certain goals.

At the same time the EL will ever broaden her (Gardner uses a female example) circle of contacts – the circle will be large and heterogeneous. The breadth of views and opinions that this gives the EL means that she will soon stand out by producing arguments and explanations that others find it hard to dispute. The EL may well have travelled widely in early life, and may have taken a decade or more to master the 'domain' in which she eventually makes a breakthrough. At the same time she must become increasingly attuned to an audience that is posing certain questions and searching for guidance – especially on issues of identity. Then, if the EL has learnt to express herself well and has worked out answers to such questions, which she can also then embody in her approach to dealing with challenging situations, she is poised for leadership. However, the less well defined the constituency or situation, the more necessary it is for the EL to invent a definite background and identity for herself and tell compelling stories – always bearing in mind the needs and limits of the unschooled mind. The ability to adjust the story to meet the changing demands of different situations is also vital.

The EL also needs to be aware of any charismatic qualities that he or she may have and to avoid stories or actions that undermine them. Here the opportunity for reflection is important and helps the EL to keep the big picture in mind. An uncluttered mind moves those obstacles that block vision and concentrates itself on the truly important variables.

At the same time there is an element of toughness and resilience. The EL is not put off by apparent failures, indeed can be energized by setbacks. However, this energy and commitment can have its down side. The EL can make overly harsh demands on followers and pay too little attention to those who should be nurtured. Paradoxically this can mean that leaders with concern for mankind as well as great ambition can undermine their own achievements even in their own lifetime.

Gardner states that the features of leadership he has examined must be viewed in the light of the nature of the world at the turn of the millennium:

● The potential for global destruction.
● Instant, often simplistic, communication.
● Absence of privacy.
● The rise of entities such as multinational corporations that transcend national boundaries.
● Nationalist and fundamentalist reactions to situations, that mainly appeal to the undeveloped mind.
● Even more technical expertise in the world – this demands leaders who retain some expert knowledge as well as the ability to communicate with non-experts.

The implications for effective leadership and for the training of future leaders are:

1 *The need to appreciate the enduring features of leadership* The key features should be part of the core training of leaders.
2 *The need to anticipate and deal with new trends* Future leaders must be aware of the new and often complex trends in society, business and technology. They must learn to consider them in the light of future changes in the dimensions of their domains and their audiences.
3 *The need to encourage recognition of the problems, paradoxes and possibilities of leadership* Leaders and their audiences must be educated about the tensions that complicate the leader's role.

Gardner draws the conclusion that if we pretend that leadership simply happens naturally, we will ensure that there will be an inadequate supply of leaders in the future. We will also make it less likely that leaders will emerge from the less dominant groups in society. If the complexities of the issues facing the world and those who purport to lead it are better understood, then it is less likely that irresponsible leadership will arise and prevail. He hopes that 'those who come to appreciate the issues, and design means of articulating them, will help to usher in a world in which leadership is less coercive, more empowering to the broad citizenry, and better able to achieve constructive ends'.

CONCLUSION

On this note of hope a complex web of psychology, analysis and biography is brought to a conclusion. Gardner has raised a number of important issues in his work, and has given fascinating insights into the minds and actions of great leaders of the twentieth century. Those in less elevated leadership positions, on the other hand, may need to spend some time deciding how best to put the sophisticated and psychological demands of Gardner's key messages into action.

Stephen R. Covey

Stephen Covey is an author and speaker, and an expert on leadership, personal effectiveness and change management. He is Chairman of the Covey Leadership Center and the Institute for Principle-Centered Leadership, both of which teach personal and organizational leadership around the world, and he is much sought after as a speaker on subjects that include family and interpersonal relationships. Covey has an MBA from Harvard and a doctorate from Brigham Young University.

Stephen Covey is author of a wide range of publications, ranging from *The Lion King* to *The Nature of Leadership*, which is a collection of thoughts about life through observations from nature. It is, however, for *The Seven Habits of Highly Effective People* (1989) that he is best known. Key messages from this massive bestseller have been extrapolated into a number of workbooks and subsequent studies, including *Principle-Centered Leadership* and *The Seven Habits of Highly Effective Families*. Covey's work is highly personal in nature in that it is very spiritual, takes a high moral tone, and approaches both personal development and leadership in this fashion. *The Seven Habits of Highly Effective People* has been accused as being a recruitment vehicle for Covey's religion, the Church of Latter-day Saints, and warning messages against it can be found on the Internet. This writer, however, can find no tangible evidence for this within the book and individual readers must make up their own minds on this issue.

The Seven Habits of Highly Effective People, with its aim of 'restoring the character ethic', contains a number of powerful messages on time management and personal development. At the same time, there are lessons in the leadership of self and the leadership of others. In order to extract the most from Covey's writing on leadership, it is necessary to explore his personal philosophies regarding principles and thought patterns.

Covey writes that during his career he became interested in how perceptions are formed, how they govern the way people see things and consequently how they behave. It taught him that one must look at the lens through which we see the world as well as the world itself, as the lens shapes the way in which the individual interprets the world. For an individual to change a situation, it is first necessary for that individual to change himself or herself; for this to happen, first perceptions must change.

In parallel, the concept of the character ethic is developed. This teaches that there are basic principles of effective living, and that people can only experience true success and happiness if they learn and integrate these principles into their essential characters. It is people's characters that communicate most eloquently with the world, because 'what we are' communicates far more eloquently than 'anything we say, or do'. From here a definite link is made between character and perception. The concept of perception is redefined as 'paradigm' – a model, or way in which we see the world, not in terms of visual perception but in terms of perceiving, understanding and interpreting it. A paradigm then becomes an explanation, or model. It becomes the source of individuals' attitudes and behaviours, and it can be seen that there are basic flaws in the personality ethic as it is pointless trying to change attitudes and behaviours if no attempt is made to examine the basic paradigms from which they flow. However, the more aware an individual is of their basic paradigms and the extent to which they have been influenced by their experience, the more he or she can take responsibility for them, listen to other people's perceptions and thereby form a fuller and more objective overview of the world. It is only possible to achieve quantum improvements if an individual addresses the root from which both attitudes and behaviour derive. Paradigms are inseparable from character, so it is necessary to work on the former before major work can be done on the latter.

Having laid down the basis of character and paradigm, Covey identifies the concept of 'principles'. These are guidelines for human conduct that have enduring value. Like fairness, integrity and human dignity, they are unarguable because they are self-evident. The more closely our paradigms match the basic principles, or natural laws, the more accurate and functional they will be. As the way in which humans usually see the problems that face them is in fact the real problem, a new level of thinking is needed: a paradigm based on 'the principles that accurately describe the territory of effective human being and interacting – to solve these deep concerns'. And this is the new level of thinking that *The Seven Habits of Highly Effective People* is about. As an approach to personal and interpersonal effectiveness, it is principle-centred, character-based, starting on the individual's inside world before addressing the outside world. The inside-out approach says that private victories precede public victories, so improve yourself before attempting to improve others. Although Covey has not yet directly addressed the subject of leadership head on, in tackling issues of paradigms he has already dealt with a major element of strategic leadership.

From here the seven habits are then put into context. The habits are:

1 Be proactive.
2 Begin with the end in mind.
3 Put first things first.
4 Think win/win.
5 Seek to understand, then to be understood.
6 Synergize.
7 Sharpen the saw.

Interlinked with the habits is a continuum of dependence, independence and interdependence, a process of increasing maturity and of increasing ability to lead. People need to appreciate the overall interdependence of all things to be good leaders as well as good team players. Interdependence is a choice only independent people can make; dependent people do not yet have the character to make this choice as they do not yet 'own' enough of themselves. However, when you think and act interdependently, paradigms can be recognized and broken far more easily.

Habits 1, 2 and 3 are about the move from dependence to independence. This gives the basis for interdependence, which is explored in habits 4, 5 and 6 – and habit 7 is one of renewal. The habits are designed to bring long-term personal effectiveness, as they are based on basic principles as well as an overall principle of natural law called the P/PC balance. Here P stands for production of desired results, while PC stands for production capability – real effectiveness lies in achieving the balance between them. The thread of principle, as well as those of ensuring a P/PC balance, runs through all the seven habits; they are of particular significance in two habits, 'Begin with the end in mind', and 'Think win/win', in which Covey most fully addresses the question of leadership.

Begin with the end in mind

This means that it is necessary to start with a clear understanding of your destination so that the steps you take are always in the right direction. It is too easy to start climbing a ladder only to find that it is leaning against the wrong wall. The right wall symbolizes those things that matter most to an individual. An individual may be very busy, indeed very efficient in what he or she does, yet that individual will only be truly effective when they work towards those things that represent their *real* definition of success in life. 'Begin with the end in mind', therefore, is based on the principle that all things are created twice; first there is a mental creation, then a physical, or second creation. It is vital to accept responsibility for both creations, especially the first, as this involves 'writing one's own script'. Successful implementation will therefore enlarge a person's circle of influence. Management efficiency is about climbing the ladder of success, but leadership determines whether the ladder is leaning against the right wall.

Effectiveness, states Covey, does not depend on the effort expended, but on whether the effort is expended in the right place. This is why, in just about every scenario, leadership must come first and management second. Efficient management on its own is like 'straightening deck chairs on the Titanic'. No degree of good management can compensate for failures in leadership, but starting out as good leaders is often hard when people are caught in a management paradigm. This paradigm can equally apply in family as in business life as people find themselves seeking efficiency before they have clarified their essential values.

The way out of this trap is to become your own creator (shades of Warren Bennis in *On Becoming a Leader*, where he asserts that leaders must invent themselves). Two human attributes that can help here are imagination and conscience. These attributes allow the individual to visualize the untapped wells of potential within, as well as to check the morality of the goals envisioned. Consequently it is possible to rescript oneself so that the paradigms from which one's behaviour flow are congruent with one's most deeply held values, as well as with correct principles. Future decisions can then be based on these values. Acting with integrity will be easier as it will be easier to stand back from the emotion of any given situation.

The best way to start is by devising a personal mission statement. This will focus on what you want to be (character) and on what you want to do (contribution), and the values and principles on which both the being and doing are based. The key to being able to change lies in holding a changeless sense of *who* you are and of *what* you value. Many social and mental illnesses in fact stem from a sense of meaninglessness, but the act of identifying a personal mission can overcome this. The act of writing one's own mission statement, essentially a right-brained process (see page 163), starts by identifying the very core and centre of one's own life and this will be the source of personal security, guidance, wisdom and power, which in turn empowers personal proactivity and gives congruency and harmony to every part of a person's life.

It is, however, necessary to centre one's life on correct principles – these are deep fundamental truths which run through the very fabric of life. Knowing one's guiding principles gives greater freedom of choice and creates a fundamental paradigm for effective living. At the same time it puts the individual in touch with an essential monitor, a conscience. Then people who have seriously undertaken to identify what really matters most in life start to think in larger terms than the mere present; they start to become leaders. Personal leadership, though, is not a singular experience; it is an ongoing process, keeping both the vision and values alive and aligning one's life to be consistently congruent with them. In personal leadership, visualization and affirmation techniques stem from a solid foundation of thought-through purposes and principles that have become the centre point of the individual's life. From here, effective goals that focus on results rather than activity, yet which at the same time giving meaning and purpose to that which *is* done, are born.

Covey expands his personalized philosophy into the realm of organizational mission statements. Everyone must be involved in their generation for them to mean anything. They must 'come from within the bowels of the organization'. Creating the mission statement will take time, patience, skill and empathy. It will also require sincerity and the application of correct principles as well as the courage to align systems, structure and the management style to the shared vision and values. Mission statements conceived in this way will affect the style of employees, managers and leaders; then every facet of the organization will become a function of that hub, that mission statement. Service excellence and productivity will both increase by leaps and bounds!

Think win/win

Covey states that the move from independence to interdependence is the move into a leadership role. You are now in a position to influence other people and the key habit of effective interpersonal leadership is that of thinking win/win.

There are, in fact, six paradigms of social interaction:

1 *Win/Win* Everybody benefits from all interactions between people. This is principle-based behaviour. It is not my way or your way; a third alternative is a better way.
2 *Win/Lose* This is the competitive paradigm. It states that if I win, you must lose. This paradigm too often blights organizations where people are graded on the basis that there is only a limited amount of success to go round.
3 *Lose/Win* Here the individual is programmed to sacrifice their own viewpoint in order to court popularity or harmony. In fact this style is destructive to all concerned, issues are not dealt with effectively and feelings are repressed. People should not repress their feelings when searching for a higher meaning.
4 *Lose/Lose* Here people are concerned that if they cannot win, nobody shall win. This is the philosophy of the highly dependent person without any sense of direction. Targets are lowered and nobody benefits.
5 *Win* Here the individual is solely focused on winning, and it does not matter what happens to anybody else.
6 *Win/Win* or *No Deal* If no agreement can be found, then it may be necessary to abandon the attempt to do business together. This can be done amicably and may result in a better start later, one that is still based on mutual respect.

The *Win/Win* solution is by far the best in most situations and if it is not possible to reach it, it may be best to opt for the *No Deal* solution until better opportunities arise. Win/Win requires the exercise of self-awareness, imagination, conscience and independent will – as well as the search for mutual benefits.

There are five dimensions of Win/Win. These are character, relationships, performance, systems and process.

Character

There are three character traits essential for setting up a Win/Win environment. These are:

Integrity, based on a clear knowledge of one's own values.

Maturity, the balance between courage and consideration. This quality balances the P and the PC. While courage may focus on achieving production, consideration focuses on the welfare of all the stakeholders. The basic task of leadership is to 'increase the standard of living and quality of life for all stakeholders'.

Abundance mentality. The paradigm here is that there is plenty out there for everybody. The attitude grows out of a deep sense of personal worth and the 'plenty' may refer to recognition, credit, power or prosperity. An abundance mentality results in sharing of prestige, profits, recognition and prosperity, and opens up possibilities for even greater prosperity based on the innovation born from everybody's greater sense of personal worth.

Relationships

These are a key focus in Win/Win. It is essential to develop trust and to make deposits into an emotional bank account with other people. Deposits are made through genuine courtesy, respect and appreciation for the other person's point of view. This requires good listening but with this also comes better self-expression, so eventually the other person realizes that a real Win/Win is the desired target in the relationship. Consequently, as a result of the demonstrated commitment to Win/Win the influence will be more powerful. This is the real test of interpersonal leadership and it goes beyond transactional leadership into transformational leadership because it involves transforming the individuals concerned as well as the relationship or business situation.

Performance

Performance agreements based on Win/Win now focus on results, not methods. People now evaluate themselves and consequences become the logical result of performance rather than rewards or punishment handed out by the leadership. The atmosphere generated is based on the acceptance of the personal integrity of all concerned, as well as relationships based on trust.

Systems

Win/Win can only survive in an organization when the systems support it. Organizations get what they reward. If they claim a Win/Win culture but support a Win/Lose culture, they will get the latter. Reward systems are vital here and must support the mission and overall philosophy of the organization.

Process

The key question is that of how to arrive at a Win/Win solution and Covey stresses that it is only possible to achieve Win/Win solutions via Win/Win processes – the end and the means are the same thing. On this basis, the following process applies:

1 Seek to understand the problem from the other person's viewpoint.
2 Identify the key issues and concerns rather than the positions involved.
3 Determine what results would make an acceptable solution for all parties.
4 Identify possible new options to achieve these results.

Of course, all these demanding shifts of thinking and action require a great deal from the individual. A further process of renewal involving physical, mental, spiritual and social/emotional regeneration is required. During the renewal the individual's life will be lining up with his or her true principles and values, a source of real peace of mind and a clearer sense of purpose. But again, the saw needs continual sharpening; being effective is a goal that can be reached, but also one that makes constant, if positive, demands on the individual.

CONCLUSION

Covey's work has been both praised and criticized, a prevailing criticism being that it is too American. One thing, however, is clear: it is impossible to ignore! The very level of book sales makes ignoring it difficult. Furthermore, as much of what Covey writes links synergistically with the conclusions of those who have taken a more data-based and systematic approach to the study of leadership and personal development, perhaps it would be unwise to do so.

Rupert Eales-White

Rupert Eales-White graduated from Edinburgh University and subsequently worked in financial services, becoming Strategic Planning Manager for Barclays Bank. He joined PA Management Development at Sundridge Park in 1990 and became a Director of the organization's Senior Executive Programme, Leadership in Management, and Leading Change-Strategy into Action. Apart from his work on open programmes, he created a sound network of in-company clients, including St Ives plc, Allen and Overy, and the Renong Group, Malaysia, before going solo in 1998 to develop his own client base, largely concentrating on the legal world.

A conference speaker and seasoned author, Rupert Eales-White focuses on helping managers and executives develop their strategic thinking, leadership, change management and team-working skills. He has published a number of successful books, including *The Power of Persuasion*, *The Sunday Times Team Book*, *How to Become a Better Leader*, *Creating Growth from Change* and *Ask the Right Question*. An author who believes in relating the theory and message of his books to how readers react, perceive themselves and work effectively in teams, Eales-White is one of the few consultants who combine management training with an academic approach to the assessment of human behaviour. Many of Eales-White's thoughts and beliefs are expressed most succinctly in *Creating Growth from Change* – a work that aptly challenges readers to reflect on their role as both leaders and recipients of change.

Eales-White acknowledges Roger Harrison and Ned Herrmann as laying down a number of the models and concepts from which he has developed his own ideas. In *The Power of Persuasion*, he developed a strategy of ways of persuading others based on individual preferences, and continued this generic approach in *Creating Growth from Change*. Here he put forward an instrument aimed at helping people better understand their own and other people's reactions to change. Based on Herrmann's whole-brain model (see page 163), Eales-White describes four different approaches.

1 *Logical detached*

A person who favours this approach will rationalize change. When it occurs they will look at the facts, evaluate what is going on, remain unemotional, analyse and look at the implications of what is happening from a logical and often detached standpoint. Usually the nature and dimensions of the change itself will not be challenged, but the implications will always be analysed. There is a strong correlation here with the A-brain thinking preference.

2 *Negative control*

Later redefined by the author as cautious control, this approach is basically negative and emotional. Change is perceived as a disruption, a threat to the *status quo*, and consequently the individual will fight to minimize the disruption of the change and to maintain as much control over the situation as possible. Key words are 'resist' and 'stay in control' – here the similarity is with the cautious, B-brain preference.

3 *People focused*

Here individuals tend to accept change rather than challenge it, and the initial reaction is not selfish but one where the person experiencing the change seeks to find out how other people are affected and whether it is possible to help them. The approach is empathetic and relates strongly to the C-brain preference.

4 *Positive creative*

People who favour this mode enjoy change, they like to take risks and are open to the possibilities that the new events may bring. They are less emotionally involved with the consequences for other people than with exploring the dynamics of the change and the longer-term implications. They take an intellectual yet excited approach to circumstances, are stimulated by vision and will always want to explore further. Here the correlation is to D-brain thinking.

Eales-White makes his message very clear, whether you are a leader or a follower: it is vital to know and understand both your own change-preference profile as well as the profiles of those around you. From this understanding will flow effective leadership together with empathetic yet effective behaviour of the leader when in the role of change agent. For someone to gain effective growth from change, whether this is personal or organizational, requires all approaches to be deployed at different times in the cycle of change. In addition, we should all recognize the strengths in each profile and value the differences.

The compelling reason for adopting the above behaviours comes from the fact that there is an essential dilemma inherent in change management. The key to success in a changing world is organizational learning; however, a fundamental issue remains. 'Inflexible means to a defined end' *versus* 'Flexible means to an unclear end'.

Balance, according to Eales-White, is the key. 'Structure and system, direction and purpose are vital. Human beings will not operate well in a climate of chaos.' So perhaps the answer lies in achieving 'flexible means to a visionary end'. From this premise Eales-White expounds his view of the leader as a sensitive, flexible change agent, someone who has the ability to interact effectively in either individual or team-based activities.

In dealing with the question of leadership, Eales-White looks at the four stages of personal development and motivation as described by Maslow (survival, security, self-esteem and growth/self-actualization) and concludes that most individuals will swing between the different stages of development while they are at work, depending on the nature of the task being undertaken. Most people who are in employment will vary in mood, from hoping to gain security, through to the development of self-esteem, and finally – if all is well – move on to personal growth. The level at which we find ourselves will also determine how we react to change, whether we are likely to initiate it, and the type of change-orientated behaviour exhibited by our leaders that is most likely to appeal to us and motivate us. Furthermore, the level at which we find ourselves will determine whether the focus of our thinking is primarily internal (concentrated on self) or external. With this in mind, he presents a chart showing the most appropriate change-related behaviour set against each of the four levels of growth.

Obviously, then, the higher a person's development level the more

Development levels and change modes

Level	Primary mode	Focus
1. Survival	NC	Internal
2. Security	NC/LD	Internal
3. Self-esteem	NC/LD/PF/PC	Internal and external
4. Growth	PF/PC	External

open they will be to transformational and visionary styles of leadership. Putting it pragmatically, the development level of the follower can be raised if the leader adopts an open, listening, praising, yet questioning approach – as opposed to taking up a blaming, fault-finding attitude.

Eales-White suggests that in the context of effective leadership in times of change, the best definitions come from asking the led what most appeals to them. There is, he says, a large core of common views on the subject that transcend culture, race or status. In making this claim, Eales-White sets out the definitions of good leadership drawn up by a number of executives working for the Renong Group of companies, based in Malaysia. The Renong view of leadership is that effective leaders will:

- *think explicitly about the leadership role* Good leaders will invest time in thinking about their leadership role and what it demands of them. From this base, they can plan their leadership strategy in all its aspects, especially the interpersonal side;
- *develop self-awareness and self-belief* Poor leaders often adopt an excessively command-and-control style because they feel insecure or uncertain whether they will succeed. Leaders therefore need to think positively about themselves before they can think positively about those they lead;
- *focus externally, listen, support, provide feedback and coach* By developing self-belief, good leaders can grow into doing what those they lead actually want – focusing on the follower;
- *display integrity in decision-making* It is necessary for leaders to

make good and consistent decisions and not to be over-swayed by politics or expediency;

• *share information* Good leaders recognize that good followers want and need to have responsibility, and so share information whenever possible in order to help them to take it;

• *direct with coaching* Any manager or follower will from time to time need both coaching and direction, depending on the nature or novelty of the task they face. The need for a questioning coach role in promoting voyages of discovery is one very close to Eales-White's heart and one that will be further expounded later;

• *delegate authority as well as responsibility* This is at the heart of good leadership and makes strong connections to the means of achieving genuine empowerment.

Eales-White, in developing his own thinking from these precepts, states that good leaders must continually focus on their own development as leaders – they must be agents of change for themselves as well as for their followers. As leaders develop, they must be aware of the style they are tending to adopt and of the implications of that style in terms of the needs of the followers. He mentions various approaches, such as that of the *visionary team leader*, or *questioning coach*, and develops those themes.

Many of Eales-White's views have been formed by his great interest in team leadership and from his belief in the power of the right question. As one of the most voluminous writers on teams today, his thoughts on team leadership (including those on the visionary team leader) are developed elsewhere. In further examining Eales-White's views on leadership, however, it is necessary to link them to his analysis of persuasion. In *The Power of Persuasion*, he reveals four main styles of persuasion. There is the use of logic, the power of incentives, the empathy approach, and finally the appeal to group norms or values. The level of commitment to change generated will depend on how, as leaders, we set out to persuade.

The lowest level of commitment generated is when the leader adopts the *stern parent* role. Here the leader focuses on the use of logic and incentives as the main weapons. The relationship is parent/child in approach – 'You must do this because . . .' This approach may be effective in the short term but is less likely to be effective in the longer term. Followers will carry out the actions because they have been told to do so but their hearts will not be in it. In dealing with the essential dilemma of change, a unidirectional approach is unlikely to be appropriate when people have different goals or targets. So the 'stern parent' approach can be both ineffective and inefficient.

The next level of commitment is that of the *strong leader*. The incentives and logic approaches are supplemented by some emphasis on group values, goals and vision. This, says Eales-White, is the classic model of good leadership, the person who comes to the rescue when things are in crisis. They move mountains and the followers' self-esteem is enhanced by identifying with their efforts. But there are dangers. From the perspective of effective change management this approach cannot be successful in the longer term as the vision is unidirectional and dies along with the leader. The leader has tried to define the future, which in fact cannot be defined in a changing world. As opposed to the 'stern parent', the strong leader has won the commitment of the followers but has not achieved their full understanding. Consequently, in the long term they will break away to follow their own dreams.

Finally, Eales-White moves on to describe his preferred role, that of the *questioning coach*. Here the approach generates the deepest level of commitment as it involves a mixture of logic, empathy and appeal to group values to achieve the desired goal. By taking the followers on a shared voyage of discovery, the leader is providing an environment where issues can be explored and findings shared with no risk of ridicule. Most important, there will be full commitment to action as all involved will 'fully understand what to do, how to do it and why we are doing it'. Eales-White does, however, add a caveat. This ideal state of affairs is dependent on both leader and follower being able to operate at the 'growth' level of development for sustained periods. The more the leader is able to create an environment that is positive to change, the easier it will be for growth to be derived from the change itself. This perhaps is where the writer makes the major link between his approach to persuasion and his change preference styles. The more the leader can exhibit the positive, creative approach and bring it out in other people by operating as a questioning coach, the more likely it is that change initiatives will succeed.

The writer concludes that it is a prime responsibility of the leader to promote discovery in those affected by the change or involved in making it happen, so that when the change does occur it will be easier for them to make connections to both the present and the past. This is all part and parcel of the key skill of managing perceptions both for ourselves and for others to ensure that the change is perceived positively. And from this positive attitude to change can come creative solutions to problems, the essential vehicles for the solution of these problems being the empowered team and the ability of the leader to promote discovery by asking the right questions.

Eales-White's approach to teams and team-building is discussed elsewhere so we will only look at his approach to promoting discovery at this stage. As a writer who is passionately interested in the encouragement of creativity in individuals and teams, he has extended his thinking on discovery and the role of the creative coach in *Ask the Right Question*. Here he focuses on what is the right question, and how we can use those questions to produce the right result. He uses the concept of what, where, when, how, why and who in open questions which when combined with effective, assertive listening become the 'discovery kings'. Although many writers, especially in the fields of interviewing technique, have explained open questions in juxtaposition to closed questions, Eales-White delves much deeper by examining the key roles of each of the questioning words. He also provides strategies and worked examples to enable the reader to use them with skill. The result is that, when properly used, the 'discovery kings' will always ensure that any conversation will result in major learning and discovery.

CONCLUSION

Rupert Eales-White states that as a result of thousands of conversations with managers during his years as a consultant, the greatest concern that most have is in the field of relationships. Relationships with the boss, with clients and with subordinates – and often it is the gaps between how we wish to appear and how we actually do come over in those relationships that is the stumbling block to achieving interpersonal effectiveness in the leadership role. In giving behavioural advice covering one-to-one relationships, meetings, persuasion and conflict management, he extends his advice to subordinates and leaders alike. A questioning approach is a key to effective leadership and good leaders will use the concept of the 'voyage of discovery' in a variety of situations.

In making these points, Eales-White has put a number of key skills within the reach of leaders at all levels, while at the same time blending well-established theories with his own ideas in a clear and pragmatic way.

Douglas Ready

In 1993 two major forces combined to produce a global report entitled *Champions of Change* on the skills and attitudes required to lead business transformations. Dr Douglas Ready, as Executive Director of the International Consortium for Executive Development Research, joined forces with Gemini Consulting to examine the challenges business leaders faced in building the organization of the future and in developing other leaders within them. Gemini Consulting is a global management consultancy firm dedicated to helping its clients achieve faster and better results through its expertise in strategy, operations, people and information management.

A major goal of the report was to assess what skills would be needed to help organizations succeed in the increasingly competitive and uncertain international business arena. Further aims were to create a debate as to how executives could build regenerative organizations, as well as how they could develop the people who would lead them. Ready and his co-researchers set out to gain a clearer understanding of the roles and dimensions of leadership required to lead the next generation of organizations and to ascertain whether organizations were doing their best to create conditions in which leadership would flourish. It is interesting to note that for many senior managers the skills and behaviours identified in the report have become more and more necessary, as mergers of already massive businesses become the rule rather than the exception, and the rate of change in technology and information steadily increases.

To collect the data for the report, Ready and his team studied the views of over 1,450 managers from around the world. They deliberately ensured that respondents came from a wide variety of sectors and distributed questionnaires in seven different languages. Respondents came from a wide range of organizations, including AT&T, British Airways, the Fiat Group, Daimler-Benz AG, Electricité de France, Gaz de France and Siemens AG.

The survey studied a number of key themes, including the following:

- How would you best describe your business's competitive environment now?
- Which organizational capabilities are most important for your business's competitiveness over the next three years?
- What are the five leadership competencies that are most important for your effectiveness over the next three years?
- What are the most effective methods for learning these leadership competencies?

Ready was interested in determining the extent of global agreement exhibited by his respondents because he felt it was vital to identify areas of common ground across cultures, as well as to understand the differences in areas such as the perception of leadership and organizational effectiveness.

Six key conclusions emerged as a result of the report, which indicated that large organizations across the world were striving to cope with change and to regenerate themselves in the midst of considerable turbulence. For the purpose of this summary, we will look more closely at those most pertinent to the role of the leader as change agent.

1 Transformation is a regenerative process, not a one-time event
By an overwhelming majority, respondents stated that their organizations were in the middle of considerable transformation. Nearly 60 per cent stated that their companies were in the middle of widespread transformation, while a further 15 per cent felt that their firms should be making major changes but had not yet faced up to the fact. Only 10 per cent felt that their organizations were stable. Almost 70 per cent stated that they themselves had experienced significant job changes over the past three years.

From the replies, Ready concluded that transformation was not a programme and not a series of restorative actions. Neither was it optional. Transformation has to be a continuous process and organizations must be committed to constant renewal in order to take advantage of new opportunities in the dynamic business environment. While these conclusions could be regarded as somewhat obvious, the report went on to make vital links to leadership. There must be vision and a future-based strategy, otherwise transformation will be mainly seen as a downsizing initiative. Successful transformation therefore requires the commitment of all staff. Behaviour and mindsets must be changed and this requires commitment and effort from the top. The capacity to manage activities that result in commitment is one of the greatest challenges for the next generation of leaders, who must view change as a continuous process rather than a single event.

2 Operational excellence is no longer a source of sustainable competitive advantage

To reach this conclusion, the researchers studied the answers to the following question: 'Which five organizational capabilities are most important in order for your business to be successful competitively over the next three years?' Answers ranked 'to be organized around customer requirements' as first, followed by 'to be flexible', 'to be a quality leader', 'to be a customer service leader', and 'to have tangible strategic vision'.

It is interesting to note that the accent on overall customer orientation has increased in most successful businesses since the report. It is noteworthy, too, that high ranking is given to strategic vision as a key ingredient not just for motivation and morale, but for organizational competitiveness. The vision that enables companies to succeed must help them combine a strong customer orientation with strategic agility, thereby elevating their core competencies to provide exceptional value to their clients. A high degree of operational excellence is already assumed.

3 Key indicators suggest that we are not prepared for the future

Here the report reached some sober conclusions. Taking the five criteria identified in the previous section, respondents identified significant performance gaps between the desired state and reality in each area. Too many organizations were obsessed with getting better at what they were already good at rather than focusing on what they should be doing in the future. While the authors were particularly concerned at performance gaps in the areas of organizational flexibility and customer focus, finding these failings to be a global phenomenon, they also discovered that the organizations were not rated as having global mindsets. Similarly, while a high proportion of respondents rated the quality of 'instilling trust between our leaders and our workers' as within the top five requirements, it was rated next to last in terms of effectiveness. The 'organizational capacity to identify the next generation of leaders' was also ranked very low.

Ready and Gemini rated the prevailing trust and expectations gap between top management and the rest of the organization as a serious cause for concern; they felt that trust was a central ingredient in successful organizational transformations. If leaders asked people to make sacrifices for possible future benefits, it was necessary for high levels of trust to exist in the organization. At the same time, if leaders stated that new behaviours were important but continued to reward old behaviours, the resultant cynicism would probably undermine the ability to achieve meaningful change. The authors' research also indicated that senior executives usually had a far more optimistic view of the performance of their organizations than did their middle managers. They concluded that when people at the top feel the need for change is less urgent than those who are faced with the realities of implementing it, it is easy to see why so many change initiatives fail.

4 *The new leadership challenge is to engage the entire organization in continuous regeneration*

In answer to the question, 'What will be the five most important capabilities that you will need in order to be an effective leader over the next three years?' respondents ranked the following as vital:

Visioning This, along with the ability to articulate values and strategy, was the clear top choice out of forty-five dimensions of leadership and top choice for most of the nine culture groups surveyed.

Empowerment This the authors defined as 'the extent to which a leader provides the encouragement, tools and authority to individuals, enabling them to utilize their full potential on the job'. They also noted that the most profitable companies listed this capability as their top priority.

Leading change The authors thought this was ranked high because most respondents felt their organizations were in the middle of widespread transformation.

Producing results This was the dimension of managing strategy into action. It was different from managing change, as the emphasis here was on producing results. Interestingly, only US respondents listed 'getting results' as their number one criterion for leadership effectiveness.

Customer focus The authors were encouraged to find this rated so high and felt that great companies had leaders who were customer enablers.

Viewed together, the authors considered that these choices signalled a change in the roles and expectations of leaders in the future. They would need the ability to articulate compelling vision with the strategic decision-making abilities necessary to achieve follow-through. In addition, they would know how to raise key resources to generate productive change. In general, they would be energized by change, not overpowered by it. The new leaders would need to master the art of continually reinventing organizational capabilities and creating mechanisms that would enable the organization to engage in continuous regeneration and renewal. The new leadership skill would be more than just having a vision, it would be that of orchestrating the entire organization in the vision to create a compelling future. It would be managing meaning, mindset and mobilization. Leadership, then, is about creating processes through which an organization will continually seek to reinvent itself.

For this to happen, leadership must be made available to as many people as possible. Yet in a global business arena leaders must be aware that fundamentally different perceptions of what constitutes effective leadership exist; with this in mind, leaders must learn how better to manage and mobilize their organization's knowledge resources.

5 *Leaders are neither born nor made. But they must have opportunity, organizational support and self-determination*

The authors wanted to know whether an organization can teach its people the new dimensions of leadership and what the most effective processes for developing leadership effectiveness might be. Responses indicated that experience was the best teacher. A close second was coaching and feedback, with performance feedback being the best vehicle for enabling leaders to develop their talents for empowering others. Although management development education rated high as a vehicle for leadership development, the vast majority of respondents stated that they themselves had the key responsibility for developing themselves.

So to develop leadership ability, the individual must be given a challenging opportunity and must act on it and accept all possible avenues of feedback on his or her efforts. It helps if the aspiring leader is given the right assignments, but it is vital that the right network of people can give coaching and feedback. The authors believe that assignments serve as the ideal classroom and that a better match should be made between the assignments given and individual development needs. The effective development of future leaders by their organizations was also seen as potentially a powerful tool in closing the trust gap the research had exposed.

6 Organizations are far less globally-minded than they like to think they are

Here Ready and his team were disappointed. Having a global mindset was rated lowest in effectiveness among the thirty-four organizational capability dimensions, and other items, such as managing transnational teams and understanding the global environment, came very low in the ratings. Ready also noted that mid-level managers appeared to rate global mindset more highly than did top management; this held out hope for the next generation of senior leaders. However, while senior executives apparently recognized that the business scenario was becoming more global, they were not doing enough to prepare their people for this new reality. If firms that stated that they were global were not actually preparing for this reality, then there would soon be a crisis. The time for change in the development of an international mindset had come.

Ready and his team found that the leadership challenges to CEOs were those of ensuring that an organization was 'continually reinventing its organizational capacity, broadening its leadership and knowledge capability, and leveraging its mechanisms for regeneration and growth'. A chief executive consequently had to be the organization's chief transformation officer – to succeed here, the CEO would need to look at gaps that might impede progress, gaps in trust and expectations, and then take action. The development of new leaders had to become a strategic priority, and CEOs had to demonstrate passion and commitment to developing leadership if for no other reason than that it increased an organization's ability to remain competitive.

CONCLUSION

Since the publication of Ready's report, innovations such as the Internet have taken powerful positions centre stage and large organizations have increasingly moved to merge and grow with each other, thereby creating monoliths with more power than many a nation state. However, its message remains valid. The strength of the report lies in the fact that it was based on sound data from a wide range of international sources and the changes in the business climate have largely endorsed its assertions. Organizations must increasingly reinvent and regenerate themselves; this regeneration must be based on sound strategic vision – and a key element in this vision must incorporate the development of a cadre of flexible, globally-minded leaders.

Robert E. Kelley

Robert Kelley's background is in the world of consultancy, and over the past twenty years he has built up a worldwide reputation as a specialist in productivity research, with the underlying premise that significant enhancement in productivity can only be achieved through people.

Kelley has done post-doctoral work at the Harvard Business School, and he has a Ph.D. from Colorado State University and an M.A. from the University of Texas. In a distinguished academic career he has been a senior management consultant with the Stanford Research Institute and a Visiting Scholar at the Harvard Business School. As President of Consultants to Executives and Organizations he has been described as an 'entrepreneur of the mind'. An author of a number of acclaimed works, he introduced the concept of followership in his best-selling book *The Power of Followership* and his *Harvard Business Review* article 'In Praise of Followers', in which he gave a novel perspective on leadership itself.

The main thrust of Kelley's ideas on followership is that the characteristics of a good leader and a good follower have much in common. Though leadership is a more glamorous concept he believes that this should not blind us to the demands made on followers, especially as most people spend a high proportion of their time in that capacity. Kelley divides followers into five types and differentiates them by their proclivity to be either passive or active, and by their display of either independent, critical thinking, or dependent, non-critical thinking. The five types are:

Sheep. Passive and non-critical in thinking.
Yes people. Active but non-critical.
Alienated followers. Passive but critical thinkers.

Survivors. They know when to adopt either active or passive, critical or non-critical approaches, as well as when to keep their heads down.

Effective followers. They have an active approach, coupled with independent, critical thinking. The characteristics shown by these followers closely resemble those of effective leaders, and good leaders need good followers to make *them* good!

Kelley's most recent work has focused on 'star performers' – in other words those individuals who make extraordinary contributions in the workplace. This concept has been developed in *Star Performer. Nine Breakthrough Strategies You Need to Succeed* (1998), which complements his *Gold Collar Worker* (1985) – a book that described a new breed of workers whose value lies in their brainpower.

Kelley states that to develop and nurture star performers is an entirely understandable goal for any organization. The main barrier to the achievement of that goal, and the focus of Kelley's research, is to identify exactly what it is that differentiates the stars from the rest, and what skills, behaviours and qualities they consistently apply to their work.

His research into star performers began in the mid-1980s, when Kelley was working with Bell Labs (a division of AT&T) on increasing the productivity among their knowledge workers. The first stage of his research attempted to identify the likely differentiating factors among Bell Labs' high-flying employees. These factors were split into four primary categories:

● cognitive – the mental requirements of any job;
● social – the interpersonal skills;
● psychological–personality – the inner drives within an individual;
● organizational – how an individual and an organization interrelate.

However, this fact-finding ran into difficulties, primarily because it became apparent that there were disagreements between managers, subordinates and peers as to who the 'star performers' in Bell Labs actually were, let alone what were their key qualities and attributes.

One trend that emerged was that managers' perceptions were heavily influenced by documented results rather than the behaviours that contributed to excellent performance – in other words, the ends or the outputs gained prominence over the means or inputs. The view from subordinates and peers was somewhat different.

Nevertheless, after further years of research, Kelley was able to identify what he calls the 'nine breakthrough strategies that you need to succeed' to become a star performer. In order of their relative importance, they are:

1 *Initiative*

There is nothing new in the notion that initiative is a desirable behaviour in any employee of any organization, yet Kelley argues that its demonstrable application is what sets the stars apart from the rest. Too often, individuals demonstrate initiative within the bounds of their existing role or job description – Kelley argues that this is simply an effective extension of what should be done in that role. Star-performing initiative extends beyond the scope of a role, benefiting the organization, colleagues and the individual.

The often-quoted examples of effective initiative are groundbreaking and significant in both their size and impact. This need not necessarily be so. Particularly for new employees, there is a need to establish credibility through 'minor' initiatives which Kelley describes as 'horizontal' – what star performers demonstrate is their ability to undertake both horizontal activities and vertical initiatives (those which are more far-reaching, and have a greater impact and visibility).

Any initiative requires risk assessment – evaluating the size and nature of the task, the capability to achieve, the extent of personal risk at stake, and the likely outcome from the activity. It then needs tenacity to take the project from the idea stage through to implementation.

2 *Networking*

We are now operating in a knowledge economy. Most people do not possess the required knowledge to perform their roles, and therefore rely on external assistance to bridge this knowledge deficit. Some organizations use Internet and e-mail technology for this purpose. Kelley argues that this is not sufficient, and that the more personal and responsive networks are more efficient, effective and focused.

The need for a broad and reliable personal network is not a new subject in management and leadership textbooks. Kelley approaches it from two perspectives: first from the establishment and maintenance of a network, and secondly from the establishment of the correct interpersonal skills and etiquette to use the network to maximum advantage.

Furthermore, networking relies on two-way traffic – the need for an individual to establish their credibility in order to be able to call on another's area of expertise.

3 Self-management

The fundamental practices in personal organization and time management have been given plenty of space elsewhere. Kelley has the refreshing view that we are all individuals who act, behave and are comfortable within a range of different business climates and practices. A tidy-desk principle may be very important to one person and a complete irrelevance to another.

Therefore we should all understand what our own values actually are – 'know thyself' has to be a starting-point. Understanding one's own strengths and weaknesses from the organizational point of view is fundamental to enduring personal efficiency.

Over and above this, Kelley argues that one has to know what is important to an individual in terms of his or her current role, their medium/long-term career aspirations, and the organization's goals. He defines this as the 'critical path'. Each of us should pursue our chosen self-management techniques but ensure that we spend the necessary time on the critical path.

4 Perspective

This focuses on the need to see the big picture, and to assess situations and scenarios from a number of different perspectives. Kelley describes these as the 'five Cs':

- *colleagues*: networking, borrowing ideas, testing concepts and seeking alternative points of view;
- *company*: understanding the decision-making process within an organization, allied to vision and values;
- *customers*: after all, they pay the bills. Too often, organizations and individuals can become introspective without seeing issues through the eyes of the very people they are seeking to serve;
- *competition*: both direct and indirect. In today's rapidly evolving market-place, tomorrow's competitors may not even exist;
- *creative*: this involves the 'blue sky thinking', putting aside the established way we do things round here and creatively challenging the *status quo*.

5 *Followership*

Kelley has here modified his definitions somewhat, although the essential thrust of his approach remains unaltered:

- *sheep* do what is required of them passively and uncritically. They need direction and tend to follow the herd unquestioningly;
- *yes-people* do what is required, usually enthusiastically; the only feedback they give their managers is good news, or what they believe their seniors want to hear;
- *alienated followers* are intelligent and capable individuals, but tend to be resentful of their leaders and the organization. Because they are passive, their resentment spills over into destructive clandestine behaviour;
- *pragmatist followers* are capable individuals whose actions are largely driven by their reading of the political climate. They tend to be risk-averse, with a 'better safe than sorry' attitude;
- *star followers* – it is these star followers that we should aspire to be – courageous, focused on organizational goals, technically competent, excellent in their self-management and independence, and with the ability to 'disagree agreeably'.

6 *Leadership*

Kelley differentiates between 'big-L' leaders and 'small-L' leaders. The 'big-L' leaders believe they have all the answers and that their role in the working context is to provide the direction, decision-making and organization. The 'small-L' leaders are not tied down by either the arrogance or the misinterpretation of the leader role. They lead only where their skills and the situation demand, letting others lead when the circumstances are appropriate.

The decision of when or where to lead should be driven by one (or more) of three areas:

- *knowledge/expertise* – based on proven capability and judgement;
- *people/interpersonal skills* – based on the ability to harness the power of individuals and the wider team;
- *momentum* – based on a focus on the goal and a task orientation.

7 *Teamwork*

Kelley is realistic in his observation that knowledge workers are increasingly required to operate in a team environment. This is not always the most productive means of getting a job, project or task done. Invariably the success or otherwise of a team will hinge on establishing the right composition of the team. This is done by ensuring that it gels with the organizational culture, measurement systems and senior management behaviour; generates the appropriate cooperative values among team participants; and is led or managed in a way which takes account of individual needs and requirements.

Above all, a team and its members must have a clarity of purpose and maintain a focus on accomplishment and achievement.

8 *Organizational savvy*

Also known as political astuteness and awareness. Kelley argues that many potential leaders find themselves in a specialist alley which serves to thwart their career progression. The answer does not lie in ingratiating behaviour, but in a proactive recognition of how the land lies in the wider organizational sense, and in using this information to decide the best means of putting oneself forward.

Other equally important means of gaining a broader perspective are by having the discipline to see things through other people's eyes, and by getting the support of an experienced and directive mentor.

Credibility in the workplace is enhanced if time is spent in developing the network through effective relationship-building skills, and by enhancing one's reputation through the development of a niche or area of expertise.

9 *Show and tell*

A straightforward concept, that star performers have to be persuasive communicators. This extends from one-to-one conversations to senior management presentations, and in many ways it is the icing on the cake. A slick presenter without substance will be found out; an excellent worker without these communication skills will be forgiven, but it remains an opportunity lost.

Kelley's advice is simple: spend time understanding the needs and expectations of the audience and deliver a message that will stick by ensuring that the content and delivery are compatible and, naturally, relevant to that audience. More often than not, this requires more consideration of human factors than technical details.

CONCLUSION

Kelley emphasizes that the nine breakthrough strategies are interrelated, and the ability to develop such skills requires considerable commitment and effort. But the carrot is there – Kelley's research has shown that identified high-flyers/star performers all demonstrate these skills. Also crucial to Kelley's many readers is the fact that those who possess these competencies are likely to be the high-flyers (and for high-flyers, read leaders) of tomorrow.

G. Suarez and J. Hirshberg

J. Gerald Suarez, Ph.D. has been Director of Presidential Quality Management at the US White House Communications Agency in Washington, DC, and has taught quality management at the Graduate School of Business in Arlington. He served in the US navy and at that time he published his first work on fear in organizations. He published 'Managing Fear in the Workplace' in the *Journal for Quality and Participation* in 1994. As an internationally recognized authority on leadership development and organizational design, Suarez is the author of various books on teamwork and quality management. He is a sought-after lecturer and speaker at international conferences, on topics which include creativity and multicultural business. The key aspects of his work are here contrasted with the upbeat message of Jerry Hirshberg in his book *The Creative Priority*. After leaving General Motors, Hirshberg founded Nissan Design International (NDI) in 1981 in response to Nissan's desire to have a leading-edge design function as a separate entity within the organization. The warnings given by Suarez can be set alongside the stretching ideas put forward by Hirshberg in setting out how he made NDI into an outstanding success. Hirshberg, like Suarez, is much sought after as a conference speaker.

Suarez bases his thinking on original work by Deming, who believed that the removal of fear should be one of the top priorities leaders should address. Unlike Deming and other writers, Suarez deals with ways in which managers can cope with fear and ways in which leaders can dispel it. First of all, however, he defines it. Fear is an unpleasant emotion caused by the awareness of threat or danger; it is not to be confused with anxiety, which is the response to a less clear stimulus. Anxiety, which tends to be more long-lasting, can have pervasive effects in an organization.

Nevertheless, leaders should pay a great deal of attention to fear as it is a distracting force that robs both people and the organization itself of their potential. It can be a motivator, but not a motivator towards constructive action; it produces short bursts of intense performance rather than long-term constructive results – as well as the wrong sort of competition within the organization.

Suarez states that fear produces questionable data because people work to eliminate the threat rather than to produce a positive outcome. Consequently it stifles creativity and innovation. Fear therefore can be like high blood pressure in an organization: a silent killer that can go unnoticed until it strikes at business results. It is a leader's responsibility to acknowledge that fear is present as well as to assess how pervasive it has become. Fear can be detected in a number of areas which span many parts of an operation. There is, for example,

- fear of reprisal, or of a poor appraisal;
- fear of failure;
- fear of success – it may damage relationships with peers;
- fear of new knowledge – it may threaten skill levels and people may not feel that they have the time to acquire it;
- fear of change;
- fear of speaking up – this can be seen as unwillingness to state what is wrong, or to admit mistakes. In both cases the organization suffers.

It is vital to take a measure of the fear level in the organization and Suarez gives a substantial list of questions a leader should ask when assessing the health of the organization in this respect. A sample of some of the most potent questions, which cover such areas as expectations, assessment, perceptions, trust, communication and training, includes:

Do you know what your peers and subordinates expect of you?
Has the organization published a statement of vision, mission and guiding principles?
Do you know what people in your organization fear?
Do you perceive that people have to do things on the job that are against their better judgement?
Do you trust your subordinates?
What have you done to ensure that your peers and subordinates acquire new knowledge and develop new skills?

Do you inform them of opportunities for individual development and advancement?

From this sample, much of Suarez's advice for creating an environment without fear is already being hinted at.

The three elements that play a vital part in creating an environment in which people can start to cope with fear are leadership, trust and vision. These arguably are all subsets of one another. However, Suarez quotes Deming in stating that any system is ultimately composed of people and that leaders must work to create an environment where employees can share information without being concerned about the repercussions of so doing, and where both ideas and concerns are responded to quickly. When leaders fail to respond, employees begin to doubt their own credibility and competence. Wherever possible, leaders must reward cooperation and innovation.

Trust is a major factor in fear reduction, and fear will reduce in direct proportion to the extent that people develop confidence and trust in their leadership. Trust itself will improve and encourage communication as people become increasingly confident that their ideas will be acknowledged. By the same token, leaders should let it be known that where no mistakes are reported they will be sceptical, as mistakes form a normal part of operations. They should never 'kill the messenger' when either bad news or mistakes are reported. In addition, the leadership should take the initiative in speaking about fear because by doing so they can improve communications and at the same time monitor people's perceptions of the overall situation. This, of course, implies good listening skills – as opposed to reacting and shooting from the hip. Good leaders are patient and understanding when dealing with fear issues.

Suarez is particularly keen on the power of the vision. A good vision statement gives out the message that the leaders of the organization are planning to be in business for many years to come. This fact in itself is a fear-buster and ensures that everybody understands where the organization is going and benefits from the constancy of purpose it provides.

The conclusion is that dealing with fear is a top management leadership issue. There are no examples of fear being minimized by initiatives from the bottom or middle ranks. This is because only top management can establish the vision, stress the core values behind it and then make policy. They must also be aware that new fears will always emerge and that they in turn must be eliminated; increasingly this elimination will come about as a result of teamwork with other levels.

In dealing with the fear factor Suarez has gone where few writers on leadership have explicitly gone before. In doing so, he has done many people a service. His work should be looked at in the light of the higher levels of uncertainty in organizations due to the ever-growing numbers of business failures, take-overs and acquisitions. At the same time, few employees can expect continuous employment, or necessarily to stay in one profession throughout their career. Notwithstanding, organizations must stretch themselves ever more dramatically in terms of both output and innovation in order to stay up with the competitive international business environment. The challenge to leaders, then, is how to ensure that fear does not take over, but at the same time to create a climate where tension and even abrasion are used as productive forces. Jerry Hirshberg provides a compelling example of how this can be done.

At one level, *The Creative Priority* is about getting ahead in the competitive world of car design. The book is packed with stories proving that Hirshberg practises what he preaches and learns from his mistakes. The writer's background has always been in car design with a pedigree that spans General Motors as well as NDI, and he takes pains to contrast and compare the two organizations. NDI itself has been a huge success with a history of awards, successful models and groundbreaking ideas. The key theme is that the leader must stress creativity as the absolute priority within the organization and take whatever steps are necessary to ensure that it happens. Hirshberg's creative priority hinges on four key principles:

1 Polarity
2 Unprecedented thinking
3 Beyond the edges
4 Synthesis.

1 *Polarity*

This is more than simple diversity, but is itself divided into three elements.

Creative abrasion The writer's argument is that friction amongst individuals is one of the most plentiful and volatile sources of energy, and by concentration on the positive elements of this friction a leader can unleash enormous creative benefits. Hirshberg encourages and fosters polarized viewpoints and seeks to get traditionally adversarial departments and individuals to work together from the outset of a project. In the case of

NDI it was the task of getting modellers and designers, engineers and marketing together. Perceptive and agile leadership is needed to recognize and mark the periods of abrasion and the leadership must recognize the opportunities springing from the friction. By focusing attention on the creative values of intersecting streams of thought it is possible to lessen the probable tension and stress.

Hiring in divergent pairs With the same aim in mind, Hirshberg always attempts to recruit diametric opposites into the organization; people with different backgrounds, interests, education, beliefs and perspectives. The guiding principle is one of expanding the business qualitatively as well as quantitatively.

Embracing the dragon The dragon is the 'reason why things cannot be done'. New truths, ideas and possibilities may be there all the time but are often rendered invisible by language and assumptions. However, by adopting the viewpoint of a complete outsider, the individual can gain a valuable new perspective. This is similar to many other writers' views on creativity. However, Hirshberg states that he made it happen in an organizational sense rather than in an individual sense, which is the more usual case.

In summary, while the concept of polarity is usually seen as harmful, the friction that may exist between individuals or systems of thought can be used to inspire innovative thinking.

2 *Unprecedented thinking*
Hirshberg insists on creative questions before creative answers. This builds on the increasingly common theme that the best solutions to problems often lie in the power of excellent probing questions. The concept expands the limits of what traditionally constitutes responsible and intelligent thought in the organization by engaging the emotional response with the logical, and the intuitive with the rational. Hirshberg gives as an example how individuals in NDI were involved in extra-curricular design work for pre-school furniture. Having conceived ideas for chairs and so on, they began to look at colours. The near unanimous view of the group was that strong, party-balloon colours should be used. Then someone asked what colours toddlers really liked. The designers tested their assumptions by looking at the type of crayons the children most often used and were surprised to find that the most popular were more adult pastel shades.

As a general principle, Hirshberg encouraged methods of brainstorming in which the group was asked to search for creative questions and to 'ward off closure' on a problem. This, in fact, leaves everyone in a state of uncertainty, yet gives time for the pre-conscious to join in the search for answers and to focus energies for a delayed but eventually better closure or synthesis.

It is also necessary to step back from the canvas, also known as 'helicoptering'. Hirshberg asserts that it works in the organizational as well as the task sense. The key is for everybody to step back at the same time; when approaching a vital deadline with much stress and tension, Hirshberg took the entire office to the cinema (*Silence of the Lambs!*). The unexpected two-and-a-half-hour break managed to re-energize the workforce. The truancy was good for morale and a collective drawing of breath put things back on track. The message is that sometimes the very act of *not* working at something is the key to moving it forward.

Then there is failing, cheating and play. The Tom Peters concept of 'managing by walking around' is given a creative context and put into the domain of all staff. At NDI everybody is encouraged to walk around and look at what other people are doing. They are encouraged to question, seek clarification and to copy – no one's work is considered to be proprietary. This is a form of disorganized *ad hoc* brainstorming and leads to results. The concept of the Pulsar – a modular car (i.e. the owner can change the shape depending on his or her requirements) – was born out of a number of doodles on one person's desk. Others saw them and the spark of the idea led on to a compelling design proposition. All these ideas were actively championed by Hirshberg, who led from the front in asserting that failure was not to be regarded as a major problem. In fact, there was no failure, only learning.

3 *Beyond the edges*

Hirshberg believes in the blurring of disciplinary boundaries. In car design there is a historic split between interior and exterior design. However, the two functions came together at NDI to develop the 'people carrier', where the perception of internal space within external limitations (the vehicle must not be too big) was the key. Through interdepartmental cooperation, designers developed the folding-seat concept and maximized the use of vertical as well as horizontal space. In order to achieve this breakthrough Hirshberg had to warn his people of the dangers of 'silo' mentalities and organizational 'stovepipes'. He also encouraged his people not to think in terms of rigid job descriptions.

It was then necessary to think in terms of intercultural creativity. There is a strong difference in cultural values between the USA and Japan, which when uncovered can represent significant obstacles. In this case a major sticking point came from the fact that none of the NDI sports car designs passed the Japanese 'test' and were rejected. Eventually the US designers latched on to the fact that the Japanese regard the front of a car as a face and that the designs being put forward were, as faces, giving out the wrong messages. The problems were eventually overcome when a number of 'value the differences' discussions were arranged that explored both individual and intercultural differences.

In the search for innovation, NDI set out to 'drink from diverse wells'. This involved taking on a number of projects outside car design. The design of boats, golf clubs, computers and vacuum cleaners was seen as a necessary broadening of horizons, which eventually resulted in the cross-fertilization of ideas and concepts in the core business. Over and above the innovative benefits of this policy to the business in a variety of fields (the Taylor Made Bubble Driver, one of the most successful golf drivers, was an NDI design), it was also very good for individual motivation as well as the firm's external reputation.

4 Synthesis

Here Hirshberg comments on what he calls 'informed intuition' and states that creativity is a marriage between passion and logic, intuition and information, and then imagination and developed skills. All are necessary, but if the organization gets the balance wrong it is all too easy to lose sight of the immediate and most vital objectives. In any creative process, it is necessary to capture pertinent information, not data and statistics, and it is the leader's role to ensure clarity here. NDI's field research on small trucks centred around truck drivers' egos and feelings, rather than cubic footage of storage, as only 25 per cent of a driver's time was spent trucking/transporting. In his comments on intuition, Hirshberg goes on to suggest that the best decision-making is usually done at home, when a combination of fact and feeling can dominate the process. However, in the work environment creativity is often superseded by the quest for data and statistics. This does not mean to say that Hirshberg is against planning. It is championed as a valuable discipline so long as it does not become a straitjacket. Planning must be porous and, by being so, involve all interested parties. The failure of the Pulsar modular car was because of poor planning for marketing rather than poor design. In discussing planning, the author echoes Warren Bennis in stating that it is not about second guessing the future but about shaping it.

CONCLUSION

Although Hirshberg does not openly stress the need for trust and vision in the same way as Suarez, it is evident that he had a vision for his organization and that he managed to create trust, stretch, friction, fun and creativity at the same time. He gives the examples of so-called 'pep talks' at General Motors which were in fact just a vehicle for delivering thinly veiled threats. After some visits from on high in which the performance of his staff was contrasted poorly with that of other organizations, he noticed that the risk and creative elements in design noticeably shrank. Fear of failure had resulted in avoidance of risks, and the closing down of creative processes in his opinion meant that all cars in the USA for a while looked depressingly similar. Breaking out from this at NDI must have been a considerable challenge for both leader and staff, although it is evident that all concerned felt that it was well worth it. Gerald Suarez would without doubt approve.

Ned Herrmann

There exists a huge range of leadership measures ranging from the practical *Leader Behaviour Analysis* through to Kouzes and Posner's *Leadership Practices Inventory*. Of all the existing measures, there is one that fits in particularly well with the Kotter definitions of leadership and management. However, it also takes the analysis further, as it personalizes what it measures beyond the purely behavioural by placing its definition of leadership in the context of the person as a whole individual with a number of talents and preferences. The Herrmann Brain Dominance Instrument and the writings of its author, Ned Herrmann, are now in a position to change the way that people think about their thought processes as well as the way they lead, manage, follow or innovate. Herrmann introduced new words and concepts into both the management and vernacular languages.

Herrmann, author of *The Creative Brain* (1989) and *The Whole Brain Business Book* (1996), was the founder of whole-brain technology and had a major impact on the development of creative thinking within the corporation. His work has inspired a myriad of articles by other writers on subjects ranging from strategy formulation to project management. Having developed the concept of whole brain thinking from his own experience, Herrmann began researching the power of the brain during his career at General Electric. He was later head of the Ned Herrmann Group, which specializes in teaching creative thinking techniques around the world. He saw creativity as reaching every level of organizational life, especially the leadership level. We therefore had here an interesting example of a consultant rather than an academic examining issues and influencing the way people think about leadership, organizations and themselves.

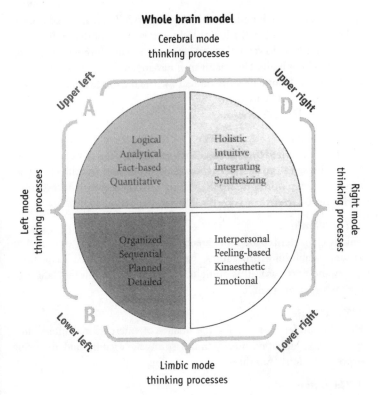

Whole brain model

Cerebral mode
thinking processes

Upper left

A

D

Upper right

Left mode
thinking processes

Logical
Analytical
Fact-based
Quantitative

Holistic
Intuitive
Integrating
Synthesizing

Right mode
thinking processes

Organized
Sequential
Planned
Detailed

Interpersonal
Feeling-based
Kinaesthetic
Emotional

Lower left

B

C

Lower right

Limbic mode
thinking processes

Figure 5

Reacting to a remark by Henry Mintzberg that it was surprising how some people could be so smart and so dumb at the same time, Herrmann researched the workings of both the human brain and the human mind in order to develop a construct that built on the emergent concept of left- and right-brain thinking.

The four quadrants of thinking, initially expounded in *The Creative Brain*, are based on the physiology of the brain as well as on a business-based concept of the organizing principle. Here all the actions and behaviours involved in business (indeed, Herrmann argued, in the whole of an individual's life) are divided into four blocks. From this Herrmann constructed his metaphor of the whole-brain model, in which the behaviours in his architecture of the organizing principle are set out against the preferred modes of thinking that an individual would display if they favoured either the left or right hemispheres of the brain or the upper, cerebral or lower limbic areas in their thinking. From his metaphor of the thinking brain, Herrmann then developed the application, which was the Brain Dominance Instrument by which an individual's thinking preferences could be measured.

The four thinking styles are:

1 *The A brain*

This is characterized by preference for logic, analysis, facts, rigour, a liking for numbers, realism, interest in how things work, and an ability to argue. A summarizing word here would be facts. In so far as we all have abilities in this region, Herrmann described this as the 'rational self'.

2 *The B brain*

This is characterized by a preference for planning, taking preventative action, establishing procedures, being precise, organized, sequential, timely and neat – as well as cautious. Herrmann called this the 'safekeeping' or 'organizing self'.

3 *The C brain*

Here the preferences are for the quality of interpersonal interaction, for feelings, empathy, music, things spiritual, teaching and for being expressive. Herrmann called this our 'feeling self'.

4 *The D brain*

The preference here is for breaking rules, being imaginative, speculating, asking 'What if?' questions. There is a distinct inclination towards integrating facts, being intuitive and pushing out the boundaries of possible action. This, stated Herrmann, is our 'experimental self'.

We all have the ability to think – and therefore act – in any of the quadrants, but we will have preferences and our preferences may consequently influence the quality of thought or action. Our preferences can be observed by what we like doing as well as by what we dislike doing.

At the same time, said Herrmann, there is tension across the model. People with high A-brain preferences will see things very differently from those with high C-brain preferences, and the same tension applies between B and D.

By looking at the model, it is clearly possible to see the difference

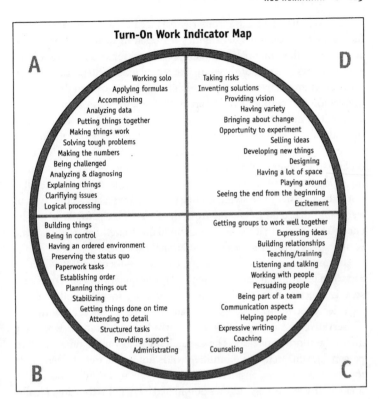

Figure 6

between leadership and management. Classic leadership exists in a synthesis of the C and D thinking styles, with a predilection for the types of thinking that most readily lead to vision creation and getting things done through the medium of people, while the A and B styles characterize management – a matter of measurement, planning and control. It is, however, principally in *The Whole Brain Business Book* that Herrmann put his thesis into action by providing advice to leaders in a number of specific areas.

On the subject of approaches and styles of management, Herrmann wrote that in the USA the subject of diversity has long been a 'hot button', but that in all the diverse areas covered there is no single mention of the most important area: that of mental diversity. Organizations are in fact made up of an extraordinarily balanced range of thinking styles; the major question must be, are they managed in such a way as to take advantage of this potential? The mental composition of an organization's workforce has never before been considered. In many situations, creativity is the difference between success and failure. At a time when the need for innovation and corporate agility are to the fore, it is a key component of competitive advantage – creativity is of the mind, and mental diversity must therefore be the key. Business leaders who understand the significance of diversity in business processes can take advantage of their organization's potential by forming teams of people with different thinking styles. This in turn requires flexibility from the leader, and the goal is not to be a master of all styles but to gain an awareness of all the styles of leadership that tend to emerge from the four different thinking preferences. This means that the leader can build on strengths and cultivate the weaker areas in order to develop situational smartness.

Herrmann went on to sketch out the typical styles of leaders who have a marked predominance of thinking in any one quadrant. The A quadrant style is typically authoritative, directive, business focused, and could be regarded as hard-hearted. The B quadrant style is typically traditional, conservative and risk-avoiding, and works best in situations where the lines of authority are clear. The C quadrant style, on the other hand, is personable, interactive and intuitive – it is not a style found often at the top as it is usually considered to be too soft to be fully effective in finance-driven business cultures dominated by A and B thinking. Finally, the D quadrant style is holistic, adventurous and entrepreneurial – but the lack of structure that leaders with this preference may exhibit can make others most uncomfortable.

The key to effectiveness is to aim for a multidominant style of leadership which can respond to a diverse set of business issues in situationally appropriate ways. To make use of this multidominance, an individual must be able to access all the styles (and variations on them) as the situation requires, and then to apply the choices frequently enough to develop an array of competencies. Although Herrmann praised consistency as such, he also advocated personal agility. He gave the example of an individual whose work requires effective management behaviour in various circumstances: in a budgetary situation; in a design review with engineering; in deciding on appropriate requests from manufacturing; in finalizing an architectural plan for the new headquarters building; in responding to the art selection committee for the main lobby; in conducting the annual manpower review with the human resources representatives – all this being done over a three-day period. Herrmann considered the range of styles that would be needed to be effective in all these different situations, which in fact use all the quadrants of the brain as well as a combination of thinking styles. He then pointed out that being situational, and flexible, is the equivalent to rising to the occasion and is a behavioural necessity for all leaders.

Having set out his stall – which backed up the situational philosophies of Blanchard, Tannenbaum and Schmidt and others – Herrmann moved on to develop his arguments in the fields of leadership, vision, mission, strategic thinking, and creativity as a process that can be led rather than managed.

From his analysis of situational approaches, Herrmann proceeded to deal with more transformational areas of vision, mission and strategy. He stated that whole-brain technology provides a method for diagnosing the 'mentality' of vision statements, corporate values statements and mission statements. He went on to say that often they are seriously out of alignment with what people really need from them. It is the C interpersonal quadrant that is most often missing – and the credibility of the leadership often suffers as a result. Herrmann asserted that it is the business world that is out of alignment with what people want of it rather than the other way round, and that different parts or functions within an organization may be out of alignment to different degrees. It is up to the CEO to diagnose these alignment issues and to do something about them. And the whole-brain approach provides a useful starting point in dealing with the cultural issues and strategies involved. When finally the organization's key leadership issues, statements and documents are in alignment with what people actually want of them, the messages become clearer and credibility improves.

After dealing with corporate statements, Herrmann dealt with the issue of strategy itself. He echoed Mintzberg in stating that senior executives often 'plunge into strategic planning because they think it is the thing to do without ever really knowing what it is or how to use it'. There are many experts on strategic planning but few on the quality of strategic thinking – which is where for the leader the process must start. Strategic thinking deals in futures, in patterns, trends and nuances, and this is where senior executives who are trained in facts, numbers and the here-and-now often come to grief. They need to go through a transitional stage in order to become truly strategic thinkers and Herrmann outlined a seven-step transition plan:

1 Understand your own mentality. That is your own thinking preference.
2 Find a way of using your D quadrant, at least some of the time. This will involve perceiving patterns, thinking in metaphors, and as a result visualizing the future.
3 Tap into and release your creative potential.
4 Be open to new ways of thinking and learning. This could involve thinking metaphorically about your organization.
5 Think deeply about your organization and build metaphoric models in order to help you to do so as well as to make connections and discover new possibilities.
6 Add to the above. Analyse the degree of alignment between the company's report, its culture, mission statement and statement of core values.
7 Take a guided fantasy into the future to help you respond to the inevitable key questions about the organization's mission, products and customers' expectations.

Herrmann stated that the above represents a short-cut to attaining the perceptions necessary to build a strategic plan. It enables the leader better to conceptualize and visualize existing relationships and future projections – in short, to become a better strategic thinker and planner.

It is, however, in the field of creativity and its application through a whole-brain approach that Herrmann was strongest. While some might argue that creativity is not a leadership issue, Herrmann, this writer and the staff of the Center for Creative Leadership in the USA would differ: they are integral to each other, and the boundaries between modern leadership and creativity run contiguously.

Herrmann said that creativity is essentially a messy business; the more you try to structure it and organize it, the more you shut it down. Indeed the very word has often been anathema to left-brain-dominated organizations. He saw creativity as grounded in originality, and innovation as grounded in already invented products or processes. Innovation is then more in the nature of an elaboration, building on the results of previous creativity. As businesses extend their product lines and elaborate on existing products they will require innovation as well as creativity

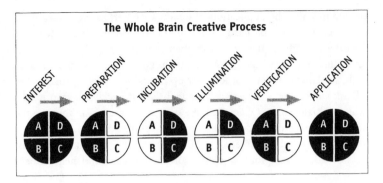

Figure 7

from their people. While Herrmann believed that many organizations were still afraid of the concept of creativity, considering it to be 'flaky', successful corporations in the future will be those that train their people in both creativity and innovation.

Herrmann went on to elaborate on the development of creativity. This is a process that follows the sequence Interest–Preparation–Incubation–Illumination–Verification–Application, as originally defined by Graham Wallas. He set it out against the thinking styles required to ensure success at each stage (see Figure 7). Linking back to leadership and teamwork, he concluded that there is a clear advantage if all four thinking styles are represented in a team (shades of Belbin) – diversity pays off. The fundamental problem of homogeneity is that it leads to quick consensus and this can be disadvantageous in the domain of creativity and innovation.

The reasons (among others) why people do not always follow the maxim of creating truly diverse groups are as follows:

* The leaders are not aware of the advantages.
* They lack ways of assembling mentally diverse teams.
* They do not understand enough about creativity to understand the significance of diversity.

From here Herrmann moved on to give advice on the supervision and management of creative people. The best way to manage 'creatives' is to be clear about the aims and objectives of the exercise from the start and then to give them space. Too many rules will inhibit the natural flow necessary for creativity. So, avoid close supervision, adherence to procedures and the application of quantitative performance measures. Although this may be hard advice for many leaders, he asserted that creating the right climate for creativity means accepting that creativity is an inefficient process, that results cannot be guaranteed and that mistakes will inevitably happen. If leaders set up places of creativity, such as the 'skunk works' that were originally established at Lockheed, then results will eventually come. Of course these successes must spread through the whole organization, and to achieve this a significant number of people must be trained in creativity. Furthermore the organization must acknowledge champions who will spread the word and help achieve critical mass.

Herrmann further defined creativity as 'an ability to challenge assumptions, recognize patterns, see in new ways, make connections, take risks and seize upon a chance'. In doing so he firmly placed the concept in the province of leadership; the connections with the Kotter definitions and the Bennis concepts are strong.

By drilling down further into his definition, Herrmann provided further personal advice for emergent creative leaders:

Challenge assumptions It is healthy to challenge the basis of statements by questioning the facts or premise upon which they are based, assumptions often being the 'filters through which we perceive the problem situation'. Eventually, however, a problem well stated is a problem half solved.

Recognize patterns When seeking to understand difficult problems we often do not recognize the existence of patterns of behaviour or opportunity that lead to their solution. Looking at problems from a distance can lead to accurate definition of their true nature.

See in new ways Here Herrmann advocated a 'problem walk around' in which the problem is viewed from the perspective of all four thinking quadrants. Since most people have their favourite ways of looking at things, this approach provides an easy way of seeing things in new ways.

Make connections Often seeking out different perceptions and then forcing a connection between them can lead to creative results; the very act of doing this is a creative process in itself.

Take risks Although those with a D-brain preference may enjoy risk-taking, people with other preferences may need to overcome their resistance. A way to do this is to manage the process by taking small risks until one's comfort level is expanded.

Seize upon a chance In the rapidly changing business environment it is necessary to be more opportunistic. Although this does not come naturally to everyone, with practice people can improve their responsiveness to creative opportunities – this in itself is vital because in most cases the situation is dynamic rather than static. Herrmann concluded that the consequence of not taking a chance is that individuals become stuck in their own mental traffic jam and there is no creative outcome.

CONCLUSION

Ned Herrmann provided a different and sometimes off-beat way of looking at leadership. However, by anchoring his approach so closely to the development of creativity he placed himself in the vanguard of modern thinking and achieved an alignment with both innovation and knowledge management. Although there are elements of a contingency approach with his emphasis on strategy development, he fitted particularly well into the field of transformational leadership. Herrmann also placed himself well outside the realms of trait theory: towards the end of *The Whole Brain Business Book*, looking at personal development, he asked, 'Can people change?' and answered his own question with an emphatic 'Yes!'

John Harvey-Jones

Long recognized as one of Britain's leading industrialists, Sir John Harvey-Jones has moved on from being chairman of the mammoth ICI to an illustrious career as consultant and TV personality. His views on business leadership were summed up in *Making It Happen*, published in 1988 and widely read by both business people and students of leadership as the testimony of someone who had actually 'been there and done it'.

Harvey-Jones's years at ICI were just part of an outstanding career. Educated at the Royal Naval College, Dartmouth, he served in the Royal Navy during the Second World War, achieving positions of command at an unnervingly early age. He subsequently worked in intelligence before joining ICI in 1956 to do work study. From there he steadily worked his way up the organization, being appointed to the board in 1973 and becoming Chairman in 1985.

Other appointments have included non-executive directorships of Grand Metropolitan, Guinness Peat Aviation, and the *Economist*. He has also been Vice-Chairman of the Policy Studies Unit and of the British Institute of Management. From 1984 to 1986 he added a European dimension to his many interests by becoming President of the European Council of Chemical Manufacturers. Harvey-Jones holds a number of honorary doctorates, as well as numerous awards from the world of commerce and industry. It was his ventures into television, however, that brought him most clearly into the public eye with the 'Trouble Shooter' series, in which he gave pragmatic and sometimes controversial advice to small businesses.

In *Making It Happen*, Harvey-Jones sets out his philosophy for business success through effective leadership. The book covers a number of different areas including boardroom effectiveness, the dilemmas in the role of the non-executive director, and the author's views of future challenges to business. It is, however, when he covers the key leadership tasks of mobilizing an organization, setting a direction, managing change, working with people and putting strategies to work that he is most compelling. His reflections on the demands that holding down the top job can make on an individual come with a unique perspective. His advice, based on his own life, of how to achieve the essential balance that has helped him to last the pace is useful and outweighs many an abstract academic treatise.

One of Harvey-Jones's first statements is that it is only when you work with people, rather than against them, that lasting success is possible. He cites the unhappy experience of having to lead the dismantling of a German dockyard in the immediate post-war years as a case in point. It is necessary for the boss to illustrate commitment, and the larger the enterprise, the harder the leader must seek to transfer this commitment to others. Harvey-Jones has on a number of occasions seen how people respond to leadership that is tuned to their needs. For this to happen, it is necessary for the leader both to listen and to rely on others. This behaviour is made ever more important by the fact that in a world of great change, it is the management's responsibility to maintain the highest rate of change that the organization and the people within it can stand. In adjusting to this rate of change, it is all too easy to treat people as groups rather than as individuals; this, though it may appear effective, Harvey-Jones maintains is an abnegation of leadership responsibility. People all over the world are refusing to be codified, and companies that ignore this fact will not attract the best and will therefore eventually die. A company is like a living organism. Cells die and need to be replaced, and the three potent forces of people, technology and competition make urgent demands for new cells, of new types. One particular demand is the increasing internationalism of the world, which demands new processes and new ways of thinking from executives. It is a great benefit if leaders can add the experience of living and working with people of other nationalities to their portfolios.

Harvey-Jones also comments on the harsh environment of competition and says that unless a company is progressing and changing all the time, it will fail. Paradoxically, it is this struggle that actually develops the best in leaders; they rise to the struggle, illustrate courage and develop the ability to live on the edge (and enjoy it). However, he points out that there are no easy prescriptions for how things should be done – leadership is an art, not a science – and he has observed many different ways of tackling problems. One thing he has found is that it is difficult to teach adults how to do things, or cope with things, but relatively easy to create the conditions in which they will teach themselves. What leaders need to do is to find a set of tools with which they are comfortable and which they can apply in different ways to the problems that confront them.

Nevertheless, an inescapable duty of a leader is to set a direction and Harvey-Jones nails his colours to the mast in support of strong, purposeful leadership. 'The business that is not being purposefully led in a clear direction which is understood by all its people is not going to survive . . .' In elaborating this point, Harvey-Jones broadens the discussion to include the sort of strategic thinking a leader should undertake. First of all, it is necessary to test the constraints of any situation – the leader must ask why it appears that something cannot be done. It is then necessary to determine exactly where the business is now. The completion of these two processes will help to give the momentum that will indicate where the business is likely to end up. As part of the initial analysis, it is necessary to know and understand the opposition. Business is like war, and reaching an understanding of the competition's leadership is a good predictor of that organization's future competitive moves.

However, the overall process of setting the direction should be one that involves everyone. The vision should be a product of discussion and debate at all levels, and this in turn will ensure the commitment of those involved in making it happen. While the ultimate responsibility for finalizing the direction lies with the board, here too there should be a high level of constructive conflict. Inadequate debate or analysis may lead to failed ventures, although Harvey-Jones accepts that in the end a level of risk is necessary, if not stimulating. 'Companies that take no risk disappear.' The process of strategy generation may be risky and at times unsatisfactory but it is better than having no process. The vision is best generated if those involved have a high degree of mutual respect, tolerance and humour. It is up to the leader to encourage this atmosphere. It must be made more dangerous to acquiesce than to disagree, and acceptable to 'dream and speak the unacceptable'. There will also be a number of political, social and technological forces at work and it is always necessary to ask whether those forces will affect the business in the future and for which its leadership needs to plan today. And in the end, this analysis must be simplified so that the future direction can be expressed simply and forcefully – perhaps in just one sentence.

There are dilemmas. Harvey-Jones reflects on his initial disagreement with statements his predecessors made about retaining ICI's position. Initially he felt the statements should have better indicated a desire for expansion and innovation. On the other hand, it is also the leader's job to ensure that the company is not endangered by foolhardy enterprises. So in the end, both the leader and the board must engage in continual iteration, to strengthen the debate by deformalizing it. The deformaliz-ation of this important debate can be achieved by taking all participants to new, non-work-based surroundings for a session of 'top down dreaming'. Those dreams for the business can be refined by a process of continual iteration that clarifies them and thus ensures commitment to the future of the company by those involved. This will achieve movement and it is always easier to switch direction when you are on the move than when you are static.

There is a further crucial element in the art of making it happen: that is the art of switching on the people involved, rather than switching them off. It means engaging the hearts and minds of those who have to execute and deliver. For this commitment to take place, people must understand what they are trying to achieve. This understanding is not achieved through the exercise of increased authoritarianism and control, which tends to lead to bureaucratic cultures where people's energies are focused more on avoiding mistakes than taking initiatives. It can also bring about a lack of openness, resulting in political manoeuvrings and sycophancy. Too often, a high level of politics in an organization can be traced to lack of clarity from the leadership as to what is expected of people, and a lack of consensus about the common aim. Clarity – often expressed by a powerful single sentence – can give ownership of the objective that will liberate people. Good leaders will have their ear to the ground and know whether that objective is being accepted, or not.

If the objective is accepted, then it is the responsibility of the manage-ment to give people the headroom to take on responsibilities, to cut away layers of hierarchy and to provide stretch. Those at the top should act as support rather than as control, and success should be given public recognition; Harvey-Jones explains that he has often sent cases of wine to those who have made special efforts. If the style of the organization is one in which the individual feels wanted, needed and recognized, then he or she will give their all. He concludes that it is 'the responsibility of the leadership and management to give opportunities and put demands on people, which enable them to grow as human beings in their place of work'.

On the same lines, Harvey-Jones states that the key to tactical success lies in people having ownership of the tactics themselves and consequently the will and determination to carry them out. The ownership of the plan must be transferred skilfully by the leader to the team. He cites the example of the transformation of ICI's Wilton site as a case in point, where the remedial actions for the ailing business were a matter of joint decision and shared responsibility. For him, Japan is a potent example of a place where the team takes responsibility and where individualism is subjugated for the common good. This in turn makes it easier for detailed long-term planning to become a core element in business processes. And to make the transference of ownership a meaningful reality, it is essential that management does not hoard information. Information is power and must be shared wherever possible.

In commenting on the leader's job of making it happen, Harvey-Jones says that the leader must accept responsibility for failure or mistakes whenever appropriate. He refers to this as 'throwing oneself across the wire'. Paradoxically, this is more likely to strengthen the leader's position than weaken it. People are likely to give the leader the benefit of the doubt, and will admire him or her for taking responsibility. The 'how' part of tactical leadership is derived from an 'enabling' style of leadership which is in turn denoted by courage, honesty and the respect of the team. Creating that respect is the leader's job.

Change is a key theme in *Making It Happen*. Change management, like all aspects of leadership, requires understanding, and sensitivity to the needs and fears of those affected by the change. In general, change is nearly always for the best, but the processes of getting there can be disruptive and require continual adaptation. While it is dangerous to go against the grain of people's feelings when planning to implement change, there is the dilemma that waiting too long, or delaying action while the minority who actually want the change become frustrated, is in itself dangerous. The greatest danger to a business lies in staying put, so the leader must ensure that there is clear and open communication about the situation. If treated honestly, people are likely to understand the need for change. They must also be made aware of the high risks involved in *not* changing. Although the future may not be totally clear, it is up to the leader to make the *status quo* appear more dangerous than the unknown. While this tactic may appear somewhat draconian, Harvey-Jones cites as an example the London docklands, where workers resisted change for many years with the result that their industry virtually disappeared.

People will be afraid of change and so the leader must understand the human forces at work. The great essentials of the successful change process are 'time, compassion and readiness to shoulder the responsibility for the action'. Symbolism is important and so it may be necessary to demonstrate that the top is changing faster than the rest of the organization. Time and money are spent on maintaining the machinery and plant of an organization; often less time and money are spent on the essential maintenance of its people's spirit and morale.

While Harvey-Jones gives some valuable insights into the skills needed to be effective on boards, both in an executive and non-executive capacity, it is when he speaks of the demands of holding the ultimate leadership position, the Top Job, that his insights are unique.

The main problem with the top job is that there are no limitations to what you should address or how you should spend your time. You do, however, need to grasp the main elements of the organization quickly, so detailed thinking about the job before you take it is vital. Essentially, the job of the chairman is to manage the organization through the board. A number of different avenues may be available, but in the end the way the board works, the processes it adopts, is up to the chairman. And the chairman is responsible for the fact that the board must be taking the company somewhere. It must have a strategic direction, and although this direction should emerge from the board itself, it is vital that the chairman should have a clear idea about the sort of company he wants to lead, and where he wants to lead it to.

The chairman is head of the board's process and consequently must invest a great deal of time in thinking about how he wants members to interact. Getting the right interaction with the board can be a tricky business; if it simply becomes a rubber stamp for decisions, something has failed. So the art of being a top leader, states Harvey-Jones, 'is one of breadth of understanding, absolute clarity of aims and lightness of actual intervention'. Many of the actions involved require courage; there will be risks, and failure to take the risks means failure to do the job as well as either you or your organization demands. Consequently the top leader's first job must be to address the composition of the board itself. The board must be moulded into a good team and one that is prepared to challenge the chairman, because the longer the chairman is in place the more likely he is to repeat one (erstwhile successful) action too often, with potentially disastrous results. It is, after all, one of the sincerest compliments and acts of friendship for one person to tell another that he has been mishandling a situation, or mismanaging another individual.

The chairman should be focusing keenly on the reservoir of talent within the organization as a whole. This means looking at who is promoted at all levels and ensuring that young talent is recognized, stretched and encouraged. If things go wrong in this area, there should be other members of the board who are ready to put the chairman right. Harvey-Jones therefore concludes that a good board should be dedicated to 'making it happen' and to dealing with delicate situations in such a way that everyone grows. 'That is actually what the board should be doing the whole time; and that is a sign that the top job is being done well.'

And what of the demands of the top job on the leader as a person? Harvey-Jones believes it is a question of time management and balance. There are skills, such as public speaking, to be mastered. There is a requirement for ruthless self-criticism and mental toughness – a search for honesty about one's own motives. There is always the danger of sycophancy and a high degree of self-knowledge can combat this.

Other key demands on the top leader are those of time and lifestyle. The art of prioritizing becomes essential. Time to work must be snatched on all occasions, but time to be with the family, or to be oneself, must be claimed with equal ruthlessness. The top leader is the key representative of the organization and Harvey-Jones says that customer-related work always came first, but at the same time he would move mountains to spend quality time at weekends with his family.

CONCLUSION

Perhaps it was this iron self-control, this keen sense of perspective, that enabled Harvey-Jones not only to hold on to but to thrive in one of the most demanding top jobs for so long. It is this fact that makes his views on leadership, while admittedly unacademic, nevertheless cogent and relevant.

Roger Harrison

Dr Roger Harrison is a writer and consultant who has specialized in organizational culture, change management and, by implication, the effects of leadership in creating and working effectively in different forms of organizational culture. His publications span a wide range of topics and include *Startup: the Care and Feeding of Infant Systems* (1981), *Strategies for a New Age* (1983), *Organisational Culture and Quality of Service* (1987), and a variety of other books and articles. *The Collected Papers of Roger Harrison* (1995) summarizes the main thrust of his work and thinking.

Harrison states that he first became fully aware of the effects of organizational culture when working on methods to help people from different cultures to work together more easily, in the Peace Corps in the 1960s. It became clear to him that a structured hierarchical structure was an inappropriate match for the stress brought about by the highly ambiguous situations in which the volunteers would have to work. In training volunteers, he developed an open learning environment that would give the students a taste of what was to come. Harrison was further influenced by cultural issues when starting to work in the UK and Europe in the late 1960s, and in 1971 he developed, with Charles Handy, the original model of organizational culture in which they identified four main forms. As a result of this collaboration, Harrison published 'Understanding Your Organisation's Culture' in the *Harvard Business Review* (1972) and Handy went on to publish *The Gods of Management* (1978).

In the 1980s Harrison started to develop his thinking when he wrote about alignment and attunement as well as of releasing what he referred to as the 'power of love' in organizations. Alignment he describes as an organization being 'lined up' in support of values, ideas and goals which excite the commitment of people in the organization. Attunement he describes as 'a sense of connection, belonging and even love' which people experience in organizations, and which emphasize human relationships and values. It can be compared to a family feeling and is often experienced in military combat teams, or high-performing teams in other scenarios. In addition, Harrison stated that there is a degree of congruence between the culture of an organization and the levels of consciousness of its members, when consciousness is approximated to the higher levels of needs in Maslow's hierarchy. Ideally, the organization must move towards providing recognition and satisfactions that truly reward its staff. Organizations will typically create climates that influence their members to demonstrate higher levels of consciousness than those in which they normally operate. It became necessary to create a model and a measure of the social climate in organizations, and this Harrison did in collaboration with the Roffey Park Institute in the UK.

The model, which does not include either the highest or lowest levels of consciousness, identified three levels, *transactional, self-expression* and *mutuality*, which exist as a hierarchy through which most organizations will develop. It is, however, all too easy for an organization to slip back to its previous state, usually as a result of unenlightened leadership.

Level One. The Transactional Level

Transactional cultures are usually very hierarchical and are characterized by high levels of command and control. Motivation is achieved by stick and carrot, reward and punishment, while individual behaviour is controlled by multiple rules and regulations. Consequently people will compete with each other for power and status. There is an immediate impact on the strategies of such organizations; they tend to be orientated towards quick gain and profit and may well react to events rather than anticipate them with new initiatives. Power may reside in the leader or leaders themselves, or it may be exercised more impersonally through systems and procedures. Arguably, this has been the prevailing culture for the majority of organizations over the centuries, but it can also be argued that organizations that are to succeed in the future must grow out of it. There are, however, some benefits: while the tendency of leaders to use personal power in arbitrary and unilateral ways is far from uncommon in business situations, a transactional organization normally provides security through a system of structures and processes which check the blatant misuse of the power of its leaders.

Level Two. The Self-Expression Culture

These are much more autonomous and egalitarian in approach. They encourage individuals and help them achieve a share of the market, or make an impact in the market-place. Consequently people in cultures such as this will be rewarded for their individual, sometimes individualistic, contributions to success or product development. There is usually a high level of internal competition in such cultures, which is often centred on such observable results as the achievement of sales targets, or success in other personal initiatives.

This approach will fit in with a firm's experimental and high-risk strategies in the market-place. Rewards will be high for the successful, especially where a direct link can be drawn between their efforts and achievement by the organization. The atmosphere, however, is often that of sink or swim, dog eat dog. On the other hand, many people who work within self-expression cultures are happy to do so because it fits in with their own ambitions. People will attempt to perform in ways that make them feel good about themselves: competent, creative, attractive, powerful, virtuous and able to make an impact. At the same time there may be degrees of irreverence, careerism and egotism. Such individuals are often drawn to entrepreneurial or start-up situations and welcome the opportunity to align themselves with a vision or ideal they regard as higher than their own interests, and which offers a path to personal growth. The highest form of self-expression is therefore often linked to vision-driven organizations. Harrison adds that there are some points that have not been given sufficient emphasis in the literature of vision-driven organizations.

People without a sense of personal autonomy and control in the workplace may learn to follow and trust a leader, but 'until they experience their own personal power and some measure of freedom, they cannot enter commitment to manage themselves in the service of a vision'. On the other hand, while the energetic and expansive aspects of self-expression cultures make them attractive to many people, there may be times when the task is complex and the vision takes on many forms in different parts of the organization. When this happens, the organization will lose focus and unity of effort and resources are wasted. Of course, organizations can be in the process of change from transaction to self-expression and here too there will be calls on the leadership. Individuals may feel lost or confused and strongly resist the change, believing they are giving up valued security for something that is of less value to them; others will be caught up in the general excitement and be looking for opportunities for advancement.

Level Three. Mutuality Cultures

Harrison describes this as the most mature form of organizational culture – the final stage of evolution. It is best exemplified by the fact that employees have feelings of mutual cooperation and recognize that all can contribute. The organization itself is likely to be orientated towards quality of response and service, as well as to quality of product. For such a result to be achievable, it is necessary for everybody to recognize that high levels of communication and trust are vital. The systems initiated by the organization must observably serve its people as well as the task. As part of it, staff will have adopted a mindset that seeks to produce excellence and innovation through cooperation rather than through competition. Teamwork and mutual support will consequently be regarded as a priority, to the ultimate benefit of the customer.

This is not an easy culture to achieve and it represents a considerable challenge to the organization's leadership to make it happen. Harrison adds that his studies have shown that most individuals would value a higher degree of mutuality within their firm's culture, and consider that they are on the receiving end of too high a level of transaction – again, a challenge to the leadership. But which form of culture is the right one to aim for if it is accepted that emphasis should be placed on innovation as a part of most organizations' strategies? Harrison suggests that the highest quality of work and the best levels of innovation emerge when people love the work – indeed when there is a high level of love in the working environment. Love is portrayed by the ancient Greek concept of *agape*, which is fraternal rather than romantic love and involves a concept of people serving one another rather than a need to receive from one another. This form of love can evoke high levels of motivation in the service of the group. This can range from self-sacrifice in military scenarios to exceptional productivity and quality in more normal work situations.

An interesting insight into the leadership elements required in mutuality cultures is that people who work in them are difficult to push.

While both output and integrity will be high, mutuality organizations are systems that the management cannot control at will. If people regard authority as being misused or illegitimate, they will not conform and will be impervious to the use of power and authority. This, Harrison concludes, may be one reason why the management in many organizations are reluctant to push the concept of self-managing teams. Managers are still for the most part power-orientated and have not yet learnt how to manage (or control) without using their authority.

The movement between cultures, as well as so many other facets of organizational life, involves change and Harrison, as a consultant, is a specialist in the processes and leadership implications of such change. There are, he states, two forms of tactics for the management of change: action tactics and healing tactics. Action tactics are those which are used to move the change forward, while healing tactics are used to preserve the social system and bind up any wounds caused by disruption. From his experience in dealing with T-groups, Harrison developed the model of the *Castle* and the *Battlefield* as an aid to developing strategies for change.

The castle is the place of safety and represents security, validation of one's personal position, protection and the ability to make choices. The battlefield, on the other hand, represents the arena of the change and is characterized by threats, challenges, wounds and opportunities. Here the threats and challenges are experienced in the present, while the opportunities are usually seen as being in the future. However, there is a positive achievement element within the battlefield represented by the possibilities of growth and learning. At the same time, almost everybody goes through life balancing their psychological need for security with their need for growth. Balancing challenge and gratification so as to evoke people's best efforts towards making the change happen is one of the most important tasks of the change manager.

A major task must be to pace and punctuate change, as well as to provide 'castle time'. A number of the tactics to reduce trauma associated with change, and by the same token promote healing, are:

- to announce the change as far ahead as possible and keep people's attention fixed on the forthcoming change;
- to engage in information overkill – this means that people will be used to the idea and ready for the change when it occurs;

- to give people the opportunity to talk directly to the change-makers and make sure that there really is truthful, straight talking – this means that what actually takes place will not appear as bad as originally anticipated;
- to create discussion arenas;
- to give special attention to groups of people who may either be especially affected by the change, or who may come out in favour of it; enable these people to become empathetic change agents;
- to give people a chance to express their attachment to the way things used to be and then symbolically to let go – this could be in the form of parties or other formal or informal gatherings.

Harrison says that change agents usually underestimate the time required for acclimatization and healing, and that consequently the other side of effective change management is to make the battlefield as attractive as possible. It is here that the real challenge to the leadership lies. When people feel excited and secure they are more likely to take on challenges and to feel more competent to do so. Consequently, managing the battlefield is an exercise in inspiration, empowerment and support; it is also a matter of creating an organizational climate that supports learning.

Specific leadership activities that help a leader to manage the battlefield include:

- being visible, leading the change from the top;
- articulating a clear and credible vision that illustrates why the change is essential;
- ensuring that top management are credible and that they 'walk the talk';
- drawing attention to the change by including it in everything the leaders say or do;
- empowering champions of change and linking them together with other supporters (both actual and potential) in order to build critical mass in support of the change;
- creating symbolic events that support the change.

Leadership, Harrison concludes, is basically symbolic behaviour. In hierarchical organizations, everyone watches and takes their lead from top management and that is why it is vital to have passionate, highly-placed champions of change; people who will be virtual 'monomaniacs' on the subject. Often it is only the most dedicated leaders who 'are willing to put in the sheer volume of time, energy and attention to detail which are required to lead the effort'.

CONCLUSION

In making these statements, Harrison reinforces attributes of leadership described by other better-known writers such as John Kotter. His writings on the castle and battlefield also provide an interesting frame in which to view the writings and actions of Jerry Hirshberg. Harrison adds considerable value to the leadership debate by his linking of change, leadership and organizational culture. Where the achievement of innovation and empowerment is seen to be a prerequisite in the struggle to ensure organizational survival, it is unwise to ignore Harrison's thoughts on the appropriateness of different cultures for different situations, or to dismiss his ideas about alignment, attunement, healing – or even love.

The Leader as Strategic Visionary

J.M. Stewart; J.A. Collins and J.I. Porras

The concept of the leader's vision is a potent one and the ability to create and communicate visions of what is possible in the future is seen by most writers as one of the key differentiators between leadership and management. It is, however, comparatively easy to talk about the 'need for a vision', but far more difficult to describe the processes that actually create one.

A number of writers, often in articles specific to the subject, have attempted to break down the components of a vision as well as the positive leadership actions required to conceive and implement it. Here we will examine two articles; they are to some extent complementary, while at the same time offering contradictory processes for reaching the same end. Both add value and contain pragmatic advice to any leader who is struggling with 'the vision thing'.

J.M. Stewart published 'Future State Visioning – A Powerful Leadership Process in Long-Range Planning' in 1993. At the time he was executive in residence at the Faculty of Management, University of Toronto, while having previously been senior vice-president at Du Pont Canada Inc. He is the author of a number of other articles in the business press. In 'Future State Visioning', Stewart writes that the process of making change happen in complex organizations can be greatly aided by future state visioning (FSV), which he describes as a set of processes for determining 'what and where you want to be in the future'. He uses examples from National Rubber (a Toronto manufacturing company) and Du Pont Canada to help make the case.

FSV is described as a method of predicting what an organization could be in the future without becoming mentally trapped by an exhaustive analysis of where it is now. It is a framework that can be applied to improve thinking about future change, and corporate, team or individual vision – or to develop new ways to address a specific situation or problem. The process starts by looking at what could be, rather than trying to plan forward from the present. Consequently, FSV encourages thinking about the possible future state of an organization. It does this by encouraging what Stewart describes as a discontinuous or step-change method of thinking by which those involved are not hampered in their thinking about the future by thinking that is preoccupied with the present. This in theory ought to facilitate the creation of a more challenging or productive future.

Stewart states that the elements making up a vision are common enough. They include defining the stakeholders, assessing the future environment, creating a vision, assessing the present state and expressing a set of values. When these elements are combined into a comprehensive integrated process, the result is a powerful tool for promoting discontinuous step-change thinking.

The key to FSV is to look at one's own organization from the vantage point of an imaginary 'omniscient outside observer', and the specific sequence of steps and imperatives is now defined as follows:

Develop a comprehensive list of stakeholders and try to view the future state and the present state through their eyes

Here there should be a discussion to identify the stakeholders and to plan their participation. The discussion will help participants to see the business from an outsider's viewpoint. They should note that different stakeholders will have different viewpoints and all should be considered. The people within the organization are also key stakeholders and therefore it is essential that opinion-leaders are involved in the process. The participation develops alignment by spreading information concerning the background of the vision, its uncertainties, its compromises and the values that underpin it, all of which are more fundamental than the vision itself. This knowledge enables people to see the vision as a flexible guide, which can be modified to meet changing circumstances. This flexibility is one of the key components of an empowered and continuously learning organization, and if participants truly represent the constituency of the organization, then buy-in and subsequent action will be assured.

Develop a broad description of the likely future environment

Stewart believes that people understand the environment better if they have struggled to describe it. At the same time it is necessary to get experts (employees) in their own field to take on this task. The exercise, however, is not one of brainstorming but should be planned around specific topics, and should use participants' abilities to research certain areas more thoroughly before decisions are made. At the same time, people must be encouraged to think several years ahead rather than becoming absorbed in the present or immediate future; they must then talk not of trends, but of predictions. These predictions can then become the hard material on which specific vision discussions can be based.

Create a comprehensive vision of what the organization could be – disassociated from the barriers of today before considering the present state

The thought processes here should be concerned with what the organization would be like if it were to be much improved in the future. Participants should consider what the customers would wish the organization to be like, and the discussion should strike a balance between high aspirations and practicalities. The resultant vision must be dynamic, stretching, and should involve the concept of continuous improvement. The future state can be viewed from both a hard and a soft dimension; these relate to the competitive position of the firm and then to the personal and organizational behaviour that will be required in the future. Most important, the future state should be described in achievable terms.

Contrast the future vision with the present state

This provides a firm basis for developing strategy and action plans and is a good starting point for a more detailed consideration of the strengths and weaknesses of the present state.

Express the values that will guide the organization as it seeks to achieve its vision

All action is influenced by values, even if they are seldom articulated. Consequently the values must be clearly stated – though it is possible that some values may need to be changed in order to attain the vision. Articulating the values will expose conflict and lack of alignment and this is the main reason why that vision needs to be stated before working to identify the values. It is necessary to involve people in this process, as they are much more likely to be turned on by values that they have helped to express. Strategy or action must be avoided until the vision and values have been created.

Ensure that the vision is expressed in terms of actionable concepts

The FSV is only going to be as good as the plan to make it happen, and if it is a good vision the plan to achieve it will already be implicit.

Stewart concludes by stating that 'what is' can be a great barrier to 'what can be'. Those who want to make progress should begin by sorting out the end – where they want to be – and then use the powerful leadership process to deliver both action and commitment. In saying this, he positions himself in the same camp as Stephen Covey and Collins and Porras. The latter, however, take the process in a different order with different emphases, and their definitions are clearer. The result is in interesting juxtaposition to Stewart's.

The main difference between this process and others that have been expounded is that Stewart regards it not just as part of a leadership philosophy but as a specific management process that can be used in a number of decision-making situations. The process stems from systems thinking, and commitment comes from striving towards an inspiring vision that one has helped to create; alignment to it comes from shared values, and the empowerment factor comes from working towards clearly understood objectives that have been created by the participants together. The process is thus clearly linked with the idea of self-management.

Collins and Porras, while dealing with the same issues, concentrate less on process and more on formulating clear definitions of concepts such as values, vision and mission. Their article 'Building Your Company's Vision' (*Harvard Business Review*, 1996) may in fact provide useful tools for recently appointed leaders who are trying both to understand and reposition their organizations in the business environment. James A. Collins is a management educator and writer, and visiting Professor of Business Administration at the University of Virginia. Jerry I. Porras is the Lane Professor of Organisational Behaviour and Change at Stanford Graduate School of Business. Collins and Porras have collaborated on a number of articles that develop the theme of visionary business leadership, including 'Organisational Vision and Visionary Organisations (*California*

Management Review, 1991) and 'Built to Last: Successful Habits of Visionary Companies' (*Harper Business Review*, 1994).

The writers state that companies enjoying continuing success have core
values and a core purpose that remain fixed, while their business strategies
and practices endlessly adapt to the changing world. Because of this, they
are able to renew themselves and achieve superior long-term performance. Truly great companies therefore understand the difference between
what should never change and what should be open to change. The ability
to manage the pressures between maintaining a level of continuity and
also making change happen is closely linked to a company's and its
leadership's ability to develop a vision. Collins and Porras go on to give
examples from organizations as diverse as Merck, Nordstrom, Sony, Walt
Disney, McKinsey, and Wal-Mart.

The components of a vision are spelt out in detail because the writers
aim to establish a new and clearer set of terms in the business vernacular.
The first component is that of the organization's *core ideology*. This defines
the enduring character of the organization, an identity that transcends
product or market lifecycles; in fact it provides the glue that holds the
organization together as it grows. The writers compare it to the essential
essence of Judaism that has held the Jewish people together through
centuries without a homeland. The core ideology is in turn made up of
two sub-components:

1 Core values
2 Core purpose

Core values are the central and enduring tenets of the organization; those
things that people believe to be essentially true. A core value does not
require justification; it has intrinsic validity within the organization. The
Disney Corporation's core values of imagination and wholesomeness are
given as examples. They stem not from market requirements but from
the founder's belief that these qualities should be nurtured for their own
sake. Similarly, service to the customer is held as a core value of Nordstrom
and is a tenet which has lasted for eight decades.

An organization's *core purpose*, on the other hand, is described as its
reason for being and will reflect people's idealistic reasons for doing the
company's work. In many respects it is the soul of the organization.
Examples of different core purposes include those of McKinsey, 'To help
leading corporations and governments to be more successful'; 3M, 'To

solve unsolved problems innovatively', and Walt Disney, 'To make people happy'. A core purpose may last for a hundred years or more as in fact it is impossible for the organization completely to fulfil it. It becomes a guiding star, forever pursued but never reached. However, in the pursuit an organization can achieve great things.

In order to place their terminology clearly within the commonly held strategic framework, the writers assert that core ideology is not core competency. The former is 'what we stand for' while the latter describes 'what we are good at'. The process of working out an organization's core ideology can be complex and is certainly an essential leadership process. From the company's perspective it is possible to ask, 'What would cease to exist if our company ceased to exist?' or 'Why is it important that it continues to exist?' Similarly, the core ideology can be identified by approaching it from the employees' viewpoint; here a potent question is 'How could we frame the purpose of this organization so that if you had enough in the bank to retire, you would still continue to work here?'

'Once you are clear about your core ideology you should feel free to change absolutely anything that is not part of it.' In making this statement the writers not only differentiate themselves from Stewart but also position themselves to describe the components of the envisioned future. This they put into two parts – abandoning the 'vision' word, the first part is what they describe as the Big Hairy Audacious Goal, the BHAG. This, they say, must be such a stretching commitment that when people first hear of it there 'will be an almost audible gulp'. A BHAG may take between ten and thirty years to complete and is so compelling in itself (like the NASA moonshot) that it does not need verbose mission statements to articulate it.

On the other hand, this huge challenge will need the second element, which is a vivid description, in order to motivate people. This vivid description will be an engaging, compelling and specific picture of what it will be like to achieve the goal. Examples given range from Henry Ford's statement that he would build a motor-car for the great multitude, to Winston Churchill's dramatic words to the British people in 1940 when he articulated what must have seemed to many an almost impossible (yet motivating) BHAG of ultimate victory. The BHAG therefore must be conceived with fire and passion, or it quite simply will not work!

BHAGs can be iterated in a number of ways. They can focus on an internal transformation of the organization; they can be quantitative or qualitative in nature; they can point towards the conquest of a common enemy, or they can direct the organization towards modelling itself on another company as an example of excellence. In all events, they should be stretching and the description vivid.

Collins and Porras bring their thoughts to a conclusion with an interesting warning to business leaders. BHAGs are not a core purpose, they are in fact mountains to be climbed. An envisaged future helps an organization only as long as it has not yet been achieved. Once climbed, it is vitally necessary to find another mountain, otherwise it is all too easy to fall into the trap of saying, 'We have arrived' and then allowing efforts to lose focus and intensity. This, the authors state, is exactly what happened in the case of NASA and also in the case of Ford and Apple Computers.

The essential leadership element in this context lies in aligning values, ideology, vision and action. Creating alignment may be the leader's most important work but the first steps for the leader will always be to recast the vision or mission into an effective context for building a visionary company. After that it will be a matter of making achievements happen. The authors state that people in truly great companies talk of their achievements and that one hears little about individual earnings.

CONCLUSION

Interesting! Perhaps in expounding both a new terminology and hinting at a new philosophy for both individuals and businesses, the authors are casting themselves in a visionary role. In all events, the need for vision in all walks of life will just not go away. Consequently those who help simplify the terminology in the context of visions and all that goes with them – as well as describing effective processes for their creation and enactment – do us all a favour.

Peter Senge

Peter Senge is an academic, consultant and author. As Director of the Systems Thinking and Organisational Learning Program at the Sloan Institute of Management, Massachusetts Institute of Technology, he is arguably the world authority on systems thinking and the learning organization. Senge is also Chairman of the Society for Occupational Learning, and as a founder member of Innovation Associates has run seminars for thousands of managers of the subject of the learning organization. His principal publications on the subject include the ground-breaking *The Fifth Discipline* (1990), its companion volume *The Fifth Discipline Field Book* (1994) and, more recently, *The Dance of Change* (1999). In addition, Senge has summarized his work in articles, one of the most pertinent from a leader's perspective being 'The Leader's New Work: Building Learning Organisations' (*Sloan Management Review*, Fall, 1990).

While there has been lavish praise for *The Dance of Change*, a book that tackles the reason why the majority of change initiatives fail, and which also explains why the majority of business leaders are rarely powerful enough to drive change successfully from the top, it must be accepted that the essential groundwork for it was laid in *The Fifth Discipline*. It is here that demands on the leader are set against a new and stretching construct of effectiveness.

From the start, Senge sets out to explain the concept of the learning organization and the five essential disciplines, or 'competent technologies', that must underpin it. While the book is not overtly about leadership, it does in fact contain more challenges and more pragmatic advice to leaders than many books that set out to address the subject head on.

A learning organization is one where 'people continually expand their capacity to create the results they truly desire, where new and expansive patterns of thinking are nurtured, where collective aspiration is set free, and where people are continually learning how to learn together'. In fact those organizations that will really excel in the future are those that learn how to tap people's commitment and be more 'learningful', as well as more dynamic, than their competitors. Senge adds that learning organizations are possible because deep down all humans are lifelong learners, and that this need, this curiosity, just has to be transformed from an individual to an organizational setting. Organizations will remain less than effective until they become more consistent with man's higher aspirations. (Here it is useful to note a parallel with the thinking of John Whitmore in *Need, Greed or Freedom* (see page 202).) The more enlightened business leaders who share these thoughts are part of a minority who can lead the way in the evolution of work as a social institution. However, what fundamentally will distinguish learning organizations from more traditional authoritarian, controlling ones will be the mastery of certain basic disciplines that in fact become the disciplines of the learning organization. These disciplines are gradually converging to create learning organizations, and though they are developing individually, each is important to the others' success.

1 *Systems thinking*
It is only possible to understand the system of anything, be it a rainstorm, a business or any other human endeavour, by looking at the whole of it, rather than concentrating on any individual part. Systems thinking enables patterns to be made clearer and therefore the ways to change them become more obvious.

2 *Personal mastery*
Personal mastery is the discipline of continually deepening and clarifying one's personal vision by focusing energies, developing patience and seeing reality objectively. People with a high level of personal mastery are best able to realize the results that matter most to them, and consequently the concept of personal mastery is a cornerstone of the learning organization. The discipline of personal mastery starts with identifying the things that really matter to the individual and the means of achieving the highest aspirations.

3 *Mental models*

These are deeply ingrained assumptions and generalizations that influence how individuals see the world and how they take action. The discipline of working with mental models begins with enabling people to scrutinize them rigorously and to hold themselves open to the influence of others.

4 *Building shared visions*

Senge states that the concept of the shared vision is the one idea about leadership that has inspired organizations over the years; measurable greatness has always come about in pursuit of goals, values and missions. However, many leaders have personal visions that are never translated into the shared visions that in turn galvanize their organizations. On the other hand, leaders must not fall into the trap of trying to dictate their visions.

5 *Team learning*

This is vital because teams rather than individuals make up the basic learning unit as well as the essential unit of production in modern organizations. Unless teams can learn, the organization will not do so.

It is vital that the disciplines develop as an ensemble – the tools must be integrated and this is why, says Senge, systems thinking is the 'fifth' discipline, the discipline that fuses and integrates the others. Visions without systems thinking end up as pretty pictures with no deep understanding of the forces that must be mastered to move the organization towards them. However, systems thinking also needs the other disciplines to realize its potential and then a learning organization can result – a place where people are continually discovering how to create their own reality.

And when that elusive concept, the learning organization, is achieved it is almost a spiritual experience for those involved. Senge describes it as 'metanoia' – a shift of mind – and to understand it is to grasp the deepest meaning of learning. Real learning is more than digesting facts and information, it gets to the heart of what it means to be human. Through learning, individuals are able to recreate themselves, and in the same way organizations can embark on generative learning that enhances their ability to create and innovate. Here Senge is developing ideas both of 'self leadership' through self-actualization (an idea also expounded, with different terminology, by Warren Bennis) and applying it in a challenging way to organizations themselves.

It is not the purpose of this chapter to expound in further detail the five disciplines (indeed systems thinking is complex). However, the concept of leadership and self-fulfilment runs through them, although the main challenge to leaders comes towards the end of *The Fifth Discipline* when Senge elaborates on the skills needed to lead a learning organization.

Learning organizations require a new sort of leadership; indeed one of the main reasons why there are not more genuine learning organizations in existence may well be a failure of leadership. At its heart, the traditional form of leadership is based on an assumption of people's powerlessness, their lack of vision and their inability to cope with change – all of which are problems that only a few great leaders can cure. But the concept of leadership in learning organizations centres on more subtle tasks and approaches. Three concepts of leadership activity are required, as leaders are responsible for building organizations where people constantly expand their capabilities to understand complexity and clarify vision. Leaders must be:

Designers
Stewards
Teachers.

These roles illustrate the fact that the leader is now responsible for learning and must take the stand of insisting that the learning organization is the vital new form. Taking this stand is the first step of leadership; it breathes life into the learning disciplines.

Leader as designer

It is up to the leader to design the organization's shape and methods of working. Although the functions of design are rarely seen, usually taking place behind the scenes, the effects of good organizational design are felt in all things. The design work is far from the traditional command and control approach; it is far more akin to one of empowerment. Systems thinking helps the leader to design the organization's policies, strategies and systems, and the essence of good design is to understand how the parts fit together to perform as a whole. Business design, however, is not just about rearranging the organizational structure, it is about understanding the company as a system in which the internal parts are not only interconnected but also connected to the external environment.

Leaders must not fall into the trap of relying on one particular discipline. They must also tackle the question of how to develop all the disciplines and ensure that there is interaction among them. This is one of the fundamental design issues the leader must cope with. Nevertheless Senge concludes that the first step of organizational design must be towards developing vision, values and purpose. After that leaders can illustrate their own personal mastery by actually living the visions through what they say and do. They must craft strategies suitable to people's needs in each situation and remember that people will learn what they know they need to learn, not what someone else thinks they need to learn. The leader's task is therefore that of designing the learning processes by which people can deal effectively with the critical issues they face and develop their own mastery in the learning disciplines. This is a new form of work for most leaders.

Leader as steward

Senge says that the leaders he interviewed had all managed to construct a 'larger story', which gave a sense of purpose to their vision. Many competent managers in leadership positions, on the other hand, were not really effective leaders because they saw no larger story. The story is central to the leader's ability to lead – the truly visionary leaders saw their organization as a vehicle for bringing learning and change to society; the story 'provides a single integrating set of ideas that gives meaning to all aspects of the leader's work. Out of this deeper story and sense of purpose or destiny, the leader develops a unique relationship to his or her own personal vision. He or she becomes a *steward* of the vision.'

In a learning organization, moreover, the leader learns to see his or her vision as part of something larger and to realize they must learn to listen to other people's visions and adapt their own. This is all part of responsible stewardship and of ensuring that the vision is fully shared by all involved. Responsible stewardship implies a lack of possessiveness.

Leader as teacher

The role of the leader as teacher is to help people achieve a view of reality. This involves focusing on purpose and systemic structure, which is the domain of systems thinking and of mental models, and teaching their people to do likewise. The leader must continually help his or her people to see the big picture and to understand a variety of interconnections. This will give a sense of purpose to the overall operation.

Unfortunately, more common are leaders who have a sense of vision and purpose but little ability to foster systemic understanding. This usually leads to domination by events and reactiveness to them, as noble aspirations are not enough to overcome systemic forces contrary to the vision. On the other hand, there are leaders who have a sense of vision as well as an understanding of major business trends, and these people are often held up as models of effective leadership and excellent change agents. However, Senge argues, the truly effective leader must be able to help people understand the systemic forces that shape change. Leaders in learning organizations develop the ability to conceptualize their strategic insights so that they become public knowledge and open to challenge and further development. Being a leader–teacher is not about teaching people how to achieve the vision but is about fostering learning, developing systemic understanding, and thereby enabling everyone (including themselves) fully to understand current reality.

A number of personal development challenges exist for the leader of a learning organization. They range from understanding the concept of creative tension and how to use it, to an awareness of the skills of systems thinking required of them.

Promoting creative tension is a tough necessity. It is the leader's task to highlight the gap between vision and reality. This gap can be discouraging, but it can also be a source of energy and endeavour. Indeed the gap is the source of creative energy. Senge uses the analogy of a rubber band. When stretched, it creates tension, representing the tension between vision and reality. The tension must resolve itself – to pull towards the vision, or towards reality (the *status quo*). The final direction will depend on whether the leader and followers hold steady to the vision. The principle of creative tension is the central principle of personal mastery. Mastery of creative tension leads to a fundamental shift in the leader's attitude to reality, and an accurate view of reality is as important as a clear vision. It thus enables the leader to identify the truth in changing situations. 'If the first choice in pursuing personal mastery is to be true to your own vision, the second fundamental choice in support of personal mastery is commitment to the truth.'

And this is the note that Senge strikes when he identifies the skills required for future leaders:

1 *To see interrelationships, not things and processes, not snapshots*
Most people have been conditioned to focus on things and to see the

world in static images. Consequently this leads to explanations of things as isolated events rather than as part of a process.

2 *To move beyond blame*
People tend to blame one another or circumstances for their problems. However, poorly designed systems cause most organizational problems. True leaders learn to understand that there is no 'outside' – you and the cause of the problem are part of the same system.

3 *To distinguish detail complexity from dynamic complexity*
Detail complexity arises when there are many variables in a situation, while dynamic complexity arises when cause and effect are separated in time and space. Consequences are therefore subtle and not obvious. Effective leadership, and leverage, lies in understanding dynamic complexity before detail complexity.

4 *To focus on areas of high leverage*
Systems thinking shows that small, well-focused actions can produce great improvements in situations if they happen in the right place. This is the principle of leverage, and the skill in tackling a difficult problem is often a matter of seeing where areas of high leverage are and thus where action, carried out with minimum effort, would produce a lasting and significant improvement.

5 *To avoid symptomatic solutions*
When something goes wrong in an organization, the pressure is on fixing the symptoms rather than the underlying causes. This usually results in only temporary relief and often greater problems arise at a later date. Often the most difficult yet most effective leadership tactic is to refrain from intervening with short-term quick fixes, no matter how popular they may seem, and to keep up the pressure on everyone to find more enduring solutions based on a systemic analysis and rationale.

Senge's conclusion is that systems thinking, personal mastery, mental models, building shared vision, and team learning are all vital to the future health of organizations. They might equally be called leadership disciplines as learning disciplines, as those who excel in these areas will be the natural leaders of learning organizations. A sixth discipline may therefore be that of mastering the possibilities presented by the present learning disciplines in order to establish a firm foundation for the future.

CONCLUSION

In matching an extremely right-brained approach to some very left-brained concepts, Senge has produced an insightful and indeed revolutionary series of publications. The one area of regret is that more organizations have not taken his advice and have remained geared to the quick fix. Perhaps like many prophets Senge has been ahead of his time, and time alone will show whether his concepts are put to work on a universal scale. The benefits could be huge.

John Whitmore

Sir John Whitmore's career has spanned a number of different fields. He has been a professional racing driver, a farmer and a businessman, and he has managed to synthesize these areas in themes that prevail throughout his written work. A keen interest in psychology and science led him to study in the USA, and on returning to Britain he used his knowledge of coaching and psychology to develop performance improvement programmes for business people. He is a member of Performance Consultants, who provide coaching and team-building programmes, and is the author of a number of books and articles. In *Coaching for Performance* (1996),which was an international bestseller and has been translated into ten languages, he expounded his theories on coaching alongside those on personal development. In *Need, Greed or Freedom* (1997), he widened the scope of his approach to include team-building, motivation, leadership, and the responsibilities of businesses within society in the future. His ideas for an integrated personal approach to the leadership of self and others must form a responsible approach to the dilemmas of the future.

Much of *Need, Greed or Freedom* is taken up with Whitmore's own philosophy, but interesting though it is, the main concentration here will be on his views about leadership and team work. The writer develops his own approach to team development with a model that runs parallel to Tuckman's process of Forming, Storming, Norming and Performing, but which adopts a more psychological perspective. These are stages, he believes, that individuals, businesses and societies will experience.

Stage 1. **Inclusion** This is the basic need to be included in the group; it is accompanied by anxiety and fear of rejection. People at this stage are likely to be more conventional than usual as their wishes focus on the need to be included.

Stage 2. **Assertion** When the feared rejection does not take place, the inclusion fears subside and the individual wants to be someone in the group. Personal recognition is sought and individuals assert themselves to achieve it. This may involve challenges to group norms or to the leadership, as individuals are in many respects competing for their position within the group hierarchy.

Stage 3. **Cooperation** Once people know where they stand within the group they become more magnanimous and inclusive. Individuals become more aware of the group's needs and so cooperate with one another rather than competing. There is now a high level of interdependence.

Throughout the book, Whitmore sets out to superimpose the model on segments of life and to use it as the basis for looking at the desired evolution of society. He also uses it as a basis for examining behaviour in business teams. It is a model that leaders cannot afford to ignore, irrespective of their field of leadership. Having set out his model and illustrated its efficacy through illustrations of both sporting and family life, Whitmore compares it with the top three levels in Maslow's famous hierarchy of human needs (belonging, self-esteem and self-actualization). There are, he says, approximate similarities with his own model, inclusion with belonging, assertion with self-esteem, and cooperation with self-actualization.

Whitmore states that a major flaw in Western society is that while it provides for material, belonging and status needs, it does little to encourage self-actualization. In fact the workplace often actually discourages it because it appears incompatible with the conventional commercial work environment. The need felt by self-actualizing people is to find meaning and purpose in their work and means of self-expression. However, the ability to do this is not being provided for – people's needs are evolving, what is motivational to them is changing, but this is not being recognized by business leaders. What these people need is not self-esteem, or money, but for their lives and work to be meaningful. If a company is to retain such people, its purpose, methods and products must be ethical and in some way seek to improve the human condition – to satisfy a fundamental need.

At the same time more and more people seek self-esteem, and while the concept of empowerment has been bandied about, it has been debased by over-use. Although fundamental culture change is the expressed aim of many boards, those who claim to espouse it would be scared of it if they understood what it really meant. Real empowerment meets the need for self-esteem, while the illusion of it frustrates and demotivates. Empowerment itself is brought about by good coaching, and this in many instances would necessitate a radical change in management style.

Whitmore expands his thinking about style when he compares the need for various approaches to business team leadership with different stages in team development. Here he concludes that the traditional command-and-control style works well enough for teams in the inclusion stage and is often necessary in order to keep control in the more turbulent assertive stage. However, as soon as the team goes beyond that and reaches the cooperative stage, it is no longer feasible. Coaching by its very nature is cooperative rather than assertive and is a more effective leadership style for a genuinely participative team. The reason is that coaching is a facilitative process when done well and uses questioning techniques that raise the coachee's awareness and responsibility. Coupled with this is the fact that a good coach, by raising the other person's awareness and responsibility levels, encourages people to do things in their own way. Within the confines of the agreed goal, they are offered choice – and choice is the key to self-motivation.

The role of good questions in the process of motivation and empowerment is expanded in *Coaching for Performance*, in which – apart from dwelling on learning circles – Whitmore outlines his questioning approach to coaching: the GROW model. This is a liberating process whereby open questions are used in a structured way to lead the person being coached from analysis, to commitment, to action. The overall format is as follows, although each element can be broken down into many more sub-questions:

T *Topic.* What topic would you like to talk about?
G *Goal.* What specifically would you like to achieve as a result of this coaching?
R *Reality.* What is happening in the current situation?
O *Options.* What options do you have in the current situation?
W *Wrap up.* What will you do, and by when?

In *Need, Greed or Freedom* Whitmore examines the function and management style of business team leaders who view their teams with an understanding of the three stages of business team leadership and who relate them to the three key areas of goals, roles and processes. A good team leader, for example, will be aware of the inclusion concerns that members of a new team are likely to have, and will address them creatively. It will be necessary to reduce uncertainty by stressing the team's purpose and goals; it is also effective to start a discussion through which a 'composite' definition of members' goals can be reached.

Roles are no less important than goals. When people are assigned a clear role they automatically feel included and the act of coaching people into their roles is in itself a major act of inclusion. The questioning approach in coaching reinforces the inclusion message: when leaders ask someone a question, they are in fact saying, 'I value your opinion.' The team leader will look to bring in any member of the team who may be potentially excluded by the formation of sub-groups or by virtue of skill or personality, and by skilful questioning will help team members find their own way forward.

The leader's role in helping the team with process matters is also a vital one at the early stage of development. Process meetings do not deal with team tasks, but with the way in which the team will meet and work. Sometimes at this stage it is useful for the leader to share the three-stage model with members because this will help them feel less confused and threatened when they experience inclusion fears or assertive behaviour that is out of character.

While a leader may find the team quite easy to handle at the inclusion stage, it is a different matter when it reaches the assertion stage. Challenges may be issued more for the sake of challenging than for any good reason. And while leaders should listen to the content of the challenge, they must be prepared to adopt a more autocratic approach, although not to the extent that the team is catapulted back to the inclusion stage again. Furthermore, at this stage high levels of conflict and stress may exist among team members and performance may be motivated by individual needs rather than by a wish for success for the whole. Consequently the team leader has to tread carefully; he or she must not crush the potential creativity illustrated by the turbulence, but at the same time must not lose personal control. If the leader can impart a firm sense of direction, then things will sort themselves out eventually. And if the leader is able to model the qualities required within the emerging cooperation stage, he or she can often deflect the negative qualities of extreme assertion as true power exists with those who use it 'wisely and sparingly'.

At the cooperation stage, where the values and principles are so different from the assertion stage, the challenge to the team leader is often that of relinquishing control. Whitmore uses the analogy of skiing and says that 'when you are willing to let go of control is the moment when you finally gain control'. A cooperative team operates in a kind of 'flow' and it needs the right sort of leadership to maintain that flow. A light hand is needed, the process-time needs of awareness, responsibility and goal clarity all require maintenance, but the leader should concentrate on the team vision and long-term issues. At the same time, the leader must be aware that any team that reaches the cooperation stage will be something of a rarity and may therefore feel isolated. This danger will continue to exist as long as the assertion stage remains the norm, yet it must be the leader's goal to propel the team through it to the higher level. The shift from assertion to cooperation encapsulates the nature of a culture change that Whitmore believes must take place in both work and society in general.

Culture change within an organization, however, is often a source of disappointment. While top management frequently send their staff on culture change and team-building programmes, they do not always attend themselves. Consequently their own behaviour does not change and staff, perceiving this, become disillusioned. Top management need to 'walk their talk', especially when culture change is on the agenda. Failure to do so means that the overall culture will remain essentially assertive. Yet successful companies of the future will be those that put the quality of working life first. When this is done, productivity, quality, and of course profits, will follow.

At present, Whitmore says, blame cultures rather than cooperation are endemic in business. Blame works against performance for a number of reasons:

- it focuses attention away from the task;
- it evokes justification and excuses rather than the truth;
- where there is no truth there can be no proper evaluation;
- blame reduces risk-taking and innovation;
- it undermines self-esteem and trust, and the ability of people to learn from mistakes.

Whitmore's view is that organizations must examine their ethical stand-point as a first step in moving towards a truly cooperative culture. A starting-point is through clearly articulating the mission statement and the values that underpin it. Ethical standpoints, however, are difficult to define and moral standpoints are often blurred by the profit motive. He believes that the only valid definitions of ethics are those views and resultant actions that 'demand that employees have a higher order of allegiance to humanity than to their company'. This may cause some to be 'whistle-blowers' when the organization is seen to be indulging in unacceptable behaviour. This whistle-blowing is likely to increase as standards rise and as 'people and society at large grow, evolve and mature'.

The ethical values in society and business are already affecting many aspects of business. These include the way people, suppliers and customers are treated, and this embraces a wide range of issues, from the way the organization sells to the way it views the treatment of minority groups within it. Any company that disregards these areas risks criticism; by the same token, any company with vision will want to be ahead of the public mood by demonstrating an ethical response. The onus on the leadership will therefore be to act as role models for their staff and to earn their respect. In addition, they must always be vigilant, as standards do not remain static but continue to rise as society evolves.

A central theme of Whitmore's work is that countries are getting smaller while corporations are tending to get bigger. Big business now controls the global economy, and a fatal flaw has become exacerbated. 'People are now in service to the economy instead of the economy being in service to the people.'

People are often sacrificed to the economy in the name of economic expediency. If the global economy were to set out to serve people's needs as opposed to their greeds, then the world itself would be a better and more stable place. Whitmore cites a number of examples, ranging from the tobacco industry to the arms trade, to back his thesis, but brings the final responsibility down to one of leadership. Business leaders and businesses, he states, have a huge responsibility to lead the way out of the inequity caused by inefficient economic systems. The pool of leadership talent is at present directed towards 'assertive means to assertive ends', but could quite easily redirect itself towards cooperation. This would incorporate a wider vision for society in general and would include a far greater say for stakeholders, employees, customers and the local community – rather than just shareholders.

There is a dilemma for leaders in all this change. They have in the past been expected to be assertive and this expectation continues. Those who have an inclination to be cooperative find it necessary to play the assertion game and leaders with a genuine cooperative philosophy are rare. However, there have been notable examples and Whitmore names Gandhi, Martin Luther King and Gorbachev, all of whom experienced varying degrees of success in coping with the contradictions between their personal beliefs and the roles demanded of them. He cites Nelson Mandela as a leader who shows great Gandhian qualities of dignity, humility, forgiveness and cooperation – perhaps the only real statesman alive today; an individual who has coped with the assertion–cooperation dilemma better than most.

And how can the ordinary individual find the personal qualities to be effective as a leader in times of change and chaos?

The answer lies with the individual. While many may feel powerless in the face of all the stresses and changes in the world, individuals can choose how they perceive and react to the external circumstances – and they can change themselves. If an individual chooses freedom as a state of mind, then the ability to cooperate will come more easily. Finding personal psychological freedom empowers the individual to adopt cooperative stances when dealing with others. A true leader, then, has been able to find psychological freedom. Total freedom in all circumstances may not exist, but it is possible to control one's reaction to them and this enables the individual to let go of both fear and the tyranny of being continually ruled by personal needs. When this state of mind has been reached, the individual is able to act by absolute choice, not as a reaction to social or any other imperatives – this is freedom. The individual is now able to act with total clarity of intention and consequently has the ability to be highly effective. Whitmore equates this state to the highest point in Maslow's hierarchy of needs, that of self-actualization, where individuals are finally able to become what they actually are. This is a process that involves the reconciliation of the opposing drives of their psychological and spiritual development and allows them to move towards finding their 'higher selves', a state where a person's life becomes a true expression of their values. When an individual knows who he or she really is, the labels that other people place on them in fact become meaningless. (Here, Whitmore's writing can be compared with that of Warren Bennis, who states that when an individual manages to achieve full and true self-expression they have enabled themselves to become real leaders.)

CONCLUSION

Whitmore links psychological freedom with the ability to give 'meaning' to what is going on in the world. There is, he asserts, a crisis of meaning, very often of a psychological nature. Western civilization is drawing slowly closer to the transformation from assertion to cooperation, and leaders will sooner or later have to take this shift into consideration. The leaders who will be successful will be those who are able to develop meaningful visions that take into account the evolving nature of human consciousness. In making such statements, Whitmore is not only commenting on the building blocks of effective visioning but also indulging in his own vision of a cooperative, leaderful future.

W.H. Drath and C.J. Palus

Bill Drath graduated in English at the University of North Carolina at Chapel Hill, and has held the post of Publications Director at the Center for Creative Leadership (CCL). He has co-authored and participated in research on a number of publications on executive development, including *Beyond Ambition: How driven managers can lead better and live better* (1991) (see CLL Study on Derailment) and *Why Managers Have Trouble Empowering: A theoretical perspective based on concepts of adult development*. Chuck Palus has a doctorate in social psychology from Boston College and is a research scientist at CCL. His major interests in adult life have been in development and executive leadership. In 1991 he co-authored *Executive Performance: A Life Story Perspective* (CCL, 1991).

Drath and Palus co-authored a major essay produced and sponsored by CCL entitled 'Making Common Sense. Leadership as meaning making in a community of practice' (1993). The title of the work itself may not appear to make much sense but it springs from the fact that CCL, despite occupying the high ground in the field of both leadership development and research, had not put forward its own definition of leadership. While the authors still shrank from offering one prescriptive definition of the concept, they did set out to develop a different way of looking at it. The concepts they developed add much to understanding the somewhat elusive concept of 'making meaning' – something that many writers on leadership have alluded to, but not developed.

The authors suggest that leadership is viewed as a social meaning process that occurs in groups of people who are engaged in some form of common activity. When a group of people start to work together, the leader may need to ask questions about what might be the most effective process of leadership for the group, and how that process might need to change as the group itself develops and creates its own shared history. The problem for the leader lies in the fact that the challenges faced by many people in organizations call for new ways of understanding leadership – what it is, as well as its limitations.

All people have a common need – that is, the need for things to make sense. But what does this mean? the authors ask. It is the process of arranging one's understanding of experiences so that one can make sense of what is happening and what has happened; one can then predict what *will* happen. In many ways, making sense is the discovery of what is really happening. As regards the relation of 'meaning making' to leadership, the authors propose a variation on this theme. Meaning making makes sense of an action by placing it within some larger frame. This frame is seen by the individual, who makes sense of the way the world is and thus is guided in his or her way of being in the world. Reality is therefore a construction. The processes of individual meaning making and social meaning making are interrelated because individuals are deeply related to the social situations in which they live. So what, then, are the implications for leadership?

The purpose of leadership is to make sense, to make meaning, and leadership can be seen to be more about making meaning than about influencing or decision-making. The process of meaning making in certain social settings constitutes leadership – and where people work together in a 'community of practice' this is especially so.

Leadership is the process of helping people to make sense of what they are doing together so that they will understand and be committed. This sense-making process itself makes the leader increasingly influential. A person does what someone else wants them to do because it makes sense to them to do so. Meaning, then, can be seen as a framework that clarifies the way things are and the way things ought to be. When the making of such a framework happens in a working community, it is possible to say that leadership is happening.

By adopting this notion of leadership, it is possible to see leadership no longer in terms of leaders and followers but as a process in which everyone in a group or community is engaged. Leadership, instead of being a force that one person called a leader can apply, becomes a community-specific process that arises in various forms whenever people start to work together. Although individuals may play various roles, some of which will involve influence and authority, authority itself becomes a tool for making sense of things (with other tools, such as norms and values), and leadership then is understandable as the process by which people put these tools to work in order to create meaning. Leadership in a community can be vastly developed if everyone's ability to participate in this process is improved. At the same time, by seeing leadership as meaning making, it is easier to see the relationship between certain human traits (such as intelligence or dominance) and leadership. The people who, by virtue of intelligence or some other characteristic, are able to express meaning on behalf of a community are those whom others may start to call natural leaders.

The writers expand on the process of making meaning. Here, the leader must reach out beyond the self to touch the hearts of others – in doing so, he or she is said to be communicating the vision. Real meaning when communicated is immediately effective because it touches what people implicitly know to be true. Churchill is cited for making stirring speeches that helped to win the Second World War, but he declared that he was only giving expression to what was already in people's hearts. He was also connecting various meanings to one another in ways appropriate to the demands of the situation. Meaning making, then, happens through such processes as 'identifying vision and mission, framing problems, setting goals, arguing and engaging in dialogue, theory-building and testing, storytelling, and the making of contracts and agreements . . . these processes are not merely important to leadership, rather they constitute leadership'.

If leadership is looked at from the meaning-making perspective, it is possible to gain new understanding of such concepts as influence, individual action, motivation and the relationship between authority and leadership. Influence, for example, is no longer the essence of leadership, rather it is the outcome of leadership. So does leadership naturally arise with the action of a dominant leader? Not necessarily; leadership is more about what people do together, as all members of a community participate in the process of meaning to some degree or other. This will have consequences for some people in positions of authority who may have to accept that in some parts of a process they will not be the leaders. Dominant leaders will still exist, and will still be very effective in situations of crisis or combat where this approach is called for. But in most cases the dominant leader is frequently called on to re-demonstrate the dominance. The shift towards a social-participation view of leadership allows different demonstrations of effectiveness to take place where the leader articulates or makes known things that were sensed, but as yet not articulated, in that community of practice.

Drath and Palus state that there are certainly implications for young people who may wish to learn the skills of leadership and the community-orientated meaning-making capabilities. The implications for development are:

(1) the capacity to understand one's self as an individual and as a socially embedded being;

(2) the capacity to understand systems in general as mutually related and interacting and continually changing;

(3) the capacity to take the perspective of another;

(4) the capacity to engage in dialogue.

The writers conclude by accepting that there are many arguments and issues concerning leadership, and the place of individual dominance within the concept, to be resolved. Whenever people are doing something together for long enough to make a community, it is relevant to think of them as striving to make things make sense for that community – to create meaning out of the experiences that occur. And this sense is usually something that emerges from the body of that community. This is the process of leadership – no matter how the process is played out and whatever the participation by various individuals.

CONCLUSION

The writers have added constructive new insights to the subject of leadership, especially to the concepts of meaning making and to the idea of participative leadership. If there is one flaw in their arguments, it is in the fact that they assume a degree of participation and benevolence in most organizations. This is by no means always the case. Many organizations currently have reorganized, restructured, flattened and changed to an extent that many employees are feeling demoralized, cynical and disaffected. They consider themselves to be the victims of change overload and as mere pawns in the game of corporate mergers and acquisitions. So what is the answer?

Paradoxically, it is for employees to understand the meaning behind what is going on. However, when changes are imposed that may have drastic effects, it is difficult to accept that they represent what was already in one's heart and mind – although not yet articulated. The answer must lie with the leaders of the businesses in the midst of these changes. Change is inevitable and will not cease, but the responsibility for carrying the hearts and minds of subordinates must fall on these leaders. Perhaps, while the most loudly expressed benefit to shareholders and the City from such changes is that of cost savings through job cuts, the accusation must be that of right ends but wrong means – that is, if they want motivation levels to remain high. It would be useful then for many business leaders to start asking themselves how they can express their actions in terms of meaning making for the communities represented in the organizations they lead.

Vision Articles

In addition to books, a large number of articles have been published on the subject of the leader's vision with emphasis on its role in transforming the organization. These come from both sides of the Atlantic, from well-known and less well-known authors. While taking different stances, these articles are largely complementary and put together they add significantly to the wealth of knowledge on leadership, vision, and the creation of stretching strategies. Three articles are examined here that deal with:

THE TASK 'Strategy as Stretch and Leverage', by G. Hamel and C.K. Prahalad, *Harvard Business Review*, 1993

THE LEADERSHIP REQUIREMENT 'Managing in an Age of Discontinuity', by John Burdett, MCB University Press, 1993

THE LEADERSHIP BEHAVIOURS NEEDED TO MOVE THE PROCESSES FORWARD 'Managing the Metaphors of Change', by R.J. Marshak, *Organisational Dynamics*, USA, 1993

Each article is briefly summarized below.

1 Strategy as Stretch and Leverage

Gary Hamel is Associate Professor of Strategic and International Management at the London Business School. C.K. Prahalad is the Harvey C. Freuhauf Professor of Business Administration at the University of Michigan. Both writers are regarded as heavyweight academics and consultants in the fields of business competitiveness. Together they have collaborated on a number of ground-breaking articles. 'Strategic Intent' (*Harvard*

Business Review, 1989) won the 1989 McKinsey Award for Excellence, and many of the interwoven strands of their joint thinking have been put into their book, *Competing for the Future* (1994). This stresses what companies must do in order to occupy the high ground. Leaders need to develop independent views about opportunities and to exploit them through the authors' definition of what it means to be strategic. This article was one in an acclaimed series of offerings on marketing and competitiveness.

The writers state that it is first necessary to understand the 'why'. Understanding the 'why' is a prerequisite for getting out in front, and the managerial frames of reference and assumptions by which a company understands itself and its environment must drive its competitive strategy. Although the frames of reference may be invisible, their consequences will be visible all the time in the companies' choice of competitive stratagems. Global competition is in fact not just competition between products, companies or trading blocks, it is the competition of mindset versus mindset – and to ensure success, the mindsets must change.

The authors assert that the idea that every company must effect a fit between its resources and the opportunities it pursues is redundant. Now the concept of *stretch* must supplement the idea of fit. Resources must be leveraged and it is acknowledged that stretch will result in a degree of organizational tension. It has become necessary to throw out the notion that 'if only we had more resources we could be more strategic' as creating a mismatch between aspirations and the resources available to achieve them. This reversal of thinking is now the most important task of management. The name of the game is that of leveraging resources, 'getting a bigger bang from the buck'! Although this may create tension, the tension itself can be energizing. This is in contrast to downsizing, which is essentially demoralizing.

The arenas of resource leverage fall into five basic categories:

1 concentrating resources on key strategic goals;
2 accumulating them more efficiently;
3 complementing one kind of resource with another to create higher value;
4 conserving resources where possible;
5 recovering them from the market-place in the shortest possible time.

In each case managers must ask certain demanding questions in order to assess the scope for further resource leverage in their organizations, whether they are financial or non-financial. The questions posed are many, yet the sample given here indicates the internal organizational shake-up and reorientation that acting on them requires.

The writers recommend a series of questions that should be asked as part of the process of designing the stretching strategy. Examples include:

Have we created a gap between resources and aspirations that will compel creative resource leverage?

Are we willing to apply lessons learnt, even when they conflict with long-held orthodoxies?

Are we willing to learn from outsiders as well as insiders?

Have we created a blend of centralists and blending specialists who can multiply our resources?

Have we created an environment in which employees can explore new skills?

Do we view core competencies as corporate resources rather than the property of individual businesses?

Have we shortened product development, order processing and product launch times?

Have we built up brands and systems that allow us to pre-empt slower rivals?

Do we understand our competitors' blind spots and can we attack without risking retaliation?

The writers conclude that the job of top management is not so much to stake out the future as to help accelerate the acquisition of new market and industry knowledge – risk recedes as knowledge grows. Strategy as stretch, on the other hand, is strategy by design in so far as the leadership has a clear view of the ultimate goal that is being pursued.

2 Managing in an Age of Discontinuity

Hamel and Prahalad do not deal with the implications of stretch for people within the organization, or with the implications for leadership behaviour. The story is then taken up by John Burdett in 'Managing in an Age of Discontinuity'. Burdett at the time of writing was Vice-President of the Lawson Marsden Group, based in Toronto. He states that in response to modern competitive challenges, organizations have attempted to implement a huge array of ideas, concepts and programmes, ranging from changes to hierarchical structures to more aggressive purchasing policies. Introducing these ideas, however, is a far cry from translating them into sustainable competitive advantage. Renewal demands new ways of thinking and a 'highly developed ability to reframe organizational assumptions at critical stages of the journey'. Organizations are having to learn not only to do things better but also to do them *faster*. Creating a learning organization is a discontinuous journey and demands management of the context, not just of people and things – a threatening idea which means that everybody, especially the leaders, must think differently. Here, the writer concludes, four questions are pivotal:

1 Is the journey really necessary? Does change have to be discontinuous? Why should organizations not stay in one territory and build organically on what they are already good at?
2 If organizational change at some point of the journey necessitates reframed assumptions, what are they?
3 If traditional training and development methodologies are open to attack, what new tools are available?
4 How do those in leadership roles move individuals or a team out of an established and often long-held comfort zone?

The final question is the vital one and is the question that impacts most strongly not only on Burdett's thesis, but also on that of Hamel and Prahalad. Burdett says that while there is still some dispute over the nature of leadership, there are areas where there is a high degree of common agreement. These include a common vision based on knowledge of the big picture; iteration of clear consistent values; crafting a culture and strategy, and the complementary dimensions of leadership and coaching. What is missing, however, is a description of the chemistry that energizes transition and makes things happen. Building on the work of Bardwick, Senge and others, Burdett refers to the tension that leaders bring to the challenge. He believes that the idea of tension is an essential part of the leader's agenda and a vital ingredient in moving the business forward.

Burdett quotes Senge in defining tension as 'the force that comes into play at the moment when we acknowledge a vision is at odds with reality'. It is nevertheless necessary to distinguish between emotional and creative tension. The former results in a lowering of the vision while the latter creates a state of arousal, an optimum level of discomfort that in turn generates high productivity. Burdett sees the challenge as essentially a push–pull model. The pull comes from an empowering vision and the push comes from raising the tension for those who want to remain in the *status quo*. Change, though, is more than just creating a potent mixture of tension and vision; the extent to which people will move out from their comfort zones will also be dependent 'on the appropriate level of appropriate skills, meaningful coaching, an openness to look at reality differently, self-confidence, the punishment/risk equation, and an ability to learn from experience'.

The writer identifies ten ways to generate creative tension:

1 Benchmarking against the best.
2 Moving the culture from recognizing seniority to recognizing merit.
3 Improving the quality of performance feedback to include both peers and subordinates.
4 Removing those who represent poor role models.
5 Encouraging risk.
6 Taking non-decision-making levels out of the hierarchy.
7 Rewarding success.
8 Destroying restrictive concepts of turf.
9 Striving for synergies.
10 Focusing on outputs.

3 Managing the Metaphors of Change

The uncertainty in the business world demands new organizational ways to view the business. They need to learn how to recognize opportunity and be equipped to move fast to maximize those opportunities – the very lifeblood of the organization must be that of speed of response, born of maximizing the benefits of creative tension. It remains up to Marshak in 'Managing the Metaphors of Change' to put the aspirations expounded in the preceding two articles into a description of effective communication that is open to all leaders.

Marshak states that organizational change can be broken down into three clear types. First of all there is developmental change. This is the sort of change that simply builds on and improves the quality of what already exists in the organization. It may streamline procedures, shorten response times and improve quality. However, at the end of the process, things are not radically different. Then there is transitional change. Here the organization will be in the process of moving from one state to another. This may involve a change of product base or the introduction of new technologies. The organization may well be still exploring where it should go and be in the process of deciding what its final state of being will be.

Finally there is transformational change – and here it is interesting to note that Marshak takes more trouble than many writers to describe his understanding of this form of change – here the organization will be setting out to change to a completely different state of being. The move may be from a manufacturing-based organization that has long prided itself on the excellence of its product to one that now sees the excellence of the service it provides, the product being the key differentiator. On the other hand the move may be from an administratively focused state to one where selling is the key. It is interesting to note that studies have shown a vast increase in the rate of growth of transformational change over the other two forms; major strategic initiatives are being enacted in every theatre of work.

It makes sense, says Marshak, that if you want people to react in a way that is consistent with the demands of the situation, it will be necessary for the leader to describe the nature of the change accurately and to reflect this accuracy in the words used. For example, if the change in hand is developmental, it is better to use language that is consistent. Phrases such as 'we must adjust' or 'develop what we have got' or 'we must get smarter at . . .' are all appropriate. When the change is transitional, that sort of language will lack the necessary power. Instead, phrases like 'explore new ways', 'leave the past behind', 'move on' are more likely to provoke the desired result as the paradigm is being bent, if not broken.

When the change is transformational, the role of the change agent – the leader – becomes more that of challenger and visionary. Here the expressions used must help others to recognize that the mould has been broken. Phrases such as 'breaking with the past' or 'the past is dead' or 'escaping from the strictures of the past' or 'moving into the light of the new' all describe what is happening in both the organization's internal and external worlds. If, for example, the organization is reinventing itself in some major new direction and it is recognized that this involves a major move in both thinking and operational style of the people involved; if this now places a considerable emphasis on new priorities and considerable stretch demanded from those people who will now be working towards these priorities; then it is not appropriate to use expressions like 'we must adjust': they are simply not powerful enough. Such words do not break any paradigms and certainly do not empower people to make a creative stretch. The language must match the situation and the resultant clarity will educate and liberate all concerned.

CONCLUSION

Marshak's views tie this short sequence of articles together effectively. Hamel and Prahalad in their influential article described the future and to some extent pre-empted the highly competitive stance most organizations would be forced into by the end of the decade. In doing so, they picked up on many of the powerful forces and trends Charles Handy had predicted in *The Age of Unreason*, in which he described the changing nature of organizations with the resultant implicit changes to work patterns and mindsets. Burdett in turn anticipated many of the cultural changes that would take place in the same time span. However, it is necessary to note that change is brought about by leaders, and that leadership is essentially about people. So in implementing change, in stretching the organization, as with so many other aspects of business life, the difference between success and failure depends on that very human factor, the quality of the communication used to describe it and motivate others to give of their best. At the time of publication, the articles covered here were considered to be quite revolutionary and visionary in content. It is interesting to note that the themes remain topical and the advice given relevant; a continuing prescription for good practice in the ever changing and ever more demanding business scenario.

Conclusion: Pointers for Future Leaders and their Development

A great benefit from compiling a book of this nature lies in the scope and overview it gives the writer. It has enabled me to take a long, cold look at the definition of leadership I made in my first work on the subject, as well as to build on some further concepts I developed in my second book. In *Discovering the Leader in You* I put forward the following definition of leadership:

> Being a leader is something you *do* rather than something you are. It is the ability to bring out a number of talents and to operate effectively through other people making them gladly accept your goals while still having the freedom to do things their way. A good leader therefore understands and meets other people's positive expectations of how they wish to be led.
>
> Becoming a good leader is something you *choose* to do through a process of action and self-discovery.

On reflection, while I still hold to what I said, I do not think that I went far enough. For example, there was no mention of the leader's vision or of the need to foster creativity and innovation. However, I did go on to put forward a mnemonic to describe the essential characteristics of good leadership. This was WIST, and the component letters stood for Wisdom, Integrity, Sensitivity and Tenacity. They seemed to hold up to scrutiny and in my second book on leadership, *The Portable Leader* (1997), I set out to define these components as competencies – leadership competencies. At the same time I wanted to examine leadership but not at the very top, as such people were often so far removed from the average manager as to be poor role models; therefore the focus of the study was on those who were quite senior, but not the Bransons, Harvey-Joneses or Roddicks.

At the same time I felt it was disappointing that one of the main attempts to define effective behaviour in business terms in recent years has concentrated solely on the sphere of management: the Management Competencies Initiative.

MCI – A FLAWED CONCEPT?

MCI was introduced on the British scene amid a blaze of publicity and instantly kindled great hopes that at last it would be possible to define exactly what managers did that made them successful, and by making this definition, enable aspiring managers to target various competencies for their own personal development. They would in theory be able to tick off competencies as 'mastered' and then regard them as portable from job to job. If only it were so easy! In fact a reading of the competencies indicates that those who initially defined them confused leadership and management, scrambling them together. It was Lord Slim who made the famous statement that managers were necessary but leaders were essential, and consequently I felt that this blurring of definitions would make Lord Slim turn in his grave. What a shame! What an opportunity missed!

I felt this loss particularly acutely, as my own definition of leadership lent itself well to a competencies approach. There was no alternative. I would have to define my own set of leadership competencies and see whether they held water as a basis for the development of aspiring leaders.

I took as an overall starting-point for defining a new set of leadership competencies my own breakdown of the talents required for effective leadership, which I had summarized under the mnemonic WIST. But now it was necessary to break down the component parts of each of these talents into competencies that were both meaningful as a description of leadership as well as being a relevant challenge for those who wanted to develop as leaders. They were further amplified in *The Effective Strategist* (1999) and it is these revised competencies that are reproduced below – although they do not in any way detract from the conclusions I reached in *The Portable Leader*.

A BREAKDOWN OF NEW LEADERSHIP COMPETENCIES

Wisdom
- able to create visions of the future and pursue them
- intuitive yet wise in the way the vision is pursued
- has thoughts and opinions on the future of business methods and the nature of work
- inspiring when necessary; capable of being a mentor at all times
- adept at influencing and persuading others
- able to see the big picture and to recognize trends
- capable of dealing with organizational politics – a communicator and a networker.

Integrity
- demonstrates to others that they are worthy of trust
- does not operate on hidden agendas
- is open and honest in dealing with others
- does not shrink from candour when necessary
- able to give bad news.

Sensitivity (in approach)
- can operate as a coach
- a good listener
- able to empower and develop others
- understands the power of teams and how to work with them
- understands what constitutes a good process and how to achieve it
- capable of continuous learning
- a facilitator of learning and of situations
- looks for future opportunities in everything that happens
- looks for opportunities to motivate others
- able to persuade and influence others.

Sensitivity (in thinking)
- conforming in approach when necessary but capable of non-conformity
- able to challenge the conventional wisdom of situations, to bust paradigms

- able to handle diversity of approach and opinion
- understands that different things motivate different people; applies this understanding
- creative, can think outside the box
- able to think strategically and to communicate the strategies by forging an overarching direction for the organization
- familiar with a number of strategic tools
- a risk-taker when necessary; adventurous and courageous.

Tenacity

- dynamic and energetic
- hard-working, yet able to balance home and work life
- capable of handling own stress as well as that of other people
- disciplined in approach; able to handle failure and setbacks
- tenacious – does not give up
- understands and copes with the pressures of power
- able to handle uncertainty and help others to do so
- demonstrates optimism
- handles change well; plans it and makes it happen.

The next stage was to see whether the competencies were meaningful and relevant as a description of what effective leaders actually did in the course of their jobs. Did leaders recognize the competencies as important? Crucially, did they exhibit them in the day-to-day performance of their jobs? In setting out to test the competencies, I deliberately steered away from examining the rich and famous as many of them have become so remote in terms of wealth, power and aspirations from the average struggling individual at work that I felt they would not serve as useful role models. Instead I chose leaders operating in the middle of organizations – people who would be subject to many of the pressures that challenged the competencies. This did not in any way mean that the respondents were either boring or colourless – taken from four continents and covering a wide range of professions, including nursing, insurance, local government, project management and kidnap-victim release, they presented a fascinating range of responses, but in essence they displayed remarkably similar competencies when they were at their most effective!

The vehicle for testing was a questionnaire based on the competencies, but it must be stated that the sample of guinea-pigs selected was never of a size to make statistical analysis viable. Instead I concentrated on the 'story' that each person told in answering the questions and used an intuitive approach to make the connections rather than science and correlation. In other words, to use the right-brain/left-brain metaphor employed by Ned Herrmann, the analysis was strictly right-brained and I make no apologies for using this approach. After all, it is in the use of the right brain, with its intuitive leaps, its ability to vision, its concentration on the 'people' element, that true leadership exists.

More important than the method of evaluation are the following questions: What came out of the interviews in terms of validation or repudiation of the competencies? What are the implications for leaders, leadership development and those who train leaders in the future?

LEADERSHIP COMPETENCIES – EXISTING TALENTS AND NEW CHALLENGES

In setting out to test the competencies, two hypotheses were made, namely that

- the more competencies in which an individual showed a strength, the more likely that person was to be considered effective as a leader;
- a shift in the requirements made of leaders is taking place, with modern leaders more often having to take on the role of facilitator for both team and individual leadership situations.

EXISTING NECESSARY COMPETENCIES

In looking at the interviews and their subjects as a whole, the following competencies stood out as both being used by the respondents as well as being considered as vital for success, if not survival, by them:

1 Having a vision
2 Being energetic
3 Having a sense of purpose
4 Able to handle organizational politics
5 Understanding teams and facilitative in approach

6 Being intuitive
7 Tending to welcome change
8 Are communicators and enjoy it
9 Able to handle stress
10 Ambitious
11 Integrity – considered it paramount
12 Keenly interested in their organizations
13 Want to continue learning.

The competencies or talents listed above are not new in any way. In many respects this is comforting, as most of the existing beliefs about what makes an effective leader still hold good. In addition, the leaders interviewed (who were already regarded as effective by their organizations and followers alike) did tend to display most, or all, of the competencies to a considerable extent, thereby confirming the first assumption. Amongst these competencies, the need for the leader to have a clear vision for the future of his or her organization remained paramount and was stressed with ardour by all respondents. On the other hand, three other behavioural needs (as competencies) came to the fore with surprising intensity. As they are behavioural in nature, they cannot be considered to be entirely novel – nevertheless, the intensity with which they governed the lives and actions of the respondents is noteworthy, especially when the implications for the development of leaders is considered.

The three areas/behaviours that emerged as having the greatest prominence in the minds of respondents were those I refer to as the 'three Ps':

1 Having a clear sense of Purpose
2 Being able to handle organizational Politics
3 Being able to manage Processes – usually by acting as a facilitator.

It is necessary to examine what exactly is meant by each of the Ps before considering the potential effect of their emergence on management/ leadership development.

1 *Purpose*

All the leaders interviewed had a very clearly defined sense of purpose. This must be differentiated from the 'leader's vision' in so far as it is not so much a case of having a quantified and clearly articulated ambition for the future of one's organization as wishing to make the very best of one's life, of seizing all the opportunities open to one and of making the most of them – in full. It can be described as 'the act of consciously applying motivated strengths and resources to projects and people that move us and in which we believe'. This is a lofty, if not intimidating, statement but can be seen in the energy and commitment that all of those interviewed applied to everything they did. Making the most of one's sense of purpose can be seen as the process of identifying the source of one's drive in order to clarify and harness it. It could well be said that the drives of an individual make up a large part of that person's personality because they force an answer to that burning question: What do I want to do with the sort of person I am? It is in seeking the answer to this question that very often both personal and business visions are born.

But what are the implications here for those seeking to develop as leaders, or those likely to train them? How do you train a sense of purpose?

In so far as all leaders must have a good level of self-awareness in order to be effective, and as most programmes of leadership development already contain a good chunk of feedback of this nature, then the emphasis must be much more on what is to be done with the information presented to the delegate. All too often programmes bombard attendees with multiple feedback and sometimes contradictory information. They are told that they are, in terms of the well-known psychometric, the Myers Brigg Type Indicator, Extroverted, Intuitive, Feeling Perceivers, that they are left-brained or right-brained, that they are plants, shapers or implementers – often without due attention being paid to what they should *do* with what they perceive themselves, or are perceived by others, to be.

The implications for leadership development programmes are that they should focus less on individualism for individualism's sake and concentrate far more on an action-based approach to personal development. There is no point in wallowing in a psychobath of narcissistically satisfying self-analysis if nothing is decided as a result of the insight. Having one's personality type identified in the minutest detail (or typecast?) may be of interest to the individual concerned, but if it becomes an excuse for not attempting certain actions, for allowing certain faults to continue ('After all, there's no point in me trying to do that – I'm a Sensing Thinker, an ST! I'm a high shaper!'), then it is quite frankly counterproductive.

Far more useful are 360 degree feedback instruments that present an emergent leader with the effects and consequences of their actions. The knowledge gained can be startling, indeed painful, but if it is combined with discussions about what could be done to make the leader's behaviour more effective then very real benefits can result. When this feedback is delivered through supportive action learning groups, the benefits are even greater, and the individual can be coached by the group on how to change his or her behaviour for maximum effect. This can be a tremendous start in the complicated process of clarifying the sense of purpose and turning it into a powerful vision for the future.

2 Politics

The ability to handle organizational politics has the dubious honour of being the competency with which nearly all those interviewed had experienced difficulty – unfortunately it is also a necessity. If organizational culture can be defined as 'the way we do things around here', then perhaps organizational politics can best be described as 'the way we do things to other people around here'! It has, of course, been around since formal organizations first began to emerge, and a long time before Machiavelli. However, with the flattening of organizational structures, with increased pressures to make stretching profit targets, with the gathering pace of change in most companies, not to mention the vast increase in the number of mergers, take-overs and acquisitions, it would appear that new and keener demands are being made on leaders to become successful political animals. Leaders will increasingly have to operate in environments where there is competition for scarce resources, where 'games' are played and where the race to benefit from shrinking opportunities becomes sharper.

Once again, how do you train people to be leaders in these circumstances? To the best of the writer's knowledge, politics does not appear on any MBA syllabus but it is the rock on which countless careers founder. Perhaps leadership development programmes should focus to a greater extent on tackling the elements of political behaviour (and antidotes to it), such as dilemma resolution, ethics, conflict management, creative thinking, breaking of prevailing paradigms, techniques of persuasion, and so on. All these are almost impossible to tackle in the conventional plenary session and so the way again seems to point towards action learning groups combined with sophisticated and sensitive facilitation from the programme directors.

3 *Process*

All those interviewed considered themselves to be facilitators of process rather than traditional leaders of the command-and-control variety. In acting as facilitators, they adopted a variety of behaviours that enabled them to extract the greatest energy from their work groups as well as to empower them. In adopting facilitative behaviours, those examined seemed instinctively aware that facilitation is allied to coaching and teaching, but is different in so far as it retains important elements of leadership within it. To facilitate is to ensure that the process works to deliver a positive outcome. What distinguishes facilitation from other forms of leadership is that it is most often done with groups where group members are encouraged to take responsibility for outcomes. The quality of the facilitation is evident in the way that the facilitative leader chooses to work with the group. In *Discovering the Leader in You*, I introduced the concept of facilitative leadership styles which were made up of the following approaches:

Intellectual command
Incentives approach
Creative group catalyst
Supportive coach.

I also stated that it was necessary for the leader to choose the best style for the situation. This is no easy task; it requires sensitivity and sufficient self-awareness not to become over-reliant on one approach but to develop a range of styles that more closely guarantee success, irrespective of the nature of the task in hand.

How to train leaders, to be facilitative, to be adept in these styles? Once again a challenge to the trainer, but perhaps a good starting-point would be for them to examine their own behaviours when most effective in a training situation. They may well find that, with mature delegates, they are most successful when acting as creative catalysts rather than when force-feeding information to participants. From here, there should not be too many steps involved in teaching would-be leaders the skills of asking probing questions, of developing good listening, and of giving constructive feedback. These may be regarded as soft skills but they can be used to facilitate the hardest of outcomes! They are in fact true leadership competencies.

CONCLUSION

In choosing just three competencies for particular attention I would repeat that this does not in any way diminish the importance of the others – the three in question are simply in the ascendance. The dilemma for emergent leaders may well be how to strike a balance between the three drives of Purpose, Politics and Process. Too great a sense of purpose may encourage some to be over-political. However, perhaps the ability to manage processes effectively, with the high level of interpersonal sensitivity required, may be the answer to that particular conundrum.

Finally, one other thing that became evident from examining the lives and work of the guinea-pigs was that many suffered high levels of stress, worked extremely long hours, and were poor at balancing work and home life. Perhaps emergent leaders should concentrate more on learning the coping mechanisms of stress management, as well as those of more effective use of their team, both for support as well as for 'doing the work'.

If leaders learn to handle better these essential elements of the working life, then the benefits would pass down through their organizations, and the working lives – as well as effectiveness of countless thousands – would be improved beyond measure. Could these be the keys that will help leaders focus on what they really should be doing? – namely, succeeding in the vital tasks of creating a sense of direction, of looking ahead at the ever-changing business and political environment, and of stimulating creative responses from those with whom they work.

Let us hope so.

Index of Authors and Authorities

Adair, John 28–35

Bardwick 218
Belbin, Meredith 77–83, 85, 86, 168
Bem, Sandras 59, 62–3
Bennis, Warren 14, 70, 99–107, 109,
    127, 161, 170, 196, 209
Blake, R. R. 7, 9, 11, 13
Blanchard, Kenneth 20, 21–7, 63, 81,
    166
Burdett, John 215, 217–19

Carlzon, Jan 113
CCL (Center for Creative Leadership)
    Study on Derailment 66–74, 210
Collins, J. A. 190–93
Covey, Stephen R. 60, 124–31, 190

Deming, W. E. 154
Drath, Wilfred H. 70, 210–14

Eales-White, Rupert 84–90, 113, 132–9
Eltedge, Robin L. 83

Gardner, Howard 116–23
Gemini Consulting 140, 143
Grant, Jan 63–5

Hamel, Gary 215–17, 218, 221
Handy, Charles 180, 221

Harrison, Roger 132, 180–86
Harvey-Jones, John 53, 172
Herriot, Professor Peter 3
Herrmann, Ned 63, 103, 132, 162–71,
    227
Hersey, P. 21, 22, 23, 81
Hertzberg, F. 14, 16
Hirshberg, J. 154, 157–61, 186
Hunt, John W. 36–41

Ingham, Sir Bernard 5

Kanter, Rosabeth Moss 108
Kaplan, Robert E. 70–73
Kelley, Robert E. 147–53
Kets de Vries, Manfred 20, 51–8, 70
King, Martin Luther 208
Kofodimos, Joan R. 70
Kotter, John 30, 42–50, 114, 162, 170,
    186
Kouzes, James 108–15, 162

Lao-Tzu 1, 33
Laskin, Emma 116
Lewin, Kurt 9
Lipnack, Jessica 91–8
Lombardo, Michael 66–70
Lorse, Jay 16

McCall, Morgan W., Jr 66–70

McCann, Dick 83
McGregor, D. M. 14–17
Machiavelli, Niccolò 19, 230
Mageries, Charles 83
Marshak, R. J. 215, 219–21
Maslow, A. 14, 16, 29, 134, 181, 203, 208
Mintzberg, Henry 162–3, 167
Morse, John 16
Mouton, J. S. 7, 9, 11, 13

Nanus, Burt 99

Palas, C. J. 210–14
Peters, Tom 108, 113, 159
Philips, Steven L. 83
Porras, J. I. 190–93
Posner, Barry 108–15, 162
Prahalad, C. K. 215–17, 218, 221

Randolph, W. Alan 109
Ready, Douglas 140–46
Renong Group 135–6
Rosner, Judy 59–62, 65

Schmidt, W. H. 9, 13, 25, 166
Senge, Peter 194–201, 218
Slim, Field Marshal Lord 2, 224
Stamps, Jeffrey 91–8
Stewart, J. M. 187–90, 192
Stewart, Rosemary 112
Suarez, G. 154–7, 161

Tannenbaum, R. 9, 13, 25, 166
Tuckman 83, 202

Wallas, Graham 169
Whitmore, John 60, 195, 202–9

Index

Numbers in italics indicate Figures.

A-brain preference 133, 164, *165*, 166
abundance mentality 130
acclimatization 185
accomplishment 152
achievement 37, 38, 46, 152
acquisitions 157, 213
action tactics 184
action-centred leadership 30–31, *31*
actions, agreeing 88, 90
adaptability 26, 69, 72
Administrative Staff College, Henley
    77, 78, 80
affiliation 63–4
affirmation techniques 128
agape 183
aggression 64, 70
Alexander the Great 32, 38
alignment 167–8, 180–81, 186, 188,
    190, 193
alliances 106
ambition 121
    and derailment 68
    for mastery 71
American Management Association
    111
androgyny 62, 63, 65
anxiety 154, 202
anxiety levels 78

Apollo teams 78
Apple Computers 110, 193
arrogance 33, 68
assertion 62, 64, 203, 206, 209
assignments 144–5
assumptions 170, 195–6
AT&T 111, 141
attachment 63
attitudes 20, 31, 135, 151
attributes
    and effective leadership 45–6
    and winning teams 82
attunement 180, 181, 186
audacity 30
authoritarianism 175
authority 46, 61, 184, 212
    autocratic 9, 10
    challenging and confronting 121
    delegated 9, 10, 45, 136
    as the means of managerial control
        16
autocratic approach *see* Theory X
autonomy 16, 17, 93
awareness 204, 206

B-brain preference 133, 164, *165*, 166
balance 72–3, 134, 173, 178
BBC 82
behaviour 20
    and change 40, 41, 47, 142

behaviour – *cont.*
  cooperative 61
  female 59
  and masculine/feminine qualities 63
  in organizations 16, 36
  and perception 125
  support 61
  unproductive 53
behavioural theories 2, 6, 7, 9–17
beliefs 26, 88, 110, 208
Bell Labs 148
Big Doubt 73
Big Hairy Audacious Goal (BHAG)
    192–3
Big Worry 73
birth order, and the will/ability to lead
    36, 37, 38
blame 200, 206
Blanchard Training and Development
    21
blue sky thinking 150
board, the 177, 178
Brain Dominance Instrument 162, 163
brainstorming 87–90, 159
'breaking free' 87
British Airways 141
budgeting 45, 79
business failures 157

C-brain preference 133, 164, *165*, 166,
    167
call centres 92
capability 151, 213
career patterns 49
Castle and the *Battlefield* model 184,
    186
chairman 177–8
challenge 17, 121
change 105
  actionable first steps 41
  approaches to 133–4: logical
    detached 133; negative (cautious)
    control 133; people focused 133;
    positive creative 133
  attitude to 72

and behaviour 40, 41
the Big Doubt 73
the Big Worry 73
commitment to 136–7
communication 176–7
creating an agenda for 44, 44
definition 40, 76
felt pressure for 40–41
initiatives for 36
introducing 39, 107
organizational 75, 76, 219–20
reasons for failure 47–9
rewards 41
rhetorical 107
significant 107
stages in successful 47
tactics to reduce trauma and
    promote healing 184–5
transformational 220
transitional 220
change management 42–3, 47, 50, 100,
    134, 173, 176, 180, 184, 185
character 29
  definition 70
  and a win/win environment 130
character ethic, definition 125
charisma 5, 32–3, 34, 56, 57, 60, 121
charting 79
Chief Executive Officer (CEO) 44, 94,
    145, 167
choice 20, 39, 120
Christianity 33
Churchill, Sir Winston 19, 38, 117, 120,
    192, 212
Churchill family 5
clarity 175, 177
coaching 24–8, 136, 144, 145, 204, 218
  five-step plan 26–7
  key practices 25
  meaningful 219
cognitive approach 117–18
Cognitive Task Analysis 78
cohesion 95, 96
commitment 15, 110, 121, 153, 173,
    211

to change 136–7, 142
to the future 175
common stake in organizational
purpose *12*, 13
communication 80, 183
about change 176–7
channels of 22
electronic 92
networks of 57
of new vision 47, 48
and trust 156
women and 63
company incentive schemes 15
company workers 79
compassion 30, 177
competence 23, 25, 97, 105, 111
competent technologies 194
competition 36, 43, 45, 74, 150, 173,
182
global 216
competitiveness 141, 142, 145
complete finishers 80
complexity
detail 200
dynamic 200
compliance 44
concrete results 93
confidence 17, 23, 53, 57, 156
conflict 40, 57, 86, 87, 205
conflict management 139
congruity 105
connections 170
conscience 127, 129
consequences 27
consideration 130
consistency 26, 27, 30, 89, 166
constancy 105
contingency theories 2, 7, 16, 19–74
Adair 28–35
Blanchard 21–7
CCL Study on Derailment 66–74
Hunt 36–41
Kets de Vries 51–8
Kotter 42–50
Rosner, Bem and Grant 59–65

control 15, 43, 62, 80, 85, 102, 109, 164,
175, 206
negative (cautious) 133
conviction 26, 53
cooperation 44, 45, 47, 63, 96, 203,
206–9
coordinating 86
coordinators (chairmen) 78, 80–81, 87,
95
core competency 192, 217
core ideology 191
core purpose 191–2
core values 191
corporate culture 49, 75
corporate values statements 167, 168
courage 4, 30, 34, 130, 173, 177
creative abrasion 157–8
creative priority
key principles 157–61: beyond the
edges 157, 159–60; polarity
157–8; synthesis 157, 160–61;
unprecedented thinking 157,
158–9
creativity 15, 17, 53, 54, 150, 161, 162,
165, 166, 205, 223
definition 170
development of 168, *169*
and fear 155
intercultural 160
places of 169–70
team 84, 86, 90
training in 170
credibility 49, 61, 112, 114, 149, 150,
152, 167
critical mass 170
critical path 150
culture
cooperative 207
corporate 49, 75, 106, 152, 168, 180,
186
the mutuality level 183–4
the self-expression level 182–3
the transactional level 181–2
curiosity 101
customer orientation 142

D-brain preference 133, 164, *165*, 166, 167, 170
D-Brain Quadrant 103
Daimler-Benz AG 141
daring 101
decision-making 41, 85, 136, 150, 160
  and chairmen 81
  and feedback 60–61
  managerial 9
  subordinate involvement 9–10, 25
decisiveness 85
delegation
  and coordinating 86
  failure to delegate 68
dependence 126
dependency 40, 47
  needs 52, 57
derailment, executive 66–74
  exposure of flaws 67–8
  reasons for 68–9
designer, leader as 95, 197–8
desire 104
detachment 51, 81
detail complexity 200
development 30, 102, 218
  developing balance 72–3
  individual 29, *31*
  leadership development programme 31
  personal 11, 100, 124, 131, 134–5, 156, 171
  personal evolution 72
  product 92
  strategy 171
  women and 64
diagnostic skills 39
difference 38
digital technologies 92
dignity 208
direction 17, 23–4, 25, 40, 41, 173, 174, 175
  clarity of 76
'discovery kings' 138
Disney, Walt 191, 192
disseminator 95

dissent 105
diversity 65, 69, 165, 168, 169
dominance 33, 81, 212, 213
downsizing 216
drive
  and derailment 70
  and desire 104
  and the expansive character 71
  moderating 73
  and shapers 81
  and team control 82
DSM III 52
Du Pont Canada 187
dynamic complexity 200

effective team-builder (ETB) 84, 88, 89
effective team-leader (ETL) 84–8
effectiveness 25, 40, 41, 45, 56, 63, 84, 104, 127, 194, 213
  interpersonal 139
  managers 39
  organizational 141
  personal 126
  see also leadership, effective
efficiency 30, 150
effort 153
Einstein, Albert 117
Electricité de France 141
emotional maturity 4, 5
emotionality 64
empathy 46, 52, 54–5, 64, 70, 133, 136, 137
employees *see* subordinates
empowerment 16–17, 47, 57, 73, 75, 88, 110, 136, 144, 185, 186, 190, 197, 204, 219
  definition 143
enablement 110, 111
encouraging the heart 110, 111
energy 4, 37, 38, 46, 55, 57, 70, 73, 85, 103, 121, 186
enthusiasm 30, 32, 61, 85, 110
entrepreneurialism 51, 54
environment 22, 61, 71, 75, 107, 112, 137, 156, 188, 189

Esso Oil Co. 11
ethical standpoints 207
evaluation 86, 130
executive champion 95
exemplary leader (EL) 121
expansion 175
expansive character 70–72
    definition 70
experience 144
experimentation 112, 113
extroversion 78

F Factor 52, 54, 57
failure 165, 221
    leader 51, 52
    reasons for failure in change 47–9
faith 105
family
    background 37–8, 119
    businesses 51
    quality time 178
fear 154–61
    areas of 155
    and change 176, 177
    coping with 156
    definition 154
    questions 155–6
    of rejection 202, 203
feedback 60–61, 80, 85, 88, 136, 144–5,
    219, 229, 230
female characteristics 62, 63, 65
feminist movement 59
field-independence 37
finishing 86
Fioat Group 141
flexibility 20, 25, 39, 41, 45, 61, 62, 63,
    69, 72, 97, 119, 134, 142, 146, 165,
    188
focusing 86, 102, 136
folie à deux 53–4
followership 119, 120, 151
    types of follower 147–8, 151
fool, role of the 55–6
Ford, Henry 192, 193
foresight 4

forgiveness 208
Fortune 500 corporations 66
forward-looking 111
freedom 15, 208, 209
future state visioning (FSV) 187–8
    definition 187
    sequence of steps and imperatives
        188–90

Gandhi, Mahatma 33, 34, 117, 208
Gaulle, Charles de 33, 34, 56
Gaz de France 141
General Motors 157, 161
genetics 5, 6
global economy 207
goals 56
    clarity of 39, 96
    cooperative 93
    effective 128
    goal direction 37, 38
    morality of 127
Gorbachev, Mikhail 208
grandiosity 52
greatness 33–4
group identity 60, 96
group(s)
    core 44
    diverse 169
    needs of the 29
    and relationship behaviour 22
    syndicate 78
    and the task size 29
    values 30, 136, 137
    see also teams
GROW model 204
growth 64, 72, 104, 105, 106, 112, 134,
    135, 137, 146, 178, 182, 184

habits, the seven 126–7
hardiness 112, 113
Harvard Business Review 9, 42, 147,
    190, 215–16
healing 184, 185, 186
healing tactics 184
helicoptering 159

higher selves 208
Hitler, Adolf 32, 33, 34, 38, 51, 53, 55
holons 95
homogeneity 168
honesty 30, 68, 85, 106, 111, 177, 178
hope 105
Human Relations School 14
humility 33, 34, 208
humour 30, 85, 174
hygiene factors concept 16

ICI 82, 172, 175, 176
idea-gathering 112
imagination 15, 127, 129
implementation 86, 149
implementers 79
impostors 54–5
improvement 26, 48
incentives 45, 109, 136, 137
inclusion 60, 202–3, 204
independence 126
individual
   development 29, *31*
   needs of 29
   role of the fool 55–6
   values 30
industry 30
influence 43, 48, 50, 115, 118, 119, 129, 212
information
   availability 94
   collecting 89
   complex forms of 118
   exchange of 60, 61, 88, 89, 136
   filtering 40
   overload 57
   peers as sources 114
   trusted/mistrusted 97
ingenuity 15
ingratiation 39
initiative 30, 149
innovation 86, 101, 106, 109, 112, 113, 155, 157, 160, 165, 168, 175, 183, 186, 206, 223
insensitivity 68

inspiration 44, 101, 111, 185
integrity 4, 26, 30, 34, 46, 70, 101, 105, 125, 128, 130, 136, 184, 223, 225
intelligence, linguistic 119
interactions 94, 177
interactive leadership 60, 61–2
interdependence 96, 126, 129
interesting work, the need to do 16
internationalism 173
Internet 92, 124, 146
interpersonal skills 39–40, 46, 60, 151
interrelationships 199
intervention 177
intimacy 64
introspection 120, 150
introversion 78, 79
intuition 103, 160
investigating 85

Japan, cultural values 160
Jesus Christ 33
job cuts 214
judgement 20, 46, 151, 155
justice 30

Kennedy, Rose 5
Kennedy family 5
knowledge 46, 88, 89, 103, 145, 151, 155
   multiple 94
   and risk 217
knowledge capital 97

Leader Behavior Analysis
      questionnaires 21, 25
leadership
   action-centred 30–31, *31*
   advice on avoiding disaster 106–7
   basic ingredients 101
   behavioural commitments 110–11
   'big-L'/'small-L' 151
   characteristics 37–8, 60, 111–12, 120–21
   compared with management 2, 30, 38, 43, 45, 46, 47, 101–2, 164

dealing with uncertainty 112–13
definition 2, 36–7, 107, 109, 117,
    211, 223
direct/indirect 117, 120
effective 90, 116, 120, 122, 134, 172;
    building networks 44, 57;
    capabilities 143–4; creating an
    agenda for change 42–3, 44; a
    questioning approach 139;
    Renong view of 135–6
the exemplary leader (EL) 121
five practices of excellent leadership
    109–10, 114
forging the future 105–6
importance of the concept 1–2, 43
interactive 60, 61–2
interpersonal 130, 135
of learning organizations 197–9
and means of expression 104
personal 128
process 97
as a process 109
qualities 30, 56
shared 93, 96
skills required for future leaders
    199–200
social 96
strategic 126
style of see style of leadership
tactical 176
task 96, 97
taught 7
training 122
of virtual teams 95–6
leadership competencies 223, 224,
    225–6
    existing necessary competences
    227–31: politics 230; process 231;
    purpose 228–30
    existing talents and new challenges
    227
    WIST 225–6
leadership genes 5
learning 85, 100–103, 112, 114, 115,
    138, 159, 167, 184

organizational 134
learning organizations 105, 195
    definition 194–5
    disciplines of 195–7, 200
    leadership 197–9
left-brain thinking 35, 163, 201
levels of consciousness 181
leverage 200, 216–17
Lincoln, Abraham 33, 34
links 90, 92, 93, 97
listening effectively 88, 105, 112, 130,
    136, 138, 156
Lockheed 169
logic 103, 136, 137, 160
loneliness 52, 119
loners 37
long-term thinking 37
Lose/Lose solution 129
Lose/Win solution 129
love 183, 186
loyalty 32, 67
Luther, Martin 118–19

McKinsey 191
making meaning 210–14
male characteristics 62, 63, 65
management
    of attention 100
    change 42–3, 47, 50, 100, 134, 173,
        176, 180, 184, 185
    compared with leadership 2, 30, 38,
        43, 45, 46, 47, 101–2, 164
    conflict 139
    definition 45
    effective 39, 46, 127
    general 42
    innovation 171
    knowledge 171
    of meaning 76, 100, 144
    middle 42, 43–4, 46, 54, 59, 143
    project 46, 86
    of self 100
    senior 43–4, 47–8, 68, 90, 114, 140,
        143, 152, 156–7
    supply-chain 92

management – *cont.*
   time 124, 178
   of trust 100
Management Competencies Initiative
   (MCI) 224
management styles
   authority–obedience 11, *12*
   'country club' management 11, *12*
   impoverished management 12, *12*
   'organization man' management 12,
      12
   team leadership 12–13, *12*
manager analysis 11
manager-centred leadership 9, 10–11,
   10
managerial grid 11–13, *12*
Mandela, Nelson 19, 32, 34, 208
Marks and Spencer 82
masterclass 28, 31
mastering the context 100–101
mastery 70, 71, 104
   personal 195, 200
Matthew, St 1
maturity 130
   emotional 4, 5
   of subordinates 22
meaning, making 210–14
measurement 152, 164
meetings
   process 205
   review 45
mental ability 80, 82
mental models 195–6, 200
mentors 72
   learning from the right 101
   over-dependence on 69
Merck 191
mergers 67, 140, 146, 213
metanoia 196
milestones, interim 88, 89
mind 116, 117, 121, 163
   the unschooled 118
mindset 144
   global 142, 145
mission 166, 168, 190

mission statements 128–9, 155, 167,
   168, 207
modelling the way 110, 111
monitor evaluators 79
moral standpoints 207
morale 142, 159, 177
maintaining 12, *12*
motivation 14, 15, 27, 37, 41, 44–7, 55,
   67, 71, 73, 110, 112, 134, 142, 160,
   181, 183, 204, 214
   theory of 70
multimedia 94
Myers Briggs Type Indicator 83, 229

Napoleon Bonaparte 32, 119
narcissism 52–3, 55
NASA 192, 193
National Rubber 187
nations 34
natural laws 126
nature versus nurture debate 6
needs
   dependency 52, 57
   group 29
   hierarchy of 16, 29, 203, 208
   individual 29
   sensitivity to 176
   task 29
negotiating skills 81
networks 39, 43, 49, 60, 91, 92, 96, 114,
   145, 149–50, 152
   social 97
Nissan Design International (NDI) 154,
   157–61
No Deal solution 129
Nordstrom 191
North American Tool and Die 110
nurture 64, 79, 121

objectives
   agreeing 88
   of a meeting 89
objectivity 41, 54
observation 27
operational excellence 142

opportunities 111, 144, 170
optimism 105, 143
options 39, 88
organization
  levels of 93
  patterns of 22
organizational learning 134
organizational objectives 15
organizational performance 12
organizations
  behaviour in 16, 36
  change 75, 76
  complexity 43
  culture 106, 152, 168, 180, 186
  goal-centred 13
  learning *see* learning organizations
  mobilizing 173
  as political systems 39, 40
  reinvention/ regeneration 144,
    146
  size of 39
  talent within 43
  transactional 181–2
  transformation 141–2, 143
  vision-driven 182
organizing, definition 45
originality 168
output 157, 184, 219
overlearning 26

P/PC balance 126–7
paradigms 125–30, 221
  definition 125
participation 60, 61, 213
partnerships 106
passion 101, 103, 145, 160
paternalism 13
patience 106
patterns, recognizing 170
Pearl Harbor 7
peers 114, 155
people
  effective 60
  refusal to be codified 173
  and virtual teams 92, 93, 97

perception(s) 125, 138, 148
performance 26, 27, 130
  and blame 206
  feedback 219
  monitoring 87
  a negative consequence 27
  no response 27
  a positive consequence 27
  redirection 27
performance gaps 142
perseverance 30, 110
persistence 81
personal development 11, 100, 124,
    131, 134–5, 156, 171
personal evolution 72
personal transformation 102, 103,
    104
personality 29
perspective 104, 113, 120, 179
  the 'five Cs' 150
persuasion 39, 43, 46, 96, 112, 133, 139,
    152
  four main styles of 136–8
persuasiveness 4
physicality 64
planning 88, 160–61, 164
  definition 45
  eccentricities of 54
  promotion 49
  strategic 167
  succession 49
  wishing to plan 85
plants 79, 82
points of view 104
polarity 157–8
political astuteness 152
political tactics 39–40
politics 230
  and change 39
  and effective leadership 36, 37, 38–9
  a high level of 175
  playing 68
  as power in action 39
  success in the political arena 39–40
potential 15

power 5, 46, 53, 57, 71, 118, 151
  abuse of 55
  centralization of 41
  desire to gain 119
  and effective leadership 36
  and information 40
  male/female attitudes 64
  and networking 43
  and politics 39
  preoccupation with 55
  of process 84
  redistribution of 41
  sharing 60, 61
  and strategy 44
  and stress 52
  virtual teams 94
  women's attitudes to 61
praise 27
predictability 27
preparation 26
primates 119
principles 125–6
  definition 125
  guiding 128, 155
process 231
  agreeing 89
  applying 89–90
  challenging the 110, 111
  and clear goals 96
  power of 84, 87, 88
  and virtual teams 98
  and a win/win solution 131
process leadership 97
process meetings 205
product development 92
production 11, 12, 130
productivity 95, 96, 129, 183, 206
  measurement 15
Professional Personality Questionnaire
  78
progress 27, 87, 145
project management 46, 86
promotion 49, 67, 178
psychological androgyny 62–3
psychometric instruments 81

public speaking 178
purpose 17, 53, 90, 198, 228–9
  clarity of 76, 152
  a distinct sense of 101
  statement of 96
  virtual team working 92, 93, 94, 97, 98
push-pull model 219
Pygmalion effect 105

questioning 85, 86–7, 88, 113, 159
questioning coach role 136, 137–8
questionnaires
  of Blake and Mouton 11
  of Blanchard 21, 22, 25
  of Eales-White 85
  Professional Personality 78
  of Ready and Gemini Consulting
    140–41
  of van Maurik 226–7

Reagan, Ronald 70–71
reciprocity, norms of 97
recognition 16
recruitment 43, 96, 106, 158
redirection 27
reflection 102–3, 104, 120, 121
relationship behaviour, definition 22
relationships 138–9
  definition 11
  dependent 47
  harmonious 11, *12*, 46
  network of 49
  relationship-building skills 152
  supportive 44
  trusting 94
  and a win/win environment 130
reliability 105
renewal 126, 131, 141–2, 144, 218
reputation 46
resistance 85, 133
resolution 103, 104
resource investigators 80
resource leverage 216–17
resources 216
  cooperative network of 44

power and control over 61
   requirements 88
   scarcity of 39
resources audit 90
respect *12*, 33, 174
responsibility 15, 16, 25, 45, 52, 102,
      125, 127, 136, 138, 144, 174, 175,
      176, 204, 206, 214
results, producing 143–4
review 88, 90
rewards 15, 27, 41, 45, 48, 97, 109, 131,
      182, 219
right-brain thinking 128, 163, 201, 227
risk
   encouraging 219
   and knowledge 217
   of power/information sharing 61
risk assessment 149
risk-taking 15, 101, 103, 105, 110–13,
      133, 170, 178, 206
Roffey Park Institute 181
Roosevelt, Franklin D. 38, 57, 117
rules 15

satisfaction 17, 32
scheduling 79
Second World War 7, 212
security 15, 26, 134, *135*
self
   deployment of 103–4
   experimental 164
   feeling 164
   rational 164
   'safekeeping' (organizing) 164
self leadership 196
Self Perception Inventory of team roles
      80
self-actualization 16, 134, 196, 203, 208
self-awareness 129, 135
self-belief 115, 135
self-confidence 4, 30, 46, 56, 64
self-control 15, 179
self-criticism 178
self-destruction 52
self-esteem 53, 134, *135*, 203, 204, 206

self-expression 101, 103, 104, 130, 182,
      203, 209
self-fulfilment 197
self-insight 57, 58
self-knowledge 178
   the four lessons of 102–3
self-management 150, 190
self-motivation 204
self-reliance 93
sensitivity 13, 176, 223, 225–6
separateness 38
servant leader 32, 33
service excellence 129
shapers 78–9, 80, 81
short-term wins 48, 49
Shula, Don 25, 26–7
Siemens AG 141
situational leadership 9, 20–23, 25
16 Personality Factors 78
Smith Richardson 66
social capital 97
social interaction, six paradigms of 129
social leadership 96
social networks 97
socialization 61
socio-tech manager 95
soft approach *see* Theory Y
Sony 75, 191
specialists 80
stability 43
staffing 45, 69
stagecraft 56–7
stakeholders 208
   defining 188
   stakeholder symmetry 106
Stalin, Joseph 38, 117, 120
star performers 148
   strategies needed to succeed 149–53:
      followership 151; initiative 149;
      leadership 151; networking
      149–50; organizational savvy 152;
      perspective 150; self-management
      150; show and tell 152; teamwork
      151–2
staying power 57

stern parent role 137
steward, leader as 198
stories 118, 120, 121
strategy 143, 166
  competitive 216
  eccentricities of 54
  future-based 142
  implementation 44
  as stretch and leverage 215–17
  visionary 76
stress 159, 205
  of being in power 52
  and derailment 68
  growth and learning under stress 112
  management 57
  tolerance of 4
stretch concept 216–17
strong leader role 137
style of leadership
  definition 22
  and expansive character 71
  factors influencing choice 23
  four key styles 22, 23–5: coaching
    approach 24; delegating approach
    25; directive approach 23–4;
    supporting style 24
  interactive 60, 61–2
  at its most effective 21
  matched to the situation and the
    environment 22
  multidominant style 166
  non-traditional 60
  S1–4 sequence 25
  and thinking preferences 165
subordinate-centred leadership 9–10,
  10
subordinates
  and change 213–14
  confidence in 57
  and conflict 47
  development 25
  interaction with 60
  maturity of 22
  motivating/directing 67
  and trust 155

subtlety 13
success 19, 37, 51, 165, 221
  celebration 114
  characteristics of a successful
    executive 67
  and derailment 67
  exposure of flaws 67–8
  fear of 52
  ingredients for 40–41
  in the political arena 39–40
  public recognition 175–6
  rewarding 219
  and stories 118
  tactics 40, 176
succession 49
support 17, 22–5, 45, 85, 86, 107, 136,
  175, 183, 185
survival 134, 135
Swift, Jonathan 76
symbolism 32, 177
symptomatic solutions 200
synergies 219
synthesis 104, 157, 159
systems 131

T-groups 184
tact 30
tactical skills 39
tactics
  action 184
  healing 184
take-overs 157
talent 178
Tao 33
task behaviour, definition 22
task leadership 96, 97
task(s) 87
  completion 11, 17, 31, 32, 87
  definition 11
  the demands of 29
  interdependent 93
  the nature of 29, 88
  the needs of 29
  value of 30
  of virtual team 93

taught leadership 7
teacher, leader as 198–9
team creativity 84, 86, 90
team design 82
team development model
  assertion 203, 206
  cooperation 203, 206
  inclusion 202–3, 204
team identity 96–7
team leader
  choice of contributors 83
  effective (ETL) 84–8
  flexibility 967
  technologically skilled 98
  types of 81
  the visionary 136
team leadership 12–13
  Belbin on 77–83
  building the team 31, 38, 68, 83,
    87–90
  Eales-White on 84–90
  Lipnack and Stamps 91–8
team learning 196, 200
Team Management Systems 83
team orientation score 85
team roles 78–83, 85–6
team strength 85–6
team task process 88, 90
team workers 79–80
Teamopoly 78
teams
  balanced 81, 82
  cohesion 32
  collated 92
  definition 76
  effective 84, 85, 89
  empowerment 88
  equality of members 33
  facing obstacles 81
  the first meeting 89–90
  importance of 30
  importance of teamwork at the top
    48
  key components in team members
    85

preoccupation with consensus 38
  renewal 113
  and successful change 47
  'think tank' type 81
  virtual see virtual teams
  winning 82
  see also groups
tech-net manager 95
technology 91, 92, 98, 173
tenacity 223, 226
tension 218, 219
  definition 218
  generating creative tension 219
tests and measures 104
Texas Instruments 108
Thatcher, Margaret 5–6, 19, 70, 117
Theory X 14, 16, 17
  defined 14
Theory X managers 14–15, 23
Theory Y 14–17
  defined 14
Theory Y managers 15, 23
Theory Z 16
thinking 88, 167
  creative 162
  group action 87, 89
  lack of original 53
  long-term 37
  a new level of 126
  patterns of 195
  strategic 69, 104, 113, 132, 166, 167,
    174
  styles 165
  systems 195, 196, 197, 200
  think win/win 126, 129–30
  thinking multidimensionally 46
  unprecedented 157, 158–9
3M 191–2
three-circle concept 29–30, 31, 32
time management 124, 178
time plan 88
Times, The 5
tolerance 174
track record 46, 67, 69
training 113, 114, 122, 170, 218

trait theory 2, 4–6, 7, 9, 29, 41, 171
transaction 20
transformational theories 2, 3
    the leader as a catalyst of change:
        Bennis on 99–107; Covey on
        124–31; Gardner on 116–23;
        Harrison on 180–86; Harvey-
        Jones on 172–9; Herrmann on
        162–71; Kouzes and Posner on
        108–15; Ready on 140–46; Suarez
        and Hirshberg on 154–61
    the leader as strategic visionary 3:
        Collins and Porras on 190–93;
        Drath and Palus on 210–14; Senge
        on 194–201; Stewart on 187–90;
        vision articles 215–21; Whitmore
        on 202–9
    team leadership 3: Belbin on 77–83;
        Eales-White on 84–90; Lipnack
        and Stamps on 91–8
transition plan, seven-step 167–8
trust 12, 15, 25, 94, 97, 101, 102, 105,
        130, 142–3, 145, 161, 183
    betrayal of 68
    and blame 206
    and fear 155, 156
    management of 100
Turn-On Work Indicator Map 165

uncertainty 112, 157, 159, 219
understanding 102, 103, 105, 118, 176,
        177, 198, 199, 211
United States of America (USA)
    cultural values 160
    taught leadership 7
    untapped human potential in 106
University of Texas 11
University of Western Ontario 5
urgency 47–9, 80

values 29–30, 46, 72, 89, 110, 113, 118,
        120, 128, 130, 143, 150, 160, 188,
        189–90, 208, 218
    ethical 207
versatility 72

virtual teams 90, 91–8
    definition 92
    leadership 95–6
    links 92, 93–4, 97
    operating as holons 95
    people 92, 93, 97
    purpose 92, 93, 94, 97
    start-up 96
virtuality 92
virtue 105
vision 40, 41, 44, 45, 47, 48, 49, 56, 87,
        89, 101, 104, 105, 106, 118, 133,
        142, 143, 144, 146, 150, 155, 161,
        166, 174, 187–93, 198, 199
    articles 215–21
    components 191–2
    definition 76
    and fear 156
    shared 110, 111, 113, 128, 196, 200
vision statements 167
visionary team leader role 136
visualization techniques 128
vulnerability 64

Wal-Mart 191
Western society 203, 209
whistle-blowing 207
Whole Brain Creative Process 168, 169
whole-brain model 133, 163–4, 163
whole-brain technology 162, 167
will, independent 129
Win solution 129
Win/Lose solution 129, 131
Win/Win solution 126, 127
    five dimensions of 130–31
wisdom 223, 225
WIST (Wisdom, Integrity, Sensitivity
        and Tenacity) 223, 224, 225–6
women
    as leaders 59–65
    psychological qualities 63–4
work
    short time-scale 24
    simple/menial 24
World Wide Web 92